# BLESSINGS
## and CURSES
### in the MIDST OF THE LAND

ROBERTA WRIGHT

Order this book online at www.trafford.com
or email orders@trafford.com

Most Trafford titles are also available at major online book retailers.

Printed in the United States of America.

ISBN: 978-1-4907-1797-5 (sc)
ISBN: 978-1-4907-1799-9 (hc)
ISBN: 978-1-4907-1798-2 (e)

Library of Congress Control Number: 2013919458

Because of the dynamic nature of the Internet, any web addresses or links contained in
this book may have changed since publication and may no longer be valid. The views
expressed in this work are solely those of the author and do not necessarily reflect the
views of the publisher, and the publisher hereby disclaims any responsibility for them.

Any people depicted in stock imagery provided by Thinkstock are models,
and such images are being used for illustrative purposes only.
Certain stock imagery © Thinkstock.

*Trafford rev. 11/26/2013*

 www.trafford.com

**North America & international**
toll-free: 1 888 232 4444 (USA & Canada)
fax: 812 355 4082

*In memory of*
*Sam and Beatrice*
*who never stopped praying for their children*

# Acknowledgments

This book was born from conversations with my brothers and sisters. My sister Cozetta was the first to suggest I do a family tree of our father. I am grateful for my brothers and sisters for their memories of years gone past. Without Sam Junior, Obadiah, Cozetta, Ruth, Lloyd, James, Alberta, Betty, and Laura, this book would not have been written.

A special thanks to my daughter, Pamela, a working mother of two who took the time out of her busy schedule and did the copyediting, which kept this book on track.

# *Dedication*

This book is dedicated to my daughter Pamela, grandson Ronelle, granddaughter Tamela, and my sister Cozetta.

# Contents

# Preface

This book is about Sam and Beatrice's struggle raising their children in the midst of the Jim Crow laws where their children were viewed as stupid nigger kids and the system that enforce that view.

In this era of Jim Crow, Sam had to maneuver his way through a maze of irrational hatred of landmines that was placed before his steps to destroy him and his family.

Here are excerpts from the World Wide Web:

- ABC News, "Baggy Pants"
- "Joe Louis's Greatest Fight: Louis Schemling"

A Closer Look
Samuel Wesley Gathing: The Husband, the Father, the Man, Poppa

Born in 1908, second of two children of John Wesley and Cynthia Gathing, Sam Wesley Gathing entered the world on April 25, 1908, in a small rural town in northern Mississippi and also into an environment of bitter hatred and hostility from the southern whites. His father was a farmer who owned five acres of land and grew his own tobacco. The boy learned early the importance of hard work and saving money. His mother, Cynthia, died when he was six months old, probably of complications from childbirth.

This journey was chartered and documented in collaboration with generations of information.

# Searching for an Answer

## 1908-1926

This is a story about Sam, my poppa, and how I remembered him who also was called by different names because of the roles he played in life. But his wife (our momma) called him Sam while his children called him Poppa. The blacks who knew him called him Reverend Gathing. Most whites called him nigger or boy. And how I remembered him—this includes some of the experiences he shared with me and with his other children also—was as a strong, intelligent man that was a leader and a preacher in the community in which we lived and his leadership through his ministers of several churches spread throughout surrounding communities. However, under Jim Crow, he was forced to play the subservient role of a boy.

His childhood was no different from those of other blacks in northern Mississippi who worked the land as poor farmers—framed house, wood-burning stove, with no electricity, no indoor plumbing.

When the fire from the cast-iron heater burned out during the night, the handmade quilts that Momma, her girls, and sometimes neighborhood women who lived up the hill or across the pasture had assisted her in making from old tattered clothing from her family that had been used and reused by older children and passed down to younger children would keep the family warm. The tattered rags were thrown in the recycle bin to be reused for these beautiful hands to make into quilts to keep her family warm.

I was an early riser like Poppa and Momma, and as I was lying in our double bed that I shared with my two sisters Alberta and Shug under several layer of quilts, I would smell coffee. The strong coffee's aroma told me that Poppa and Momma were up. It was still dark outside. No sounds in the early morning. The familiar sounds of the crickets and the occasional hoots of the Mississippi owls were silent. It seemed that between dawn and before sunrise there is complete silence, a stillness and peace on the farm that could not be found anywhere else. Even before the break of day, the ancient sound of the rooster, a friend to humans, would awaken me and my family to the sound of its cock-a-doodle-doo—a sound that has been around since the beginning of time. For millennium, before the clocks or radios woke up man and beast, the rooster would usually perch on a high place, protecting the hen yard that he thinks belongs to him with his head lifted up to heaven. Its mouth wide open, it would sing cock-a-doodle-doo as though he is trying to wake the whole universe, that it's time to rise and shine. When the rooster crowed, every animal and man seemed to respond to this sound. From the barnyard, the cows would start to moo, and the calves would respond. The horses would neigh, the pigs would snort. The whole family knows it's time to rise and awaken from the night of sleep and slumber.

Although the rooster hadn't crowed, Poppa and Momma were up, preparing for the long workday ahead. I eased out of bed between my two sisters, trying not to wake them and thinking that I could have a few moments alone with Poppa while my siblings are still sleeping. I knew too how Poppa loves to talk to his children, giving the dos and don'ts about life, trying like most other parents to protect their children and try to stop his children from going in the wrong direction by explaining to them some of his own life's experiences: "Save for a rainy day that's sure to come. You will reap what you sow."

As I entered the living room, Poppa was sitting in his green recliner reading his Bible. The living room felt warm and comfortable from the fire he has made in the cast-iron heater with the long pipe extending through the ceiling to the chimney, emitting smoke outside from the wood that one of his boys had brought into the house that they had cut from the woodpile out back.

Poppa looked up from his Bible when I said, "Morning, Poppa."

Upon seeing me, his face became warm, glad to see me. "Morning, girl. You are up early, aren't you?" More a statement than a question, I replied, "Yes, sir."

Poppa said, "I was just thinking about my poppa. He was born in 1882. Remember, he died in 1957. I dreamt about him last night."

"What was it about?" I asked.

"I've had this dream before. I see in this dream my birth mother is walking away from my poppa as he's holding another woman's hand. I never see my mother's face, only her back."

"Oh, Poppa, that's a sad dream," I said.

Poppa continued, "My poppa, John Wesley, was a small dark man who seems to be always working from sunrise to sunset on his five-acre farm and demanded the same from his five children. My only sister Mary were the firstborn from my mother Cynthia, and I was the second child. You know I was six months old when she died. Roberta, I will tell you something about men. Most don't want to be alone. Don't want to raise children without a woman. That's just the way most men are. Now when my mother died in 1908, she was a young woman, only twenty-four years old."

As Poppa was telling me this, a thin veil of sadness just for a moment covered his face. If I hadn't been paying attention, I would have missed his brief moment of sadness. Poppa continued. "During this time, it wasn't unusual for complications to occur during childbirth. Women gave birth at home with the presence of a midwife. I was told that's what happened to my mother. Historically, many died in childbirth. Their husbands remarried. My mother didn't die right away from my birth, however she never did recover."

"No one can replace your mother."

"I grew up with two different stepmothers. My sister Mary and I called her Momma. Millie was her name, and we knew that she wasn't really our mother, that she was that woman who slept with our poppa. I don't remember much about her, though. After giving birth to two of my half brothers—Emerson in 1911 and Booker T. in 1912—she also died young like my mother. My brother Emerson was a hard worker like our poppa, was a drinker of alcohol, but not a heavy drinker like our brother

3

Booker T. Booker T. was nothing but trouble. He fell into the bondage of alcohol. Couldn't stop drinking, drunk himself to death.

"My poppa's last wife was Etta, had a plump, full figure. Dipped snuff loved flowers. Enjoyed working in her flower garden. A good cook, too. Momma Etta and my poppa had one child. A baby girl, a pretty little girl, they named her Iola. I saw the way Momma Etta loved Iola the tender care she gave Iola. I never felt what I saw; I would watch Momma Etta whole her. Nurse her. This made me miss my own mother more. Roberta, I have never told anyone else this. This was so very hard for me I was only six or seven at the time. I used to go behind this big oak tree on my poppa's farm and sit on the ground under this old tree and cry. I had a deep aching longing in my spirit for my mother. Still do."

As Poppa continued to talk about his early life, I smelled the biscuit baking that Momma had made from scratch and the homemade sausages that she had preserved for a time like this.

Poppa talked often about his life. He would tell his children how he and our mother met and how they grew up together. His family was close to Beatrice's family. There was not a time when he didn't know her, and he and our momma played together as children. "Your mother was a pretty little girl. She would laugh a lot. Still do."

"So Momma have always been that way, Poppa?" I asked.

"Yeah. People don't change much, Roberta. It just seemed that she was meant to be my wife. Consequently, when I finished my eighth-grade education from the one-room school house for Negro in 1923 in Marshall County, Mississippi, I wrote to my uncle Luscher (my poppa's brother) and asked him if I could come to Madison, Illinois, to live with him?

Poppa left Mississippi when he was eighteen years old to find work in Madison, Illinois. While living with his uncle Luscher, Poppa found employment in a steel mill. The young man saved every penny that he could because he had made up his mind that he would return to Mississippi when he had enough money saved to marry his childhood sweetheart, Beatrice. December 22, 1929, in the state of Mississippi, Desoto County, Sam and Beatrice became husband and wife.

For a wedding gift, Poppa's father gave him a mule named "Rock" and a big red cow. Poppa bred this red cow, and over the years, her offspring produced over seventy-five cattle and calves.

# 2

# *The World Our Poppa Was Born Into*

Poppa, like other people of his era, has seen triumphs and tragedies. He has witnessed wars, revolutions, and social upheavals.

The year 1908 when our poppa was born, one hundred Negro men were lynched by the Ku Klux Klan, a legalized white terrorist group of white men that had its beginnings in 1867. This was the most ruthless political terrorist group in American history.

World War I began in 1914 when Poppa was seven years old. Germans unleashed a horrific new agent of poison gas and attacked a British liner that went down in 1915 with 128 Americans aboard. Congress declared war in April 1917. By 1918, 4 million fresh U.S. troops were over there. The Depression came in 1929; Roosevelt took office amid the Depression.

Hitler's Nazi Germany in 1930-1940 exterminated over 6 million Jews and no whites in the Holocaust gas chambers. Our poppa was twenty-two at the beginning of this horror.

Poppa said that the news that had seeped through the BBC (British Broadcasting) on the horror of Adolf Hitler's Germany and the killing of millions and millions of Jews by putting them in gas chambers—and even 15 million civilians were killed by this murderous and racist regime, including Germans of African descent—were forcibly sterilized.

General Dwight D. Eisenhower was the army general during the Hitler regime from 1930-1940. When he and his army landed on the beach of Normandy, this was the beginning of the end of Hitler's regime. The American soldiers had arrived.

It is written that when General Eisenhower first saw the heaps and heaps of charred skeleton remains, it was so overwhelmingly shocking that the stench could be smelled at a great distance. The depth of it was beyond any earthly imagination. The general gave orders for pictures to be taken of the ghastly manner of death of these people. Eisenhower was being quoted as saying, "If I told the public, they wouldn't believe it. We have to take pictures; they have to see for themselves."

Poppa said that tension and fear gripped his stomach when he saw these horrible shocking heaps of skeleton images in the newspaper. He feared the horror would come upon them and that the lynching of our people may not be the end for us. Hitler's gas chambers maybe next. We feared copycats of the gas chambers would be used by the KKK.

"I have seen charred bodies," Poppa continued. "Sometimes after lynching, the KKK would burn their victim's bodies." He probably couldn't imagine anything worse until now. Poppa saw a direct link between lynching and the gas chamber—they both were fueled by hatred. Poppa reasoned, "If a white man can do these horrible crimes against a people that have white skin and straight silky hair like himself, what on earth is he capable of doing to a man he thinks is subhuman?"

Hitler writes in *Mein Kampf*: "It is criminal lunacy to keep on drilling a born half-ape until people think they have made a lawyer out of him, while millions of member of the highest culture—race must remain in entirely unworthy position; that it is a sin against the will of the Eternal Creator if His most gifted beings by the hundreds and hundreds of thousands are allowed to degenerate in the present proletarian morass, while Hottentots and Zulu Kaffirs are trained for intellectual profession. For this is training exactly like that of a poodle."

At the war's end in 1941, Hitler committed suicide, leaving a mass of rubble and millions upon millions dead, maimed, homeless, and without food or shelter.

On December 7, 1941, the Japanese attacked Pearl Harbor.

In August 1945, the United States dropped bombs on Hiroshima and Nagasaki.

The tragedies of living under the dark cloud of fear of breaking one of the Jim Crow laws included being aware of it all the time that blacks had no right and that a white had to be respected, including the white's women and children. Poppa learned early that whites expected and demanded total obedience from Negroes as though the Negroes were small children.

Our poppa's oldest teenage son was raped by some members of the Ku Klux Klan (more about this in a later chapter).

## Triumphs

As Poppa continued to grow and develop, taking an active role in the southern Baptist Convention, they would meet in different American cities, like Chicago, St. Louis, even as far west as California. This opened a door for our poppa craving for travel, perhaps to flee from the bondage of Jim Crow, although for just a little while. Maybe he felt as though he was on vacation before returning back to the physical and mental restraints that Mississippi held for their Negro citizens and his family and his farm. Gradually through his leadership, he became in 1950 the moderator of Sardis East Baptist Congress. As moderator, Poppa held the gavel, seeking ways to solve internal disputes these churches encountered.

Before 1954, there were no public schools for blacks in Mississippi that went beyond the eighth grade. Poppa played a major role in the building of black schools and churches by organizing committees and support group through his pastoral platform, appealing to large groups of people for financial support.

In 1952, he bought his own hundred and fifty acres of farmland in northern Mississippi. This blessing freed him from leasing land from sometimes racist whites.

In the 1930s, Poppa and Momma were forced to move several times as their young family grew. Sometimes these leases would last for four years. Often as soon as the lease was up, our poppa wouldn't renew his lease because the whites would change what was written on the lease. White men had total control of the laws with the controlling power to change laws that enforced their desires and wishes—laws that were against the interest of the blacks. These racist men belong to the "white man only" club. Blacks, when leasing their land, were forced to shop in the landowner's store. And in these stores, the merchandise, food, clothing, etc., had high markup. These store owners used abusive business practices. Many tenants never got out of debt. Blacks knew whites were cheating them, and the whites knew that they knew. However, whites knew that there was nothing the black could do about it because there were no laws that would protect them. Subsequently, Poppa and Momma had to tolerate racist landowners to lease their land.

These conditions placed in Poppa a far-reaching in sight that no matter what, by any means necessary, he had to own his own land. Poppa was *from a family of landowners.* No way could he and his family continue to live under these injustices. *Saving money for that great day of landowner ship became his top priority.*

# 3

## Reconstruction

P oppa told his children that he was standing on the shoulder, proverbially speaking, of two generations of landowners. His grandpa Bill Gathing, born in 1828 into slavery, bought land during the Reconstruction. His own poppa bought five acres of land in the early 1900s in Byhalia, Mississippi.

Poppa said that after the four bloody long years of civil war was over, there was a period what was known as the Reconstruction (1865-1877). President Abraham Lincoln tried making amends to some of the horrible effects of hundreds of years of slavery, even giving ex-slaves land in South Carolina. Blacks all through the South started buying land left and right. This made the Southern white very nervous, especially here in Mississippi.

"Girl," Poppa continued, "whites knew the power in landownership, wars are fought over land. During this time, Negro didn't have the right to vote. Roberta, it would be almost a hundred years after the civil war, in 1965, when the voting rights act was passed during the Johnson administration before the blacks had that right."

"You must be kidding! That long?" I stated in amazement.

"That's true. It's in the books. You can read about it."

Consequently, whites started passing laws that would increase the black's land taxes beyond what they could possible pay. The clock is turned back after Reconstruction. All rights for blacks were undone through one means or another. And economic progress was thwarted. Life grew increasingly more difficult in the South. Subsequently, many blacks started losing their land, especially here in the Mississippi.

These men of color knew where their hope was sealed. It had to be in God, for they had experienced disappointment, counterfeit hope before and during the Reconstruction in 1867-77. W. E. B. DuBois call them the "mystic years." Ten years of freedom before the white existing power structure changed their minds and reversed the freedom they had given the Negroes after the civil war. For ten years, the United States establishment accepted and fulfilled the constitution of the United States. Thomas Jefferson wrote in 1787, "We hold these truths to be self—evident, that all men are created equal."

These glorious ten years of sunshine, of freedom, and loosened chains actually set free the Negro to be fully human. A rush to feel their God-given humanness, the American Negro took full advantage of it. Lerone Bennett Jr. writes in *Before the Mayflower*: "In Mississippi, South Caroline and Louisiana, black lieutenant governors were sitting in power. A black was secretary of state in Florida; a black was on the state supreme court in South Carolina. Nor was this all, Blacks and whites were going to school together, riding on streetcars together and cohabiting, in and out of wedlock. Never before—never since—has there been so much hope."

Once Reconstruction was put into action, white slave owners panicked. When slaves were set free, what and who was going to fill the void that's left? Who's going to work the land? The whole southern system for over three hundred years was built upon slavery.

W. E. B. DuBois writes in *Black Reconstruction in American 1860-1880*:

> As slavery grew to a system and cotton Kingdom began to expand into imperial White domination, a free Negro was a contradiction, a threat and a menace. As a thief and a vagabond, he threatened society; but as an educated property holder, a successful mechanic or even professional man, he more than threatened slavery. He contradicted and under

minded it. He must not be. He must be suppressed, enslaved, colonized. And nothing so bad could be said about him that did not easily appear as true to slaveholders.

Farming the land spoke the same language to all farmers black and white and what they talked about the most. Raining on the just and unjust, they all had the same concerns: How will the crop be this year? Depending upon the weather, both prayed for rain, prayed that it stopped. During the 1900s to the 1950s, farmers were devoted to raising cotton—the chief cash crop of the times.

Blacks and whites alike depended on the weather for a productive cotton crop; however, blacks had an additional worry: Will the white landowner be fair at harvesting time? Will they get a fair price for their hard backbreaking labor, working from sunrise to sunset, walking behind their mules plowing, breaking ground so they could plant their cotton crop, stopping only for lunch?

There are many long days between sowing and reaping for a farmer and many worries, too. Farmers' worries actually begin before planting season in March and April. Sometimes we would see Poppa walking across the fields where he planned to plant his cotton, looking at the soil. We children would hear him talk to our momma about the soil.

"Bracey (that's what he called our momma), the soil look's rich. If we get the right amount of rain, we are going to have a good crop this year, If the Lord's willing." The worries didn't end until the last boll of cotton was picked in the early fall. The cotton plant is waist high or above when it reaches maturity, overflowing with beautiful white flowers that turn into pure white fluffy cotton. Cotton like all plants has its enemies, but it seems that the cotton plant has more than its share that attracts all kinds of creeping things: aphids, bollworm and boll weevils, cotton bollworms, and armyworms. Harvest is in September and October. The anxiety about the uncertainties of farming, of whether the crop will survive all the challenges Mother Nature throws at it, was a prayer, a wait-and-see question all throughout the sowing and reaping.

Poppa rented three hundred acres of farmland from the Nicholas place during the early 1940s. Mr. Nicholas was a jovial, friendly man with rosy cheeks. Sometimes he would have a pocket full of candy for us, candy that he had gotten from the general store that he owned and where the Negroes who lived on his land shopped. Although Mr.

Nicholas seems to be a nice man, we still saw him as a white man. A man that was superior to us. Sometimes when we children were sitting on the wooden steps of our framed house sucking on the lollypops and blowing bubble gum that Mr. Nicholas had bought us, we watched and listened to Mr. Nicholas and Poppa talking. Mr. Nicholas did most of the talking, and Poppa bowed his head rapidly in agreement (yes'm) with him being a nice white man, maybe even a Christian man. He probably had the white Jesus picture hanging on his living room wall. Poppa had the same picture on his living room wall too. We never did hear him call our poppa nigger. Mr. Nicholas only called our poppa boy and sometimes by his first name Sam.

Not like the way Mr. Wilkin used to do when Poppa leased land from him. Poppa's children hated Mr. Wilkin. When Mr. Wilkin pulled up in his old 1934 Ford pickup truck with the Mississippi red dust trailing behind, Poppa's children would say, "Here he comes." We all knew who "he" was. Dread and fear would come with him. Mr. Wilkin was known as a member of the terrorist group the KKK.

We would be playing outside having a good time laughing and playing. Just having fun. But when we saw his truck, all the fun left. Our dog Fido would start barking. Just seeing him stole our joy. We saw a change in our poppa too—a change from being our poppa who was in control of his family to someone who was timid with fear and afraid. Our poppa had to pretend to play this game with Mr. Wilkin because if he didn't, Mr. Wilkin would tell the whites that our poppa was an uppity nigger. During these times, having the reputation of an uppity nigger pretending to act as though you were a man equal to white men was the worst crime of all. You or one of your boys may be lynched because of it.

Mr. Wilkin would sometimes park his pickup truck on my sister Cozetta's flowerbed of beautiful viola, marigold, zinnia and petunia. Cozetta said her flowers were so pretty they attracted passersby. People, blacks and whites alike, would stop to look at their magnificent blossoms in rich enchanting colors.

After the civil war that ended in 1865, the war that outlawed slavery, the southern whites, ran by the KKK (Ku Klux Klan), used fear to keep the southern Negro in bondage. In the 1930s, when our poppa, a young man in his thirties, was raising his young family, he and our momma were living in Mississippi, the most terrorist state in the United States.

Fear would arise when the Negro heard about a black man being lynched and which was the intended purpose of the KKK. Blacks would keep wondering if they would be next.

Although Poppa had to always play a subservient role around whites, he couldn't completely cover up his ability as a leader. When our poppa leased these farms, he often had other Negro tenants under his control. Sometimes two or three families would live on these leased farms.

With his leased land, he was allowed to sublease to other farmers. The farmers were called "sharecroppers." A sharecropper was a person who farms land owned by another and gets part of the crop in return for the use of the leased land.

In today's time, it is hard to imagine the life that our poppa was forced to live. For this young man was born to be a leader. In the presence of Poppa, you could sense his power to influence and persuade. However, with his strong character around white people, Poppa had to play the role of a boy around white men, women, and their children also. I am sure the whites could see his strength. The racist whites knew he was not stupid. But under the Jim Crow laws, this outrageous role was played for years. The Negro man was not allowed to look or make eye contact with a white man. Negro men could not work on the same job with a white man. The black man or any black person could not drink, eat, or sit where whites did. Throughout this period, it was acceptable for whites to call any black person "nigger." Nigger this, nigger that! By calling our poppa boy and nigger, they were using the worst possible slurs. It was a daily struggle for Poppa to keep his heart from being contaminated with the spirit of hate. It was hard for his children to witness their strong, intelligent poppa pretending before white folks that he was inferior to them, talking to whites with downcast eyes because blacks wasn't allowed to make eye contact with whites, saying "Yes, sum or no, sum" and hearing whites call our poppa "boy."

# 4

## "The Big Yellow Pencil"

After all the animals were in for the night and we have all eaten supper and most of Poppa's children were just sitting in the front room waiting for bedtime, our poppa would sit in his chair and Momma would sit in hers next to him. Then out of the blue, Poppa would say, "I will tell y'alls a story the way it was told to me." And he would begin.

"Well, my poppa could barely read that the little reading and writing that he learnt in 1892 from Mrs. Taylor, a nice white lady that wore her hair brushed back into one long braid that hung down to her waist. My poppa as a ten-year-old boy used to cut wood for her. Although Negroes weren't allowed into white people's houses, unless they worked inside as maids or cooks. Poppa said that while his poppa was cutting wood, he would look up and see Mrs. Taylor looking out the second-story window of this huge antebellum house watching him chop wood. Poppa said that his poppa told him that when he knew Mrs. Taylor was watching him, he would raise the ax higher and cut the wood with more force.

"When he had finished cutting wood, Mrs. Taylor would let him sit on her back stoop's lower steps, and Aunty Brown (Negro women who cared for others were called "aunty"; they were never shown the respect of missus), the cook, knew it was her responsibility to give him iced tea from a tin cup. Mrs. Taylor felt a friendly interest in little Wesley's welfare.

"Then one day, while he was sitting on the back lower stoop, he smelt a sweet unfamiliar scent. Her unexpected present startled him, he almost dropped his cup of iced tea. 'Wesley, I have been watching you, you are a smart nigger. I am going to teach you how to read and write.' With that being said, she gave him a big yellow pencil and a table with lines spaced far apart. Mrs. Taylor patted him on the head and said, 'Boy, you can do it.' He held this big yellow pencil as though it was an expensive piece of jewelry. This big yellow pencil became his chief treasure. Years passed and Poppa said his poppa always talked about that big yellow pencil.

# "A Call to Preach"

**P**oppa's children heard stories of his family history many, many times while they were growing up. In fact, these stories still lives on in them, and they share them with their own children.

Our poppa grew up in church. His poppa, whom Poppa also called Poppa but whom his children called Grandpa Wesley, had a strong resemblance of our poppa. They both were of medium height and of very dark complexion. Grandpa Wesley made sure his family went to church every Sunday; he taught Sunday school. Consequently, the Bible was a large part of our poppa's spiritual growth. Poppa told his children that he knew at a young age that church was where he belonged.

Poppa said that at age nine, after receiving Christ, he knew he was called to preach. "I remember the day like it was yesterday. I was sitting on the wooden bench in this small white-framed church, reading silently, following the words as my poppa, the Sunday school teacher, stood before his class of about ten Negro boys and girls in his dark tweed suit. The stern, resolute look on his near-black complexion reflected the seriousness of his teaching. And as his poppa was standing before the class, reading to them aloud from his small worn Sunday school book that was once used by the white church, he would read from

Ephesians 4:11: 'And He gave some Apostles, some Prophets, and some Evangelists, and some Pastors and Teachers.'

"The word *pastor* completely passed my mind and went directly to my spirit. The spirit of the Lord came upon me greatly. Oh my God, I'm going to preach! This message left no doubt I was going to preach."

Poppa said that even at a young age, he felt comfortable speaking before groups of people. At age nine, he stood before his Sunday school class, reading from his small Sunday school book. "I was never afraid of people, always felt at ease standing up before people."

The elders of the church saw his ability to lead and started giving him more leadership roles in the church. The more our poppa read the Bible, the more he wanted to know about the ancient world. The Scripture opened up his mind to a larger meaning of life, that there was a bigger meaning to life than the life Mississippi portrayed. In 1920, when our poppa was twelve, he said he started reading the Bible and was remembering scripture that made him aware of the ancient world. That life didn't begin and end in Mississippi. There were times when a white would call him nigger and he would think of Moses and the Israelites and how they were held in bondage and God brought them through. And that the Jews hated the Samaritans in the Bible, even calling them dogs: "The Jews had no dealing with the Samarians." Our poppa saw some similarity to these scriptures in his own life.

From the study of the Bible, this increased his desire for an even deeper knowledge of the world in which he lived. Sometimes "the Quakers" would bring biblical literature and leave it at the Negro churches. Poppa would be one of the first to take these books home to read.

Although our poppa didn't have much formal education that went beyond the eighth grade, he had a strong desire to seek and find; as the Bible says, "Seek and you shall find."

Through word of mouth and as time passed throughout Poppa's early twenties, Poppa's gift as an orator spread throughout the area, and he was given more honorary duties that he may have some place and post in the house of the Lord. Poppa was asked more and more to speak at different churches.

During these times, the only requirement to preach was to make a public announcement that God had called you to preach, and the church would shout, "Praise the Lord!" Once the announcement was made, this young inexperienced preacher was blessed to sit in one of the tall-backed red velvet clergy chairs in the pulpit that was reserved for preachers. He was now seated where God placed him, wearing a black suit and tie, spotless, shining freshly polished black shoes with Bible in hand. If the new men of God had the "gift of glib" and didn't give the women anything to gossip about, they would easily have a large group of spiritual hungry followers.

At other times, however, there would be a vast army of men who were drawn by the allure of power and authority that comes with being a preacher; and he would make the announcement, "God has called me to preach." And by this announcement, other preachers even having doubts about this calling would yield to the calling to this new preacher. In reality, who has the right to judge the "calling"?

Moreover, the label jackleggy preachers started creeping into the Negro's vocabulary—preachers that didn't have the gift of glib. These young men, some without character and obviously not fitted to be seated in a place of authority and honor, piggyback on the power of other preachers, never having a church of their own.

Our poppa wasn't one of them. The demands for his gift of preaching grew by leaps and bounds, and he became the guest speaker at churches in the area. Although at age thirty, our poppa didn't have a church of his own, he had the gift of an orator when he talked. Everyone listened, his words floating over the sanctuary packed with worshipers, where in the Baptist churches the parishioners weren't too sophisticated to show their emotions. Most had a tendency to shout. The shouting, halleluiahs, the amens were their expressions of feeling totally free for a short while, happiness that came in waves that flooded their whole being. When they shouted, Jim Crow wasn't on their minds.

Our poppa would give his listener hope by telling them about the Israelites' struggle, how through the mouth of Moses they were led through the wilderness, how some died there because of lack of faith. Hitting the podium with his fist, sweat running down his face, this illustrated the emotive force in the deep belief of our poppa that "God will lead his people and take them where they should go."

Momma told her children that once our poppa told her "Bracey, God has called me to preach."

"Of course, I saw it coming, but when he actually said it, the reality scared me. Me, a preacher's wife?" Momma said she has been around preachers' wives all her life. Her own momma was a preacher's wife; her poppa did the same thing our poppa did. One day out of the blue, he told her, "Roxie (that was her momma's name), God has called me to preach."

"Just like that, she became a preacher's wife. Men don't ask their wives; they just tell them. I'm going to do this, I'm going to do that. As though to say I'm the head you are the tail." She really didn't have a choice in the matter. Our momma wasn't comfortable being a preacher's wife. She was never one to want public attention. By nature, she was demure, and this gives us an idea of Momma's reserve.

Poppa was able to travel to different churches because he was one of the few young men who owned his own car. In 1938, at the age of thirty, our poppa owned a 1938 Chevy.

Poppa had traveled the ten-mile drive from Byhalia where he and his family lived at the time, often to Mt. Sinai because he was often asked to preach, doing some of their services, and this wasn't an easy drive. It was a drive on a bumpy, primitive dirt road. When it rains, you could not get in your car or truck and drive on it. You had to wait sometimes for the rain to stop because of so many mud holes where you may get stuck. And at other times the hard rain would wash the road away. Dirt roads came before gravel. This ten miles' drive from Byhalia, Poppa would occasionally pass antebellum houses sitting way back on their tremendous huge lawns that present calm and tranquility through the weeping willow and magnolia trees, with veranda that wraps around the front and sides of the vastly huge house that had all the reminders of slavery with wooden framed shacks nearby that poor Negroes lived in as they worked for their ex-slave masters.

During the planting and harvest season on this drive back in the "boondocks," as our momma would say, we would see Negro workers plowing, planting, chopping, or picking cotton. When a car passed, the workers would stop briefly, stand motionless, and give a friendly hello wave and a friendly goodbye wave with two sweeping motions at the passengers in the passing car before continuing their labor; we would all wave back. In Mississippi, all Negroes waved. No one passed and wasn't greeted with a friendly greeting.

As our poppa was driving his family to Mt. Sinai Church on this warm Sunday morning in early May of 1940, the roads and fields were eerily silent with the absence of workers in the fields. The landscape was blanketed with stillness that only Sunday could create because Sunday was considered a day of rest (Exodus 34:21): "Six days you shall work, but on the seventh day you shall rest." The expansive pasture was spread out on both sides of the dirt road. At a distance, herds of cattle, some standing, others lying, are comfortable under shade trees. Even further in the distance, horses were grazing on grass in the pastureland.

Momma was sitting up front with her husband. She had one small child in her lap and another, as we used to say, "in the oven," meaning she is pregnant with another. Momma used to say, "Get ready, we are going back into the 'boondocks.' Way in the backwoods where there is little appearance of civilization."

In 1940, Momma and Poppa had seven children—Cynthia, Sam Junior, Obadiah, Cozetta, Ruth, Christine, and Alfred. Consequently, when they took their children to church, the car was crammed full—three or four sitting on the car's backseat and each one has one of their siblings sitting on their lap. This was acceptable years before the invention of seatbelts. During these times, the safety of children was the parents' responsibility.

With their children crammed in the backseat, there would be hushed talk in the front between Poppa and Momma, with Momma leaning over closely to Poppa so she wouldn't miss any of his words and their children in the backseat couldn't hear grown folks' business.

Poppa said, "Grown-ups should be careful what they say around children because children are listening and they will tell others what their parents said. You know, I wouldn't be surprised if wars have been lost or won by children repeating what they overheard what their parents said and telling other children and those children telling their parents who were in the enemy camp. Children just don't have the ability to judge what should or shouldn't be said in public." Sometimes we would be real quiet. We may hear a name in their hushed conversation, like Mr. Wilkin, then we would hear soft whispers, leaving us children wondering what Mr. Wilkin had done. This would always be a mystery to us young children.

When Poppa approached this hill, Mr. Powell, a member of Mr. Sinai, was approaching the same hill in the other direction with his mule-driven wagon. Neither one saw the other coming; during these time, wagons and cars shared the road. The mule responded to this sudden and unexpected car and was frightened and started jumping and bolting. Mr. Powell pulled on the horse's halter.

"Whoa, mule! Halt! Whoa, Nelly!" Even trying to control the mule with the bridle and bit, he had great trouble bringing the old mule under control. The mule continued his jumping and bolting, standing on his two hind legs. Poppa's children in the backseat of the car started screaming, thinking our poppa's car was going to collide with the out-of-control mule and wagon. Momma said, "Oh my God, Sam! Be careful, you are at the extreme edge of the ditch!"

Poppa raised his voice to his panicked and frightened children in the backseat of the car. "Will y'all be quiet! Y'all are making matters worse!" Twelve-year-old Ruth sitting next to the back passenger door looked right up at the horse's two front uplifted legs as they appeared to be coming right down on top of the car. She covered her face with her hands and shrieked in fear, "Oh nooo!" The mule's two feet landed on the ground, missing the car by inches.

For what seemed like forever, the scared old mule calmed down. Mr. Powell afterward was, like the rest of us, very shaken as he and his old mule drove off, leaving clouds of dust hovering in the air. Poppa said with a little trembling still left in his hands as they still held a tight grip on the steering wheel, "That man knows that old mule is too old and sensitive to be pulling a wagon, too easily spooked. He ought to know better. That mule would do the same thing if a snake or anything crossed his path. Some of these animals haven't gotten used to the modern invention of cars. Some people haven't either, I must add."

Poppa had been taking his family on this ten-mile drive to Mt. Sinai for a while, to this old dilapidated framed church that was propped up by two by four to keep the church from falling. Tin buckets were spotted in several places inside the church, which were used to catch the water from the leaky tin roof when it rained; the church was built in 1884. The first structure was destroyed by fire and rebuilt in 1893. When Poppa announced that he had been "called to preach," this calling qualified him to sit in one of the clergy chairs with the pastor of the church, Reverend Suggs. Our poppa said that Reverend Suggs had told him that he was getting too old to carry on the responsibilities of the church and he thought that our poppa would fit the requirement.

Lloyd, Poppa's fourth son, said, "Poppa told Reverend Suggs that when he becomes pastor of Mt. Sinai, he will rebuild the church. In 1940, at the age of thirty-seven with the authority invested in them, the deacon placed our poppa as the pastor of Mt. Sinai Baptist Church.

Staying true to his word after becoming the church's pastor, our poppa pledged the first $300 to the building fund, which set the pledging in motion. Another building was constructed as rapidly as funds would permit. In 1946, the second corner was laid.

Our poppa therefore was granted more freedom of speech, and with the authority as a preacher, this gave him more influence in the Negro community. With the authority of persuasion, Poppa had to be cautious of what he said to his own people, be aware of his words. He should not sway them to anger against the white social order, to make them stay in the framework of humility and peace. Knowing the safety valve that Jim Crow had placed around, the Negro can easily rupture. Don't rock the boat, so to speak. "Vengeance is mine, I will repay," says the Lord.

As Poppa's popularity grew, the demands on him increased. Reverend Roger Person, an older preacher who was the pastor of Second Baptism Church where our poppa was a member and later became a pastor there himself, took a liking to our poppa and took him under his wing, so to speak. Our poppa knew that as a young preacher, he did not know how to handle all the growing demands that was placed upon him. God gave them both an example in the Bible to live by because they both read their bibles daily. They both read many times in Timothy 1 and 2 how the Apostle Paul gave Timothy advice. Reverend Roger Person knew Poppa would face all sorts of pressures, conflicts, and challenges from the church and surrounding culture.

Like Apostle Paul who gave Timothy fatherly advice, warning Timothy about false teachers and urging him to hold on to his faith in Christ, Rev. Roger Person gave our poppa the same advice.

Our poppa over the years had seen too many preachers get in deep trouble with the white authority when they started dipping and dabbing in southern politics and tried to tell whites what the Negroes think and feel. Most whites really were not interested in our feeling or what we think.

In 1917, when our poppa was nine years old, the Negro churches had constantly grown from its beginning in the 1700s. *The History of the Negro Church* by Carter G. Woodson writes,

> The first people proselyted by the Spanish and French missionaries were Indians. There were not any particular thought of the Negro. It may seem a little strange just now to think of persons having to be converted to faith in the

possibility of the salvation of the Negro, but there were among the colonists thousands who had never considered the Negro as belonging to the pale of Christianity. Negroes had been generally designated as infidels; but, in the estimation of their self-styled superiors, they were not considered the most desirable of this class supposedly arrayed against Christianity. There were few Christian who did not look forward to the ultimate conversion of those infidels approaching the Caucasian type, but hardly any desired to make an effort in the direction of proselyting Negroes.

Consequently, the Negro church like all of Black history in American was a long and difficult struggle to grow and survive against the greater White culture in America.

Our poppa often talked about the church, which held his greatest interest. The conversations of his father, his grandfather, and his great-grandfather Bill Gathing were all about the church and that their only hope was in God.

However, though, as time unfolded and Negroes were surrounded by writers like W. E. B. DuBois, Booker T. Washington, and Carter G. Woodson, who wrote *The Mis-education of the Negro*, and circumstances made it necessary for Negroes to travel more, they compared their lives to other who didn't live under the constraints of Jim Crow. Through these writings and travel, the Negroes started seeing the whites in a different light, seeing some of them as not being fully human. "Why are they so mean?" our momma used to say.

Of course, we will never know for sure how extremely difficult for our poppa to read these books and still walk the tight rope of Jim Crow. But one thing we do know, there had to be many depressing moments for our poppa to know the truth of himself and pretend that he didn't know the reality of himself as a child of God. Gandhi said, "The woes of Mahatmas are known to Mahatmas alone." Some pains are so deep in the soul of a man that words cannot express them. The expressed word will probably cause the sufferer to weep. Someone has said, "A man isn't supposed to cry."

# 6

## They Bought Land

Once our poppa became the pastor of Mt. Sinai, the ten-mile drive from Byhalia became more frequent. To be near to his church, he started thinking of buying land near the church. Poppa and Momma had been discussing buying their land even before their ten years' marriage and before their ten children. Our poppa said Mrs. Helen Echols, a widow and one of his church members, wanted to sell her 150 acres' land right across from Mt. Sinai. To our poppa, in 1952, this was the perfect location.

Breaking the news to our momma probably wasn't easy because Momma had made it clear that she didn't enjoy the ride back in the "boondocks."

Our poppa said he knew that Mt. Sinai or the land he was considering buying wasn't in the best location. Some things Momma had said about the location were true. The roads had to be one of the worst in the area. However, in 1952, the land that our poppa wanted to buy was approximately twenty-one dollars per acre. The four-bedroom log house with three fireplaces would keep his boys busy cutting wood to keep his family warm in the winter months, and the house was large enough for his growing family. The property also had several apple, peach, and pear trees. Nearby were blackberries, figs, wild plum trees, and grapevines.

Within a short time, Momma knew she couldn't resist her husband's decision even moving back in the "boondocks." Our momma's close-knit family of two brothers and eight sisters doubted the decision of her husband to move back yonder. Considering the times in which they lived, both of my parents' families were considered middle class, owning their land on which they lived. Owning land was a status symbol of success. "Why back there?" they asked because they all lived near the convenience of the nearby towns of Byhalia and Oliver Branch.

Our poppa and momma were moving from the rented land and house within walking distance of Byhalia. The small town had the typical post office, general store, a doctor too.

The town is laid out with the railroad tracks running straight alongside of the town. We could hear the whistle bellow as the train rolled through. Even with the overcast of Jim Crow, this southern town had a quite calm peace if the law of the superiority of the whites wasn't forgotten. On the outskirts of town, there is the feeling of farm life, where farm animals are gazing in their pasture.

Before our poppa bought his 150 acres' farm, Me, Shug, and Alberta would climb to the top of the slope bordering the train tracks and sit there. As the train passed by, we waved at the conductors, and they waved back at us. Roberta would often lead her sisters into the fancy of jumping the train and going all the way to New York to an exciting city life. She had heard and even read about the life of a hobo.

"We can just jump the train like I read once about these hobos, who would get on the train and sleep in one of the empty cars without anyone knowing they were there and ride all the way to New York City," Roberta said.

"Girl, you are crazy! No way will I do that," Alberta said.

"That sounds like a good idea to me. We will never have to chop or pick cotton again," Shug said. And our daydreaming would continue how we could pack all our belongings into a pillowcase, tie a string around it, and tie it on a long stick just like the hobos Roberta had read about, getting off the train at one of its night stops so we won't be noticed, finding work during the day so we could have money when we get to New York City. After arriving in New York, we will have enough money to get a small apartment and be free at last!

Of course, reality pulled us back for now. The dream never did really leave Roberta. The more she read, the more she knew she would see a larger world. Geography and history always held her interest; the study of other people, places, and land held a strong passion in her to visit these unfamiliar cultures. China, Middle East, Africa, Brazil—cultures that were different from America. Even daydreaming about these faraway places freed her consciousness to a larger world far beyond Mississippi. The books she read pulled her imagination to the exoticness of faraway places.

Years later when she had migrated up north in the 1960s, working in a factory, this gave her enough money to buy many books she wasn't able to buy before. James Michener became one of her favorite authors. How could she not want to go to Hawaii after reading James Michener's very descriptive, extraordinary, thrilling panorama and fascinating detail writing on Hawaii? His book on Alaska was so vivid, the scenery so very, very pretty. It took her through the history of an ancient land, and she knew she had to experience it: "In the valley down which the glacier came ended at the shoreline, the towering face of ice would come right to the edge of the ocean, wherein due time fragments of the glacier, sometimes as big as cathedrals, sometimes bigger, would break away with resounding cracks that would reverberate through the air for many miles as the resulting iceberg crashed into the ocean, where it would ride as an independent entity for months and even decades."

Books became a big part of her life. Immediately after picking up a book, as the title suggested that it might hold her interest, in her mind she would start searching for a quiet spot that's at times difficult to find. Getting away from external noise and distraction was nearly impossible where sounds weren't far away. Sometimes Roberta would fantasize about living in a log cabin in the woods where the only sounds were birds chirping, occasional hoots of a distant owl, maybe the sighting of deer with one of James Michener's books pulling her imagination into another time and place, finding refuge in a separate world, unlike her own.

However, in the 1950s, at twelve years old, Roberta hadn't been introduced to big books. She found comfort in reading *Reader's Digest* and *True Love Story*, a women's magazine that brought inspiration to the closeness, intimacy, and friendship of males and females, family, and friendship. The comic strip in Poppa's Sunday paper was her escape for now.

The night before October 18, 1952, was filled with anxious excitement tantamount to Christmas Eve for a small child. We could hear our poppa talking throughout the night. Momma was silent because our momma, unlike our poppa, didn't let expectations disturb her sleep. "Bracey can sleep through the worst of storms." Because of the upcoming signing of the final paper on the ownership of their land, Poppa experienced trouble sleeping.

Earlier that morning during breakfast and after Poppa had blessed our food, he opened the conversation by saying, "I want to tell you what I dreamt about last night." Our poppa was a big believer in dreams: "God speaks to man through dreams and visions."

"I dreamt that I was standing on my own land looking across a large green pasture that had many cattle of different colors. And I looked up into the sky and there were dark clouds and white clouds."

Roberta asked, "Poppa, what do that means?"

"I think, girl, that this land is going to bring success and problems. I'm telling you, children, that's the way of the world. The Bible says we will have trials and tribulations as long as we live."

Poppa continued. "The road has been long and sometimes rugged with hardships and troubles that come with life. Life can be stormy sometimes, but we must praise God in the midst of our troubles because blessing can be found in storms."

On the morning of October 18, Momma and Poppa were in their bedroom. Momma was assisting her husband as though he was dressing for church. The room smelled of cigarettes, Old Spice, and the sweet smell of our momma' perfumed dusting power. The wrought iron bed has been neatly made up, covered with an egg white bedspread. On the dresser was Poppa's worn leather-covered KJV Bible.

Poppa had on his dark suit trouser, white starched shirt that Momma had ironed the day before, and spotless black shoes that Momma had polished the night before. Momma, as usual, was standing a few inches shorter than her five-foot-eight husband tying his necktie. Next, she got his suit coat that was lying on top of their made-up bed. She had already inspected the coat for lint and was now assisting him with his coat as though he was a small boy. Once his suit coat was comfortably on, she gave him a gentle stroke on each shoulder as though brushing off a missed speck of lint, but in reality was her final touch of approval.

It was Momma's turn to get dressed once she was satisfied that her husband was properly dressed and has met her approval. Momma's dressing, unlike her husband in which she is the only participant, is a family affair. All of her children who are present had an opinion on what she should wear and how she should look once dressed. Poppa was dressed and sitting comfortably in the front room reading his Bible because it was his wife's turn to get dressed. Seeing our poppa dressed was a signal for Cozetta to put aside the large pan of green peas she was shelling, for Ruth to stop sweeping the kitchen floor, and for Cynthia to stop washing the dishes and go in our parents' bedroom to assist our momma in dressing. Not that Momma needed their help; they just thought they knew best. Five-year-old Peggy sitting on the floor near the cast-iron heater rubbing her golden cat Tommy suddenly leaped off the floor and followed her sisters into Momma's bedroom and climbed into Poppa and Momma's bed because she loved being in her parents room, even enjoying the smell of it and especially enjoyed seeing her older sisters helping her momma get dressed.

Ruth reached for Momma's black dress. Cozetta said, "No, not that one, she should wear the blue dress which would look good with her black hat." Cynthia said, "Momma can't wear the blue dress because her hat wouldn't match it." Cozetta won the first round; Momma put on the blue dress. "No, not that purse, it won't look right with those shoes," Ruth said.

If anyone had asked Momma how she felt about all this attention, she probably would have said, "Young girls know more about dressing than older women."

They knew they were going to receive the blessing that God had prepared for them. Momma's daughters had dressed her beautifully for this very special occasion in a blue long-sleeved dress that hung about three inches below her knees. Her black low-heel shoes were accented by silk seamed socking, the stocking seams running down the back center of her legs. "Momma, your seams are crooked."

Poppa reached for his hat on the kerosene lamp table near his old wicker chair near the heater. Momma had her purse, meaning they were all ready to go to the title company. Their children were gathered in the front room to see them off on this memorable day in their lives. Standing near Momma, Peggy looked up at her. "Mommy, can I go?"

Looking down on her baby girl with warm feelings of love, she said, "Baby, you can't go this time. The next time, I will take you with me, okay?"

Peggy said, "Momma, you look so pretty."

"Thank you, baby," she said as she bent down, giving her a hug, Peggy smelling the sweet scent of Momma's perfumed dusting powder as her face was pressing against Momma's neck, feeling downhearted because Momma was going away. Momma said that whenever she had to leave Peggy, she had to struggle with the feeling of abandonment; it was always painful to see the sad look upon her little face.

On this October day, the sun was shining as though the universe was in agreement with the blessings our parents were getting ready to receive. The ten-mile scenic drive from Byhalia to Holly Springs was unusually quiet for Momma and Poppa. Probably, everything that needed to be said has been said already.

Poppa removed his dark gray hat and held it uneasily in his hand before entering the title company office. He had a stern, serious look on his face. As Momma looked at her husband, a look that only a wife could discern, she knew her husband was extremely nervous. They both walked nervously into the title company office. In the entrance hung a large picture of President Dwight D. Eisenhower and a picture of the governor of Mississippi, Hugh L. White. He probably could feel the power of the men as their eyes stared down upon him. Our poppa probably wanted to stop briefly as though in a museum and reflect upon this moment because he had read much about both of these men. He knew it would be disrespectable to keep the title company waiting, so this moment in time was bypassed.

Poppa probably had to resist the urge to hold his wife's hand, remembering that colored people weren't supposed to show emotions in public.

Upon entering the title company office, a pretty blond white girl about twenty looked up from behind her desk and greeted Momma and Poppa with a warm smile. "Good morning, Sam, and you too, Beatrice."

"Good morning, ma'am," Poppa and Momma said at the same time.

"Why, Sam, this is a big day for you and your wife."

"Yes-sum, it sure is," Poppa replied.

"Y'all can sit." The girl pointed at the two chairs right in front of her desk. With them comfortably seated, the young girl handed Poppa a big Bic ballpoint pen and several pieces of papers to sign. Poppa may have felt uncomfortable signing these legal documents before reading them, but to read them would be showing the white establishment disrespect. Our poppa was probably hoping the trembling in his hand wouldn't show.

With our poppa signing and Momma's signature right below his, they became landowners. The pleasant young woman stood and shook their hands, congratulating them. Momma and Poppa looked at one another with great joy. Momma said, "Thank you, Sam." Poppa probably wanted to jump up and shout like the way he does when he was preaching. Praising God!

On this pleasant fall day in November, the leaves were putting on their fall colors of red, golden brown, and yellow. Our poppa carried away all his thirty heads of cattle and all of his goods that he had gotten in Byhalia from his rented land to his own land ten miles away: "Your wife, and your little ones, and your cattle shall abide in the land I have given you" (Deuteronomy. 3:19).

Poppa and Momma's large family of fourteen children began their life in their log house with electricity, but indoor plumbing hadn't arrived yet. Our water source was an outdoor dug well from which we draw water by using a rope with a bucket at the end of it, using a pulley to pull the rope with the bucket full of water from the well. Water from the well was brought into the house for our daily usage. We usually took baths once a week. Saturday was considered bath time using water that was heated on the wood-burning stove in a cast-iron tea kettle. The same tin tub that our family used for washing our laundry on a corrugated tin washing board was also used for bathing. Because of the labor that was required to get water, several members of the family used the same water because water wasn't wasted. "Whose turn is it to draw water?" Momma would ask.

When Poppa's children, especially the girls, reached the age of sixteen, which was considered the age that boys could come to visit, they were being chaperoned by Poppa and Momma by sitting on the front porch while their daughters are sitting with their boyfriends in the living room or the front room, as we used to say. If the girls had taken a bath the day before, to make sure they smelled fresh for their boyfriend, they would probably take a sponge bath, which we called a washup. They did this by heating a small amount of warm water and putting it in a bowl-like pan and bathing the necessary parts of their bodies to smell fresh.

The ancient use of night pails and outhouse was still in usage waiting for indoor plumbing. The night pail was a tin bucket with a lid to control the stink that was usually kept under the bed for night use that the family used as a substitute toilet, which was call a "slop jar." "Whose turn is it to dump the 'slop jar'?" The outhouse looks like a modern-day portable potty built from faded scrap wood with the seat having the same design as a modern-day toilet commode without the lid, also made out of the same faded wood sitting over a manmade hole to catch the excrements. Once inside, the stink was overwhelming. If you are lucky while sitting there, someone has left a newspaper because toilet paper hadn't reached the "boondocks." Washing your hands wasn't a convenient option because water was only found where Mother Nature put it; the resources to transport water from its sources to where it was needed wasn't available.

The serious consequence of not washing hands was unknown to the uneducated, the educated, the rich, and the poor alike:

> Dr. Semmelweis in 1847discovered that cases of puerperal fever, a form of septicaemia also known as childbed fever, could be cut drastically if doctors washed their hands in a chlorine solution before gynaecological examinations. At the time, diseases were attributed to many different and unrelated causes. Each case was considered unique, just as a human person is unique. Semmelweis's hypothesis, that there was only one cause that all that mattered was cleanliness, was extreme at the time, and was largely ignored, rejected or ridiculed. He was dismissed from the hospital for political reasons and harassed by the medical community in Vienna, being eventually forced to move to Paris. (I thank *Wikipedia* for the information on Dr. Semmelweis.)

No one can imagine the inconvenience of living without indoor plumbing unless you've lived during a time before it existed. Imagine if you can, going all day even more sometimes without washing your hands. Washing hands wasn't even thought to be important. When blowing their nose (some men would rub the excess snot on their dirty clothes they had on), they would just take their dirty hand and blow their nose, aiming at the ground with some of the snot (mucus) getting on their hand. No big deal, they would just wipe what's remaining on their clothes using their clothing as a handkerchief—coughing and sneezing, no hankie, shaking hands with each other's dirty hands. How did we live to tell about it? Only through the grace of God.

# 7

## The Mourner's Bench

Our poppa was very much aware of his children approaching the age of accountabilities, meaning they are accountable for their sins. They must have increased knowledge in the awareness of God and the price Jesus paid by dying on the cross for their sins.

When the children reached their preteens, they were expected to go on the mourner's bench, seeking forgiveness for their sins and asking Jesus to be their Savior. A mourner's bench was a bench that's in the first pew in front of the sanctuary that's reserved for the soon-to-be converts to Christ, where they will be throwing themselves to the mercy of the Lord: "Lord, please have mercy on me a sinner."

On this warm day in August 1954, everyone was excited about the upcoming revival. The night before revival is bath night.

It was time to get her hair fixed, and Roberta prepared for this process by sitting comfortably in a chair near the stove with a towel across her shoulders with a slight bend of her head downward while she put one hand on each ear, bending them slightly so that her sister won't accidentally burn them with the hot pressing comb. Cynthia, our older sister, was standing near the cast-iron stove where she was using the heat from the wood-burning stove to heat the pressing comb to press Alberta's and Roberta's hair the night before. She had a white rag folded on top of the stove near where the pressing comb was heating to test the comb to make sure it wasn't too hot. By laying the hot comb on the white rag, if the hot comb burned the surface of the rag, this let Cynthia know that the comb is too hot and would burn Roberta's hair like it burned the rag. As she was pulling the hot pressing comb through Roberta's kinky hair, trying to straighten it using Royal Crown Hair oil, smoke was rising from the hot comb like smoke from incense, carrying the odor of the hot hair oil when the hot comb hit the hot hair oil on Roberta's hair, melting the oil that ran down to Roberta's scalp.

"Ouch! You burned me!"

Cynthia popped her gently in the head. "You better be still or you are going to get burned again!" Cynthia loved to sing when she was busy. As she was pressing Roberta's hair, she was singing, *"Like a ship that toss and driven battered by an angry sea . . . when the storms of life are raging, the Lord will make a way, somehow."* She stopped pressing Roberta's hair and started singing and dancing the foxtrot to her own singing.

Roberta said, "Cynthia, hurry up, you take too long."

"Girl, don't sass me." Their hair was straight and smelling like Royal Crown pressing oil after Cynthia finished pressing their hair. Their routine after getting their hair "done" was to get their homemade brown paper bag rollers that had been cut up in strips about one and a half inch wide and about six inches long, twist each strip, and use them as rollers. These rollers were reused many times; the oil from their hair after each use made them easier to handle.

On this day of preparation, our house was bustling with activities. Christine would holler, "Somebody has one of my stockings!" "Anybody seen the big black comb?" Seven-year-old Lloyd would speak loudly, "I can't find one of my shoes!" "Where is the black shoe polish?"

Our house of fourteen children was a very crowded nest—full of lively hurly-burly. "Who stole the last cookies?" "Save that last piece of chicken for your poppa." "Somebody cut a big slug out of my cake that I was saving for Sunday's dinner." "Whose turn is it to tote some wood in the house?"

Roberta and Alberta were anxious, nervous, and excited about the week of revival because at eleven years old, it was their turn for the mourner's bench. They were in the girls' room getting dressed in their brand-new Sunday clothes Poppa had bought them for the exciting event. Poppa and Momma had taken them to Holly Springs and bought them everything new—new underwear, new socks, and pretty black patent leather shoes. Each of the twins had identical black polka-dot dresses. As Alberta and Roberta were getting dressed, Roberta was standing behind her sister, buttoning her dress because young girls' dresses had a row of buttons running down the back just below the waist; and when she finished, she would tie the ties that hung down from each side of the waist of the dress, forming a bow in the back of her waist. When Roberta finished buttoning and tying her sister's bow, it was Alberta's turn to return the favor. Roberta looked at her twin and asked, "Alberta, how did you get that black spot on your dress?"

"Oh, Roe, I was hoping you wouldn't notice it because of all the black dots. My pretty dress is ruined, ain't it?"

"No, Alberta, it's barely noticeable between the black dots. How did it happen?"

"Well, yesterday, I tried my dress on when we came from Holly Springs, and Momma had given me a dime to polish her shoes. I didn't want to take my pretty new dress off, so I polished Momma's shoes in my new dress, and some polish got on my dress." Roberta looked at her twin and hugged her because she thought Alberta was getting ready to cry.

Onlookers would say, "Oh, there are the twins, aren't they cute?"

Typically, when a child enters the beginning of his or her teens, church members put focus on him or her because this is the age when a child usually begins to feel a draw by the Holy Spirit and recognizes that he or she must seek salvation from sin. However, a person can feel this draw at a much younger or older age—once a year, the church would do a revival service. Members met nightly for a week. The church believed that a young person must be drawn by the Holy Spirit to seek God, and that salvation isn't automatic (1 Timothy 3:8-13).

Alberta told Roberta later that the spot on her new dress hurt her to her soul. After we all arrived at church, she told Momma she needed to go to the toilet. "Hurry, child, you can't be late."

"Yes-sum," Alberta said. She hated going to the outhouse because the stink made her sick. But she had to go and pray. So she took a deep breath before going in so she wouldn't have to breathe once inside. It was awful, Alberta said, no one had cleaned it in a long time. The floor and the seat were covered with filth. She quickly begin to pray, "Jesus, save my soul and wash my dress as clean as snow."

"*Jesus will wash you as clean as snow,*" that was the song she heard Poppa sing. *Jesus will wash you clean as snow.*

On this very special event, the ten or more boys and girls were all dressed in their Sunday's best. They were waiting in the church foyer for their grand entrance for they were the reason for this very special event. The bench up front was reserved for them. Their parents had turned them over to the church. Before going into the church, their mommies and papas had given them a gentle hug.

"May God bless you, child." Our momma leaned over to her eleven-year-old twin daughters. "Roberta and Alberta, I love you, but God loves you more." She gave them a gentle hug. With the hug came the sweet smell of our momma's perfumed dusting powder.

"Yes-sum, Momma." Now they were in the hands of the three ushers in the church's foyer dressed in white dresses, gloves, shoes, and hats that looked just like what nurses wear in the hospital.

When the choir started singing, "*I'm going through; I'll pay the price* no matter *what other do . . . I'll take the way that the lord told me to, I'm going through,*" this was the usher's clue to bring the young people in, leading them to the front bench. As they were walking in the crowded church with teary eyes, everyone stood to welcome them.

The children that the Holy Spirit called would all sit on the front bench, a bench that was called the "mourner's bench." Our poppa was the pastor of Mt. Sinai and was sitting in the pulpit in one of the red velvet clerical chairs with legs crossed. Two guest ministers sat by our poppa's side, one to his left with the other one to his right. A large picture of the white blue-eyed Jesus hung high on the wall behind the pulpit, looking down on the sanctuary. The choir was sitting in its reserved pew. Several of Poppa's daughters were members of the choir—eighteen-year-old Ruth was directing the choir while Cozetta, Christine, and Shug sang with the choir on this Monday night.

Poppa, with Bible in hand, rose slowly out of his clergy chair. "Lord, we thank you for this revival, for the saving of souls. Jesus, we are asking you for your mercy and blessings all through this week of revival meeting. May we feel Your Holy Spirit throughout the week. Come, children, give your heart to Jesus." Reaching out his hands, he said, "Won't you come? Jesus is waiting, please come. You don't want to be lost in hell's eternal fire where there will be burning and gnashing of teeth."

As our poppa was standing at the podium looking down on the mourner's bench, his Bible was clenched in his fist. "You are all sinners like we were before we came to Jesus." Mumbling in agreement ran through the congregation. "And as sinner, you are condemned unless you give your heart to Jesus! You can't wait until tomorrow because you could be dead tomorrow." Roberta looked at Poppa and remembered all the funerals she and her sisters and brothers were forced to attend. Old dead people, people she didn't even know. We were just going to church with our poppa when he preached at a funeral. As Poppa said those words, she wondered how many of those old people were in hell and how many were in heaven. She knew she didn't want to die and go to the everlasting fire of hell. "Lord Jesus, save me!" she prayed.

Roberta used to try to understand a place where time didn't end. No matter how hard she tried, she always saw an end. Her thoughts were that everything had to end sooner or later, doesn't it? Once, she asked Poppa, "Poppa, how can anything don't have an ending?"

"Girl, if God says there will be no end, then it's the truth."

"But, Poppa—"

"Girl, you ask too many questions."

When our poppa finished preaching, it was now time for the four or five elders of the church to come and pray and sing to the mourners. Many old people came and knelt, also standing, as they sang while clapping their hands, singing spiritual songs of joy.

Alberta was sitting on the bench next to Roberta with the other mourners, and as the elders were clapping their hands so close to the mourners' faces, the mourners could feel the air that was forced out between the elders' hands as they were clapping and singing.

*I got rid of my heavy load.*
*Somebody got rid of their heavy load on Monday.*
*Somebody stand up today and say they got rid of their*
*heavy load.*
*On a Tuesday I got rid of my heavy load.*

and

*Come on mourner in the army of the Lord*
*You've to die in the army of the Lord.*

As the singing and praying continued, Alberta said something came over her. She felt a warm feeling of love cover her like a blank. The love was so strong that she started weeping. The elders saw her crying, and they gave more attention to her. *"Come on, mourner, in the army of the lord."* Alberta said she felt light as a feather and then she started shouting and praising and thanking Jesus. Momma, as usual, was sitting in the pew that was reserved for priority seating. Once Momma saw Alberta weeping, our shy momma was overcome with emotions as she started weeping, reaching into her purse and pulling out her pretty white cotton handkerchief trimmed in flora pink and blue lace that Cozetta had given her for Christmas, crying with joy that another one of her children had been saved from eternal damnation. Poppa stood up from his clergy chair, "Lord Jesus, the angels in heaven is shouting and glorifying God because another soul has been saved."

On this warm Monday night, the very first night of the week-long revival, Alberta's prayers were answered. Jesus heard her prayer in the foul, stinking outhouse. One of the ushers led her to the bench that was reserved for the new converts. When she sat down, she was surprised to see the ink spot still on her dress. *"You will be washed white as snow."* She said she didn't feel as white as snow because her dress wasn't clean. She wondered why Jesus left the spot on her pretty dress.

On Wednesday night, the fourth of August, Roberta was sitting on the mourner's bench before the elders started to sing and Poppa was still preaching "as a sinner you are on the way to eternal hell fire. Today is the day of salvation."

Roberta was sitting on the mourner's bench when she remembered the vision she had the night before as she was lying on the girls' wrought-iron bed that was shared with her two sisters, Alberta and Betty Joe, beneath a quilt that Momma had stitched by hand. Her place in bed being near the window, she looked out the bedroom window, gazing at the full moon's night sky, which was often done with her sisters and brothers when they were playing outdoors on those warm Mississippi nights to escape the stifling indoor heat. These were the nights of summer where we would occasionally see falling stars. Look, pointing to the sky, look yonder, see the falling star! Hurry, make a wish! Way up yonder was a playground for our imagination—where God lives, where Jesus lives, sending down blessing, and where angels lived, too. The streets there were paved with gold. We felt a strong connection to the universe. We thought that someday when we get to heaven, we will walk and play on the Milky Way.

Roberta was completely engrossed in thoughts of heaven and hell. It seemed like grown-ups were always talking about heaven and hell. "If you won't be good, you're going to hell. You want to go to heaven, don't you?" She said she thought that if she could stare into the night sky long enough, Jesus would show her the third heaven like He showed Apostle Paul: "caught up to the third heaven."

She kept this gaze while she was propped up on her pillows. It was easy to imagine that the universe was teeming with life; the reflection of the full moon was the only light present in the room, and the room was quiet as she lay in bed that was shared with her two sisters. Once her two sisters had finished with the tossing and turning—"Get your cold feet off mine" "Stop breathing in my face" "You're breathing in my face too" "Get off my pillow" "It's my pillow too"—they finally were asleep with the sounds of their breathing and the sucking sound coming from six-year-old Betty Joe as she sucked on her right hand's two middle fingers, using them as her pacifier, the only sounds in the room.

Roberta felt the presence of love pull her attention from her preoccupation with the full moon starlit sky, and when she slowly turned her attention to the foot of their bed, there stood an angelic being, cloaked in a glowing white soft chiffon garment. For some reason, this didn't frighten her. The presence of this angelic being radiated love and peace. She looked at me and faded away. I knew that the Holy Spirit had sent her to comfort me. Even at eleven years old, I knew that.

At breakfast and after the family was all sitting around the table, Poppa blessed our food, and as usual, Poppa opened the conversation by asking, "What did you all dreamed about last night?" Some remembered, some didn't.

"Poppa," Roberta interjected. "I saw an angel at the foot of my bed last night." Everyone stopped eating and looked at Roberta.

"What?" Fred said. "You mean you dreamed about an angel?"

"No, I was wide awake because I had been looking out our bedroom window at the stars, hoping to see a falling star, and by it being a full moon last night, the room was partially bright from the light of the moon. I felt a warm sense of love, and I turned my head and looked at the foot of my bed, and there stood an angelic being dressed in glossy white garment."

Lloyd said, "I believe you, Roberta, because I was out in the woods hunting for rabbits one night and I saw this bouncing light that looked just like a basketball, bouncing right along all by itself."

Fred started laughing. "Man, that make me think of the time I was in the woods and I saw this old man looking just like Rip van Winkle. His long white beard was hanging below his waist, and he walked straight through a big old oak tree just like it wasn't even there." Everyone laughed.

Poppa looked at Roberta. "I believe you because the Bible speaks of angels, speaks of angelic beings visiting people on earth. An angel came to Mary, the mother of Jesus, in Luke 1:31: 'Behold, Mary, you shall conceive in your womb and bring forth a son and shall call His name JESUS.' God sent an angel to minister to Jesus."

Poppa continued. "The Bible speaks of angels in many places. The cherubim who are angelic beings were in the Garden of Eden, they guard the tree of life. Everyone who love the Lord, God has assigned them an angel. Angels are real, Roberta, and don't you forget it."

"Yes-sum, Poppa." No one laughed. After a few seconds of silence, as an afterthought with a somber expression on his face, Poppa, while holding his fork of eggs in midair, paused and asked, looking across the table at Roberta, "Did the angel speak to you, girl?"

"No, sir, the angel just stood at the foot of our bed, didn't say nothing, and slowly faded away."

"Lord, that's something, all right," Momma said with a slight giggle.

"I don't know about seeing things that can come and go and disappear at will," Shug said. "Momma, I'm in agreement with you. I don't want to see anything that can disappear."

The conversation about ghosts and angels continued throughout breakfast.

Poppa and Momma would often ask Roberta to tell them about her vision; they pondered upon it and discussed it among themselves. At church, as Roberta walked past, she would hear a grown-up say, "Is that the one who saw an angel?"

Roberta said, as she was sitting on the mourner's bench, the remembrance of the vision of the angelic being was strongly with her.

"I could feel his presence even as I sit there. When the elders started singing, *something got ahold of me, oh yes, it did. I went to a meeting one night, something got ahold of me. I was on the mourner's bench, they were sing come yea who love the Lord and I thought they were singing to me. The same God that laid His hands on my mother laid his hands on me.*"

Roberta said that as the singing continued, she felt lighter and lighter, felt that she could actually fly. The words were ringing in her head, and she heard the words of her Poppa: "Come to Jesus, today is the day of salvation." She felt not on her own volition but overwhelmingly divine in nature, the pull of love that surrounded her poppa. Although the sanctuary was filled with hallelujahs and praises to God, Roberta said she felt a hush silence fall upon the church. She was only aware of the presence of her poppa in the pulpit; it seemed to her that the very presence of Jesus Himself was in the pulpit standing right beside her poppa.

*Come little children, come to Jesus*—she was caught up in the Spirit, and she felt like she was flowing by divine intervention toward her poppa. She felt as though her feet were gliding right above the surface of the floor. "*Something had a hold of me, oh it must be God.*" Roberta said later, "I remember being lifted up, up, and not on my own accord, and the next thing I remember, I was in the pulpit with Poppa hugging me and him and the whole church was praising God."

More of the mourners would begin to shout, signifying that they had received the Holy Spirit. The whole church would rejoice with them, shouting and praising the Lord that a soul had been saved. And when the new convert had finished shouting, they would be placed near the altar, meaning they have come to Jesus. This ritual would continue once a year for a week.

# Baptism

O n this hot and sultry day in July, Cozetta's and Momma's flowerbed of zinnia, peonies, coreopsis, and marigolds were in full blossom and provided a brilliant burst of colors near the front porch of our old faded log wood house, which accented our house along the ground of the full length of the front porch that runs the full length of our log house. The fresh delightful sweet fragrance from their flowers was a welcome greeting. Alberta and Roberta were feeling that they were truly a child of God. That if they died this very moment, they would go to be in heaven with Jesus. They both knew they came to Jesus.

Preparations for baptism started in the Gathing household right after revival. The week-long wait was very eventful. We heard the pedaling from the foot-pedaled Singer's sewing machine as our momma was doing the final touches on our white robes that she was making from white fabric she had bought from the department store. Once we were baptized, our sinful old garment would be replaced by our white robes of purity and now we would be married to Jesus. With the background noise of our momma pedaling her Singer's sewing machine, her twin daughters were in the girls' room waiting upon the finish of their white robes.

The night before, the talk was all about the baptism. Alberta and Roberta was in quiet chitchat about the closure of their commitment to service God and obey Jesus. The children who had gone before warned them about how cold the water will be.

"Girl, the water is ice cold," Shug said, "and y'all better be careful when y'all walk into the water. The floor of the pond is muddy, mushy, and slippery with mud swishing between your toes. When Fred was baptized, the deacons had to lift him up because he almost fell."

Ruth overheard this as she was on her way into the front room to do some writing for Poppa. Entering the room, she walked over to her two little sisters, standing between them and putting her arms around their shoulders. "Shug, stop trying to scare them." Pulling her sisters close to her, she said, "Don't be afraid, baptism isn't nothing to be afraid of. Jesus isn't going to let nothing happen to y'all, okay?" This gave Roberta and Alberta a small amount of confident and reassuring.

Ruth's mind and heart was on Poppa. She had her lined note tablet and a big yellow pencil in her hand, looking forward to taking notes for Poppa as he sat comfortably in his green leather chair in the living room with a serious, intense look upon his face, in deep thought because he took his messages very serious, pondering and collecting his thoughts. Ruth pulled up a chair and sat close to Poppa.

"Okay, girl, you can write that down." With the smell from his tobacco pipe permeating the front room, Ruth took a few notes for him, which she frequently did, regarding his sermon as he was preparing his sermon for baptism.

These were always precious moments for Ruth. She loved being near her poppa. Parents recognize all the special gifts in their children at their young and tender age, and our poppa was no different. His eighteen-year-old daughter Ruth was his secretary doing all of his routine work that he needed in writing. "Now, girl, read that back to me. Yep, that sounds good."

Finally, the sewing machine was silent. Momma had finished. Cynthia and Cozetta were standing near Momma, waiting for the final touches on their sisters' robes. Once Momma had cut the last thread with her scissors, with a sigh of release, she said, "All done." Cozetta and Cynthia came in the girls' room with the finished product of their sisters' white robes draped across their arms.

"Here they are, girls," Cozetta said with a big smile.

Alberta and Roberta both were filled with awe and overwhelming sense of the love of Jesus upon first seeing their pearly white robes, actually fighting back tears. Cozetta and Cynthia were both aware of the spiritual significance of the event for they had experienced it themselves; their remembrance of their own baptism was frozen in their minds.

A few weeks after revival services, our poppa, family, and church members, the choir also, would stand on the grasses' bank of the pond, which served as a staging point for baptism, like penguins near the ocean shore with the rest of us. Old and young men shaking each other's rough, calloused working-man hands dressed in their Sunday's best, even standing on the grasses' bank of the pond, their black shoes sparkling through the tall grass. The soft, pleasant greetings of "So good to see you, how are the kids?" could be heard. The warm summer breeze carried the sweet fragrance of cheap perfume and Old Spice from the close-knit crowd. Momma and her children were standing in front of the background chatter in the crowd behind them. Out of respect for their pastor, the very front of the crowd was reserved for their pastor and his family.

Momma was dressed in a pretty pink floral dress and was wearing a beige hat with a matching purse that has met her daughters' approval. She has a soft, gentle, bashful look as she held five-year-old Peggy's hand. Momma had seen several of her children baptized, and each time, with each child, the experience was new and great, intense spiritual emotion would swell up in her deep inner being. Once she saw one of her children dunked and raised up out of the water with water dripping off his or her face gasping for breath, breathing in the new life of Jesus Christ, she would start to weep with joy. Momma's children would gather around to comfort her with Cozetta leading the way, and they would weep also.

Before our poppa led the converts into the water, a deacon would assist him with his robe, and Poppa would preach a short sermon. "Jesus was baptized in water before he started his ministry, now listen closely." He spoke to the converts. "Once you are baptized, don't take it lightly. Old things are pasted away, meaning you don't do the sinful things you used to do, you are now a new creation. Do you understand?" All eight of the children said, "Yes-sum." After a brief prayer, the choir sang.

*I looked over Jordan,*
*And WHAT did I see,*
*Comin' for to carry me home,*
*A band of angels comin' after me,*
*Comin' for to carry me home.*

After the singing, the deacon assisted our poppa with one deacon on his right and one on his left to lead him into the pond and also to make sure he didn't slip and fall. The new converts were standing on the bank, all eight dressed in their white robes, anxiously waiting their turn to go into the water. The caretakers of the converts were taking the opportunity during this time for last-minute preparations for their young loved ones. Cozetta and Ruth were tying a white cloth that made one think of Aunt Jemima around Roberta's and Alberta's straight oily hair that still had the strong scent of Royal Crown Hair oil from Cynthia's pressing their hair the night before. Their white robes were now on, covering their blue jeans and long-sleeved blouse beneath. They would be leaving their sandals in the care of their two older sisters, of course, entering the water barefooted.

Alberta and Roberta were standing next to each other as they were waiting to go into the pond. Roberta's attention was pulled to the activities of the buzzards hovering low in the distant sky. This made her think of death, knowing that if an animal died, the buzzards were there to hover, suspended in midair, anticipating their next meal. She said later that she was going to ask Poppa if there was a heaven or hell for animals.

Alberta said later that all she could think of was the things Fred had said about almost falling. She whispered to Roberta, "I hope we don't slip and fall."

"Me too," Roberta responded softly. It would be many years before churches had indoor pool for baptism. Two of the deacons of the church had gone into the pond before our poppa to measure the depth of the water and test to see how far our poppa could bring the new converts for their safety.

Once Poppa had walked the allotted distance into the pond, the two deacons with him signaled for the two deacons waiting on the bank to bring in a convert. Alberta was the first chosen to go into the water. Deacon Miller was a tall, dark, slender man who sang some of the songs to the mourners. *"Wade in the water, children, God gonna trouble the water."* Walking toward Alberta with great humility with years of experience, he knew the converts would be nervous in this new experience and a nervous moment for them all. Reaching for Alberta's hand, he leaned over, speaking softly to her, "Come, child, Jesus loves you. Don't fear, we are not going to let you fall."

"Yes-sum."

Even going into deep water was a new experience for Poppa's girls because we weren't allowed to go swimming where the only available water was in the open outdoors—the lake, pond, or a nearby creek. When our brothers went swimming, this was acceptable; however rules were different for his girls. He felt that wet, clinging clothes on his girls' bodies during and after swimming made them too provoking, which would incite unfavorable attention from the boys that were present. Consequently, wading into the pond of waist-deep water was a first time for Roberta and Alberta, just like their older sisters when they got baptized.

We didn't rebel against these rules of the times because Negro girls and women weren't allowed to wear shorts in public. It was against Jim Crow laws.

Roberta was standing on the bank of the pond in front of the crowd, waiting for her turn with the other converts. Poppa's family was standing very close to their momma like baby chickens to a hen, watching Alberta with Deacon Miller cautiously wading deeper and deeper into the pond. Roberta was saying a silent prayer that her twin wouldn't slip and fall, aware also that her sister, like herself, had never been in deep water before. Roberta knew her twin sister well, knowing she wasn't fond of any new experiences. Alberta was more comfortable with the familiarity of the soil; unfamiliarity weakened her confidence. All eyes were on Alberta. Her twelve-year-old body swayed just a little as the water rose a little above her waist and her white robe began to float, rising above her waist, trying to swim without her. She was trying not to fall and trying to keep her robe from floating above her body.

"Oops," was heard from the crowd. She and Deacon Miller were close enough now for our poppa and Deacon Suggs to reach out their hands. "Come, child," Poppa said. Finally, Alberta's wet hand touched our poppa's wet hands, and she began to weep, probably feeling relieved to truly and finally be at last in the security of her poppa's strong hands where safety truly lies. We all could feel the energy from the gripping of their hands. Murmuring of "Thank you, Jesus" went throughout the crowd. Tears were slowly rolling out of our momma's eyes down her cheeks; if you weren't looking at her, you wouldn't have known. Ruth pulled out a white laced handkerchief from her black clutch purse and handed it to Momma because when there was any emotional event relating to Momma, her children always looked at her to see how she was coping. "How is Momma doing?"

Alberta looked into her poppa's face as he held her gently with one hand cupped in the back of her head with his right hand and his left hand along with Deacon Suggs supporting her back with his hands. "In the name of the Father, the Son, and the Holy Spirit, I baptize you." Then our poppa and his deacon submerged her into the water. Just as quickly, they brought her up, gasping for breath with water dripping off her face. Alberta said later that when she looked at her poppa through the water dripping off her face and eyes, she only saw love in a gentle man that she had never seen before. The strong-authority man was replaced by a gentle, mild-mannered man of love. It was as though a veil had been lifted, and she saw the real man.

Alberta's experience paved the way for Roberta and the eight other converts. She had built their confidence in her wade in the water.

The choir sang "Old Time Religion" and "It Was Good Enough for My Father and It's Good Enough for Me."

Roberta had no doubt that she was a brand-new creature in Christ. The revival and the baptism really did wash her as white as snow. She had a strong awareness of the presence of God. Nightly she would take her Bible to bed with her, reading it. Sometimes her poppa would come to his girls' room and stand at the doorway. "What are you reading tonight, girl?" he would ask with pride in his baritone voice.

"The book of Matthew, Poppa."

"Child, if you have any questions, just ask."

"Yes-sum, Poppa."

Roberta said that after Jesus purified and cleansed her, she saw God in everything. She had a heightened awareness of all of God's creations. There were times she would be outside with her sisters and brothers playing on a mild warm day, and when a warm breeze would blow, she would stop and stand still because in that breeze, she felt the presence of God. She would start to weep. Shug came near her. "Roberta, what's the matter with you?"

"Shug, I love God."

"What?"

"I said I love God."

Sometimes, as children we would lie on the ground looking up at the huge white clouds slowly moving above, and our imaginations would create different images from the shapes of the clouds. Roberta would point up and say, "I see angel in that cloud." "Girl, that's not an angel, that looks more like a bear to me," Shug said. Alberta would say, "It looks like a big old fat man to me."

Much later, the strong worldly impulses would, with great regrets, pull Poppa's children into a world of whiskey-drinking, smoking club-goers. Like a fish swimming in its environment, the fish's focus is shifted from the water and is focused on a hook with a big fat worm on it. The fish is now caught. The worldly music was for Poppa's children the worm of worldly music. "*It's your thing, do what you want to do, I can't tell you who to sock it to.* Leave that music alone because that type of music you listen to has a strong attraction, be it spiritual or worldly. Lucifer was the minister of music in heaven, and when he rebelled against God, God kicked him out of heaven and he became the minister of music down here on earth."

And we fell into the arms of good-looking men who didn't love us after turning eighteen and graduating from high school and fleeing Mississippi, shaking the dusk off our feet to join the great migration where the north beckoned, for all its usual reasons with the other Negroes catching the train or Greyhound bus that was driving away from Jim Crow for a freer, better life where we didn't have to chop or pick cotton to earn money. And finally we cut the tight controlling string of our poppa's teachings and preaching, also the spiritual songs that we loved to sing in church, at home, and while working in the fields in exchange for the flittering burst of colors from the strobe lighting in nightclubs and basement house parties, moving, gyrating, and grooving on the music of Isaac Hyzen.

*If you come back to stay, I will never drift away*
*Every nerve in my body is immersed in your body.*

And Aretha Franklin's

*Rock sturdy baby, you make me feel so good, let's call
this song just what it is.*

Entering the bright city lights and the high, abundant energy for
them was like being calves released from their stall that "skip with joy."
Poppa's children loved the attractions the world offered. With the night
life came men that held us tightly in standing-room-only crowd thick
with cigarette smoke with a small tang of marijuana in the mix while our
head leaned on their shoulders, taking in their male cologne blending in
with our sweet perfume. *"Just move your hips from side to side."* The
strobe light dazzled us. We were caught up in it.

"Roberta," Poppa once said, "there is a big difference between
love and lust." Before his children would reunite to their roots of their
poppa's teaching, experiencing with worldly life and taking a long
vacation from God only causes heart aches and pain. Roberta said she
learned the hard way that her poppa knew what he was talking about
when he said, "Some men aren't worth two dead flies."

But for now in 1951, our poppa's new converts at twelve had their
eyes on God, believing strongly in heaven and hell, right and wrong.
The Greyhound bus hadn't arrived to pick them up and take them away
from their life of innocence, leaving their weeping momma and their
praying poppa into the hurly-burly of city life.

As the influence of the Negro church continued to grow, this was a
compelling positive force in the Negroes' lives. The sweet smell from
the ladies' cheap perfume and the men's Old Spice greeted you when
you entered the church sanctuary, with ladies wearing their hats; it was
important to them that they wore their Sunday's best. Men young and
old dressed in their suit and tie. The ladies knew and the young men too
that they were expecting to see their favorite person at church because
the church was the center of their lives. It was a meeting place for friends
and family. They did not have access to amusement parks, theaters.
Everyone looked forward to Sunday's church for this became the big
social gathering for the week, where boys met girls. Sometimes when a
young man was walking his young lady from night services, he would
try to woo his sweetheart into marriage for he knew her well. They went
to school together, he knew her parent, he even knew her grandparent.

The church was also the business center. Men talked about the price of cotton. Women shared and exchanged recipes there.

When our poppa has delivered his sermon to the standing-room-only sanctuary, he would sing a few verses of his favorite song "May the Lord be with you until we meet again." The crowd would start their greetings and give the familiar faces handshakes and hugs, talking about the sick, the death of one of their members, their children. Even Poppa would still be standing in the pulpit, smiling, talking with one or more of his fellow ministers who came as guests and who would always sit in the pulpit in one of the tall red velvet high-back chairs. Their black shoes were spotless that they were probably polished the night before. During services, while our poppa was preaching, they would be cheering, enthusiastically rooting him on while they held their own Bible in their hand, swinging the Bible with arms lifted high in agreement with Poppa with their Amen! Halleluiah! Preach, brother!

Poppa was socializing in the pulpit with his white teeth sparkling against the background of his very dark complexion. Talking with fellow ministers, he was still very aware of his wife sitting where the ladies of honor sits in the front pew with the same dignity of special guests sitting in the box seat in the opera house. Our momma, as the wife of the pastor, was unusually shy and timid in public. Under these circumstances, she would never go on her own to meet and talk with people. After church service, members of the church would come to where "Sister Gathing" was sitting. It was obvious our momma felt uncomfortable with all the attention. As one of the members reached to shake our momma's hand and Momma would make an attempt to stand, the member would say, "Please don't stand, Mother Gathing." We all could tell this was an awkward moment for our mother. Our momma and poppa were emotionally opposite. Poppa was very open and reaching out to people, enjoying the attention of the public. Momma was bashful, shrinking from too much public attention. Even with their differences, it was obvious love was there.

Poppa was also aware of his daughters Shug and twin daughters Roberta and Alberta. Who were they talking with? Who are they planning to leave church with? Poppa didn't allow his teenage girls to walk along with a boy. However, if two or more of his girls were walking together and he knew the boy's family, that mile walk to his house would be okay.

Poppa's daughters loved the walk under the stars, listening to the Mississippi night sounds of a distant coyote, tree frogs, the occasional hoots of an owl blending with the sounds of crickets. Our sweethearts would hold our hands as we walked on the side of the dusty road. They didn't forget who they were walking with—the preacher's daughters. There was probably no night brighter than a full moon on a Mississippi night; we could actually see our shadows beneath the full moon.

Roberta was walking with Willie, Alberta with Joseph, and Shug with her beloved Marshall. That was a wonderful year on that warm July Mississippi night in 1958. We didn't know at the time that nothing we will experience in later years would come close to the times we walked home from church on those warm nights with our sweethearts. Even looking back on those years, knowing that we were in Poppa's heart, that we had his protection, just him being in our lives was protection enough.

Willie was going to Rush College in Holly Springs, studying to be a teacher. Joseph's looks along was enough for Alberta. The same went for Shug; Marshall's height, copper-tone skin, and curly hair were pleasing to Shug.

We didn't know it then, but those warm Mississippi nights on the dusky road were the highlight of our lives.

We loved those boys, but after high school graduation, we left them for the lure of a better life up north to St. Louis and Chicago, where there were no cotton fields or Jim Crow. Poppa's beloved daughters married strange men from a strange tribe, from strange families. Like the tribe of Joshua 11, "the Amorites, Hittites, Perizzites," we met such men at work or at a house party who, unlike our poppa, didn't know how to pray. Most of his children's marriage ended in divorce court.

When the reality of these bad marriages set in, Poppa's daughters would reminisce of those innocent years with our Mississippi sweethearts. What if we had stayed and married our first love? What if the hate for the cotton fields and the Jim Crow laws hadn't blinded us to the potential of a very strong family life? Mississippi was where our momma and poppa could have had an intimate relationship with their children and grandchildren.

# 9

## A Door Was Opened

In 1954, Poppa and Momma were living in the small town of Byhalia, Mississippi, where everyone knew their place. The whites and their Negroes both played by the rules that society in which they lived had built into their laws. There were laws for whites and laws for Negroes that had deep roots in their culture, and when these laws were violated, there was a high penalty.

Citizens, Negroes and whites alike, lived in a quite calm peace. The beautiful two-storied antebellum houses that were visible through the shade of huge weeping willow and magnolia trees bursting with beautiful pink flowers in early spring, which when a warm spring breeze came brought with it the refreshing scent of the magnolia blossom, on their rolling manicure landscape presented a picture of peace and tranquility. Sometimes passersby could spot a Negro man with his straw hat pulled low covering his face to protect him from the Mississippi blasting sun, paying special attention to detail that's pleasing to his white master.

Travelers who weren't familiar with the state of Mississippi, passing through this picturesque perfect town of serenity and beauty, couldn't imagine what was behind this façade of the tranquil country place—the terror of the night, the lynching, the cross burning that was used to terrorize the Negro families. And by the lack of outrage, most whites gave their approval.

The Negroes knew how to say yes-sum while not looking the Whites in their eyes because for a Negro to look a white man, woman, or their children directly in their eyes revealed to the Whites "I'm as much human as you." If this law against eye contact is broken, this Negro would have earned the reputation of being an upper nigger. No Negro in Mississippi ever wanted that label because they may become a target of the dreadful, feared KKK. This, of course, seems difficult to accept to us present; but due to the spirit of that day, this attitude was accepted as just being "that's just the way it is."

This quite peaceful-looking town would sometimes be disturbed by the KKK as a reminder that they were still a powerful, threatening force. And to make sure those niggers wouldn't forget who was still in control. Like the time when Willie Earl, the teenage son of Mr. Johnson, a deacon at our local church, was walking with a couple of his friends along the side of the road and a car with several white men pulled up along and started calling them niggers. Mr. Johnson's oldest seventeen-year-old son looked at the driver dead in the eyes, didn't even blink. This scared the white driver because he hadn't ever experienced anything like this before.

"Boy! Who do you think you are looking at!"

"At you, sir." His two friends, as they told the story later, said that they almost wet their pants from fear. Before speeding off, the driver screamed through the open window, "Nigger, you will be sorry, you damn uppity nigger!"

Upon hearing this, panic that was fueled by overwhelming fear flooded Mr. Johnson because he knew this was a serious problem and that these men were capable of lynching his son. Mr. Johnson told his wife, "We have to get Willie Earl out of Mississippi tonight!"

Mrs. Johnson started crying, "Oh Lord, no, not our boy. Jesus, please show us mercy."

Willie Earl was sitting at their kitchen table with his head hung down. He was so scared. As silent tears rolled down his cheeks, he wondered how could he have done such a stupid thing. "Pa, I'm so sorry, am just so tired of these white folks."

"I know, son, we all are, but until God wants change, it will not change. Go, hurry now, we're going to your uncle Peter's house in

Memphis. He would know what to do. Hurry now, we don't have much time." With extreme haste as though their house was on fire, they grabbed a few of the essential things, some clothes, their battery radio, a few jars of food that Mrs. Johnson had canned for the winter. Mr. Johnson with his family in his 1952 Studebaker rushed off in the night of 1953 and was never heard of again.

Poppa had rented a small farm a short distance down the road from his parents' five-acre farm. His stepmother "Big Mamma" and his two half brothers and half sister Shug all lived nearby. Poppa's only full sister Mary, a schoolteacher, lived right across the railroad tracks that ran parallel to Byhalia. We called Poppa's oldest brother Uncle Tussie and his younger brother Uncle BB. To us Poppa's children, they were part of a network of kinship that appeared to be close-knit.

Sometimes we would gather there after church where there was a three-tier system—women in the kitchen, men on the front porch, and children out playing on the bare dusted front yard. The men would be sitting on the front porch debating the current issues and bouncing off points of beliefs against opposing points of philosophy—*The Soul of Black Folks*, first published in 1903, *Uncle Tom's Cabin, The Life of Booker T. Washington*. As their children played on the grassless bare front yard, there were always issues being discussed by the men sitting on the front porch, and they would engage in highly charged emotional opposing points of views. There were no winners or losers in these debates; feelings and opinions were rarely changed.

Our poppa was a strong supporter of Booker T. Washington, advocating that his stance on the education of the Negroes were the best way. "It was foolish for Marcus Garvey to think he could find success in Africa, and also how in the world did Nat Turner think he could kill all the white people he felt had wronged the Negroes?" His brother Tussie interrupted. "Just tell me, Sam, why are Negroes the only race of people who have to turn the other cheek?"

"Nat Turner probably could have pulled it off with better planning," Uncle BB said. "I think W. E. B. DuBois is right. Negro men need to start thinking like other men and stop thinking like boys."

When our poppa was in a discussion with his brothers, his conversation would inevitably lead to the importance of landownership. "If the Negroes don't buy land, he will be working for the white man," we heard our poppa say. His two brothers would just look at him as though what their brother said had no value. Their inaction and lack of interest showed that they were content living their life as a sharecropper not desiring more than they had.

"Okay, BB, you just said that Negro men should stop thinking like boys. Well, buying land is a pretty good start, don't you think?" Poppa had a stern, unyielding look on his face, the deep furrow on his forehead more pronounced, the passion in his voice expressing his deep feeling on the subject. "Our time has come. Negroes are buying land left and right, it's now or never!"

Poppa looked at his two brothers and saw by the calmness, the absence of emotions, that they didn't get it. This was very difficult for our Poppa to accept. He had hoped that he and his two brothers could buy a farm together and tighten their family bond—his children and their children, their wives on the same land. Poppa had learned from years of sharecropping that there was money to be made on the land. The 1940s and beyond was the age of agriculture. Mississippi and other southern states was the king of cotton. The demand for beef, dairy, corn, and all types of vegetables was at its peak. Poppa said, "The only way a man can stay poor is he has to be lazy. Don't want to work because anybody who is willing to work will not be poor." How can a man have anything if he thinks he can spend a big amount of his time under a shade tree drinking corn homemade whiskey half the day like his brother BB?

Poppa continued to try to persuade his brothers on the importance of landownership. "Now is the time before the winds of change start shifting in another direction, in which it most surely will. BB, you and Tussie have gotten comfortable in your position as servants. Don't want to take the opportunity to become independent men, men I say! Not whining boys!

"Men and women too must think about the memories they are going to leave once they get old in age and is dead and gone. We have to think about the life we live. Drinking whiskey under a shade tree with your buddies, don't you know your name will be covered with darkness as you age and even after you're dead and gone, buried in your grave? In fact, the life of drunkenness and slothfulness will increase by words of mouth. For generations, these ugly things will be talked about. Even after death, gossipers will continue to discuss your life, the way you have lived. These memories cannot be swept under the rug; the one who comes after you will remember, the one you love the most won't forget. Damn you forever to the cesspool of filth."

These debates could continue with the aroma of the southern dinner of fried chicken, a big pot of greens seasoned with ham hocks, corn bread, and chocolate cake that stimulated our appetites. The big glass picture of iced tea is ready with slices of lemon flowing on top. The men weren't paying much attention to their chatter; however, they couldn't ignore the laughter of their wives. When our momma and our aunt Annie Mae and aunt Duchies got together, there was always laughter in their midst. Both women were tall, light-skinned women with long pretty black curly hair that hung below their shoulders.

Men are always in a state of seriousness, it seems, when the outdoor work is done and they have time to sit and discuss the threats that surround them out there. They are always aware of impending danger to themselves or to their loved ones.

The women's world is in their home, under their feet, so to speak. They had lots of laughter just loving their family, the work of their hands. Their hands were always busy whether they were standing or sitting. Standing with their aprons on, they are preparing food, or with broom in hand, they are sweeping around their husbands' and children's feet as they sit near the fireplace.

"Don't sweep my feet, it's bad luck."

"Well, move your lazy feet out of the way." And when these women finally got around to sitting, will say, "Will somebody go and get my sewing basket? I need to sew on missing buttons and mend those socks." But no one moves. Poppa may say, "Shug, go and get your Momma's sewing basket. Do I have to tell you children everything?" As Momma is sitting with sewing basket near her chair and sewing on missing buttons on one of her boys' shirts, she says to no one in particular, "Men work from dawn to dawn, women's work is never done."

We heard a lot about President Truman and how he was opening up jobs for Negroes, made it a law that the federal government had to stop discriminating against their Negroes and requiring equal opportunities in the armed forces and also for various branches of government jobs.

Roberta remembers the first time she had seen a colored mail man. The year was 1951, and she was eight years old. Her poppa had told her to go to the mailbox and get the mail. She and any one of his children had done this almost daily. While Poppa was sitting on the front porch knowing it was time for the mailman, some of his children would be playing out front. When our Poppa sees the mailman, he would call out the first child that comes to mind.

On this warm fall day, when Poppa saw the mailman's vehicle come up the road, he said, "Roberta, go and get the mail." "Yes-sum, Poppa." So she ran at the end of the long dirt drive way just before the mailman drove off. Expecting to see the same white man that was usually there as the mailman with his arm extended was getting ready to put mail into the mailbox, Roberta reached the mailbox, expecting to get the mail directly out of the white man's hand.

"Oh my, you are colored!" African Americans were called by several different names throughout American history. Slaves were considered as "those black savages doing slavery," "those infidels by the Christian whites, later were called "those niggers" from "those Negroes." Next sometime in the 1950s, they went from Negro to those colored people. Many colored people didn't like the name *colored* and find it to be offensive. "Why do we have to be called colored? We are the only people that don't have a definite color." Then out of the blue, colored people started calling themselves black people; there were some blacks who didn't like that name neither. "I ain't black." And finally to connect them to their African roots, they were called African Americans. By the way, these names weren't accepted by all African Americans. Some said, "I am not an African. However, in 1951, African Americans were called "those colored people."

The mailman gave her a big old smile, showing his pearly white teeth. "President Truman says they have to hire colored folks now."

"Glory to be! Wait till I tell Poppa!" Roberta ran as fast as she could with the mail and with Poppa looking at her with alarm, wondering why she was running so fast. When she reached the front porch, Poppa stood up. "What's the matter, girl?"

So out of breath was she that she could hardly speak. "Poppa, we have a colored mailman!"

"Are you sure, girl?"

"Poppa, he is the same color as you. It's President Truman who did this. It's him, all right, Lord have mercy. I read that he was going to do this. I thought it was too good to be true. Bracey!" As he was walking into the house, Momma was in the kitchen frying chicken.

"In here, Sam." Poppa entered the kitchen with joy mixed with amazement. "Bracey, we have a colored mailman! President Truman said he was going to do this wonderful thing and it is done. Lord, when a president speaks!"

Momma looked at her husband, doubtful about this amazing news. Colored men down here in Mississippi can't force a white man to do anything he doesn't want to do. Perhaps finding it hard to imagine a colored man replacing a white man's job, Momma asked, "Sam, do you think they are going to lynch that man?"

"Bracey, the president of the United States did this. They have to obey the president."

"No, white man is going to let a colored man take his job," Momma said. Momma couldn't comprehend the power behind the president's words. However, as the days and weeks unfolded, more and more colored people were visible in government jobs. Colored people were popping up like day lilies in the spring. We would walk into the post office, and where whites once stood, there was a colored standing right beside him, standing upright and proud in his khaki uniform. The dignity that he so proudly showed he had learned during his time spent in the military.

Our poppa sent Alberta and Roberta, his twin daughters, into the post office for the first time to buy stamps while he went to pay a bill in Byhalia. Handing us a $1 bill after he had parked in front of the post office, he said, "Alberta, you and Roberta go and get a dollar's worth of stamps. I'm going to the general store and I'll be right back."

"Yes-sum, Poppa."

"Be good now." Although they both had seen a colored mailman by now, they had never seen them actually working behind a counter.

Roberta said later that as she and Alberta were walking to the entrance of the post office, Alberta was walking closely behind her because Alberta would use Roberta as a shield, proverbially speaking, when she felt approaching danger because Roberta was more aggressive than she was. Roberta felt anxious also; however, she had a strong will, even forcing her legs to take her where they didn't want to go. Down deep in her conscience, she knew she was born to be free. She didn't know how or when, but she knew that there was only one God for all people, and the definitions the whites had of her wasn't the real her. Even in this state of mind, inferiority would sometimes creep into her spirit. "I'm just as good as they are," she would have to reassure herself. The feeling of inferiority was so pervasive that without "divine assistance," we couldn't overcome it.

Just the thought of facing white people unnerved them, especially white men, because like all people of color, they had experienced hurtful words before, strong, penetrating words that entered the spirit of a child: "There are those black nappy-headed niggers. We don't want them in our schools, churches, or neighborhoods!" When she and her sister walked into the post office and the tall, dark-colored man looked at them with a welcoming smile, this was the first time she didn't feel inferior when in the presence of whites. Didn't feel like just a nappy-headed nigger kid. Just his presence standing side by side with a white man made her feel for the time fully human.

The door that President Truman opened for the colored people of that day was an important force in the colored community. The president opened a door of growth beyond their familiar lifestyle as maids, servants, even schoolteachers to their own children, preachers in their colored churches. Where they were boxed into their prescribed order of Jim Crow's lifestyle and didn't step outside of this customary mode of procedure where everyone knew their place and stayed in that place, everything was "peaches and cream," so to speak.

President Truman made it possible that for the first time, colored people could actually get jobs that whites wanted.

# 10

## Feeling My Poppa's Shame

Roberta said that on this pleasant spring day on a Saturday in June 1958, she was sitting on the stoop of their front porch reading *Native Son* by Richard Wright. She heard a car pull up, which drew her attention from the book she was reading. She recognized the car as Mr. White's, a white man that would come by to collect money from our poppa for life insurance. She wasn't aware that this scene she was getting ready to witness that her memory would return to this very scene the remaining of her life. However, at fifteen, Roberta didn't know this; how could she?

Mr. White parked his car, and after he got out of the parked car, Poppa appeared from the back of the house, walking fast, almost out of breath. Roberta wasn't surprised about her poppa rushing because she knew that it was against Jim Crow law for a black man in Mississippi to keep a white person waiting.

Poppa walked up to Mr. White, saying, "Howdy, Mr. White."

"Morning, Sam."

Roberta said she doesn't remember the words that were being said, but she would never forget the respond from her poppa. As Mr. White was talking, Poppa's eyes were on the ground, saying, "Yes-sum, yes-sum, Mr. White," while rapidly bowing his head in submission.

Roberta said that as she witnessed the degrading scene, she actually felt the pain and humiliating angst her Poppa must have been feeling at that moment with his teenage daughter watching him. Roberta said tears welled up in her eyes. She slowly closed her book and walked into the house and went into the girls' room, lying across the wrought-iron bed on top of the quilt that had the history of their lives through the patchwork that Momma had patched together. After lying there for a while, she decided to sit up in bed to try to continue to read. She quickly closed the book again because she still couldn't concentrate on what she was reading. The words of *Native Son* were spinning around in her head:

> "Naw. But I just can't get used to it," Bigger said. "I swear to God I can't. I know I oughtn't think about it, but I can't help it. Every time I think about it I feel like somebody's poking a red-hot iron down my throat. Look! we live here and they live there. We black and they white. They got things and we ain't. They do things and we can't. Half the time I feel like I'm on the outside of the world peeping in through a knot-hole in the fence."

And that's exactly the way she said she felt. The same way Bigger felt in *Native Son*.

For some reason, as she sat up in bed, her eyes were drawn to the patchwork in the quilt that she was lying upon, the patch from the black and white polka-dot dress that she and Alberta wore five years ago when they were ten. They were pretty dresses, but she never liked dressing like another person even if it was her twin sister. "Here comes the twins, ain't they cute?" There was a patch from Poppa's blue shirt—that was his old workshirt. Even in her tears, she smiled when she looked at the patch from Shug's old striped sun back dress that she once wore to church that showed too much of her shoulders and Momma made her walk all the way back home to get the little top that went with the dress. She said she lay there scanning the patchwork, recalling the days of her early childhood.

They were happy days, days before she took life seriously and when the only things that were on her mind was to go outside and play with her sisters and brothers. Now at fifteen, she was beginning to pay attention to the ugly side of Mississippi.

At fifteen, Roberta said she had seen our poppa many times while growing up in Mississippi acting like an uneducated Negro around whites. But this was the first time his inferior role troubled her. Now she was beginning to see the ugly side of Mississippi. The spirit of anger was creeping in. This was probably the beginning of her fury over social injustice. She had to strongly resist the urge to give Mr. White a piece of her mind. However, she knew that if she did that, the consequences of her action would be huge. For today, crying would be enough, and the awareness that she hated Mississippi and white people too would stay with her.

With the gift of remembering dates, times, and places, Poppa often talked to his children about some of his life's experiences, usually oral history and teachings of his past, about knowing that what we are taught and accept will chart the course for our lives, be it good or bad. Like the generations before him, the ancient path was words by mouth. The same way his forefathers did, a path leading back across the ocean to our homeland of Africa and they were in the cargo of the slave ships. And how we Negro slaves came out of the packed belly of this human cargo in the early sixteen hundreds and was viewed as subhuman dropped like anchor with chains on foreign soil. "The slave trade was a black man who stepped out of his hut for a breath of fresh air and ended up, ten months later, in Georgia with bruises on his back and a brand on his chest," Lerone Bennett Jr. said.

"Once I was in Holly Springs, the year was 1942," Poppa said. "I went there to pay my taxes and to pick up some things your momma needed from the general store there. I took my two boys Plaite and Junior with me. Plaite was about nine years old, Junior was about eleven years old. They would always ask me when they hear me tell your momma that I was going to Holly Springs, 'Can we go, Poppa?' 'Sure, sons, go get into the truck.' They both ran and put their shoes on their dusky feet from playing outside barefooted.

"The boys loved the ten miles' drive in the back of my 1940 Ford pickup truck. I would be watching them through the rearview mirror. Roberta, it was never a time when I didn't worry about them. All parents worry about their children, black and white both. But the worries down here in Mississippi is worse, more intense for blacks. Lynching and all that horror, aware too that they were born into a land fraught with violence, difficulties, and danger. And how all of us are influenced by our surroundings. Knowing how living under this system of Jim Crow has affected my own life. I read once in the *New York Times* that a white man was lynched in New Orleans in 1895, but down here in Mississippi, they only lynch Negro men and boys. My grandpa Bill, born in 1828 in slavery, talked about men he knew who were lynched."

Poppa continued. "My own poppa, your grandpa Wesley, who died in 1957, knew two men during his lifetime that were lynched. And I've gone to two funerals of men who were lynched.

"Most people when they hear the word *lynch* don't know the full meaning of it. Most lynchings were led by a mob. KKK would hear about a black looking at a white woman, and they would with a "hearing only," no trial, as the accusation was enough. The mob sometimes consisted of a preacher, a farmer, and several others would capture their intended victim usually at night. This mob would beat him beyond recognition. Put a rope around his neck and hang him on a tree until he's dead.

"When I arrived in Holly Springs on this warm spring day in 1942, I told the boys to stay in the truck while I go into the store. 'Be good, now, I will be right back.' 'Yes, sum, Poppa,' they said.

"When I came out of the store, these men, two white men, were making fun of my sons. 'Hey, you nigger kids. Here comes your pappy.' And as I was walking toward them, this man looked at me. 'Sam, we know you are one of those uppity niggers. Always wearing a suit and tie. We know you are a preacher, but to us you're just a boy, you are still a nigger preacher.'

"The shame, the deep pain of that experience will never leave me. You know a father values how their children see them. For my boys to see this, I felt a shrinking in my spirit, a terrible smallness at that moment. Not being able to defend my boys, knowing that the safety of my family depended on me not to respond to this. Consequently with this pain inside of me, I even had difficulty breathing. I heard myself say yes, sum," Poppa said.

"Plaite asked me later why I didn't defend him and Junior. My only answer was, 'Son you are too young to understand now. You will understand when you get older.

This experience with his children as witness built up resentment against the whites and what they stood for."

Over time, this resentment became a deep and bitter anger that eventually weakened or destroyed their playful childhood spirit, which is part of the story.

Poppa' boys were full of fun and good spirit when they were young, telling jokes about the simple things in life, about the fox chasing the rooster, or what would happen as they were sitting on their stool milking Bessie the cow and how Bessie would whip them in the head with her tail as she was trying to whip the flies off her back. My brother Lloyd told about how he was out in the woods hunting and his favorite hunting dog Fido was chasing a snake instead of chasing the target rabbit.

Even in their old age, their playful childhood attitude about life has not restored. As Poppa's boys got older and they had a greater, more frequent encounter with the southern white males, the fury over social injustice and inequality slowly grew into resentment and anger. They stopped talking and joking about the simple things in life. Their conversation took on a different tone, a tone of anger about their experiences, seeing how Poppa was being treated. At every turn, they started paying attention to the injustice in their environment. The anger of Poppa's children, especially his boys, was stemmed from the injustices in the social and cultural forces that shaped their life.

My brother Plaite said he remembers it so plainly. The year was 1948; he was fifteen years old. He was standing in line in the grocery store at the checkout counter, and a white man and a white woman came in line behind him. My brother said he was told by the cashier, "Boy, get in back of the line. You see those people in back of you?" "Yes, ma'am," he said. Plaite said that as he walked to the back of the line, the bitterness of anger moved up into his throat as he was looking down. When he walked past the white couple, he felt an acidity burn in his stomach as he stood there looking at the back of their heads. A strong compulsion surged up within him as he stood there looking at the two liter bottles of RC Cola that was on the counter that the white couple was getting ready to buy.

He said, "I thought to myself I should pick up that bottle of soda pop and hit that old white man in the head. Then just as quickly, I thought of Poppa. They will kill my Poppa. That thought left me, but the anger never did leave.

"After I got back in the truck with Poppa, he asked, 'What's troubling you, boy? You're awful quiet.' I didn't tell him about the incident in the store because I knew there was nothing he could do about it. So I asked him, 'Poppa, why do you worship a white Jesus? And why do you have his white picture hung in our house?'

"Poppa didn't answer. For a while he was silent, and then he looked at me. 'I'm going to let God answer that for you, son. God will answer when he knows you are ready for the answer.'"

Plaite said that the incident in the grocery store at the age of fifteen was the first time he remembered being angry all day. This feeling was something new for him. He hadn't been angry at anyone that long before.

The anger our Poppa's boys had slowly turned into hatred for the southern whites. This hatred and anger had an erosive effect upon their lives. This loss of joy in their lives makes us all understand why Jesus said to forgive your enemies.

Most of Poppa's children saw the Jesus that Poppa preached about as an unloving white man that was related to the evil white men because the Jesus that they saw looked like a white man with white skin and straight silky hair. How can this Jesus be a friend to these evil white men and be a friend to the black man too? they asked.

On a daily basis, the opposition from the whites grew worse as Poppa's boys got older. White males saw them as a bigger threat to the southern white authority.

I don't think there was ever a time while growing up in Mississippi when a white driver with his buddies would not stop and have some "fun with these niggers" when passing or approaching blacks walking along these isolated country dirt roads. So there was Poppa's three oldest boys Junior, Plaite, and Alfred, teenage boys just laughing and talking. Junior saw the blue 1946 Ford approaching them. He knew this spelled trouble because he recognized the truck. These men had terrorized them before.

The truck pulled up alongside the boys. They were so afraid with the thought of lynching running through their minds. *Are they going to kill us? Drag us behind their truck?* Poppa's boys had heard that sometimes white men did these terrible things.

Today wasn't a day for lynching, but it was a day to have some fun and keeping the nigger boys, soon to be men, in their place down here in Mississippi. You have to show these younguns before they become men or these niggers will try to run things.

The driver slowed the truck to a stop. The driver stuck his head out of the truck's window and spat on Junior and pressed his foot on the gas pedal and speeded off with him and his buddy laughing. The dust from the dirt road caused the spit on Junior's face to stick to him even more. The spit and dust formed a gluelike paste on Junior's face. Even after washing and rewashing his face, he couldn't wash the feeling that the spit and dirt were still on his face.

This day in 1947 was the day that Junior couldn't shake it off, and the anger stuck, so to speak.

The horror for Poppa's three boys along with the hatred and fears intensified as they got older. They still joked and did horseplay as teenagers. However, their negative experience with the whites slowly started became the things they talked about more and more and less and less about the simple things in life.

# 11

## *Our Poppa Told Us Stories*

Poppa's great-grandpa Bill was born in South Carolina in 1809. He lived through slavery, the civil war, and Reconstruction. The story of his life was passed down through three generations: our poppa's Grandpa John, to his Poppa Wesley, to our poppa who talked often about the men that influenced his life.

Great-grandpa Bill lived to be 106 and was married three times.

Our poppa would say before he started telling us about his life history, "You know, people should know more than their names. They should know some history behind those names. I'm going to tell y'all the story the way it was told to me." Then he would begin.

These were times when women died young, often of complications from childbirth. Grandpa Bill had three wives; all of them died young long before their hair turned gray. At the turn of the century, women's life expectancy was forty-six.

### Isabella

Who were these faceless women, real women who had real lives, real worries, and real fears? Women who had been taught since childhood that "a woman must obey her husband"? She remembered those words in her marriage vows. She was told by her own momma that "a wife's task was to bear children, to serve her household, and obey her husband and always do her wifely duties." These women who had been taught how to be dependent and meek didn't forget the vows their husbands took at their wedding: "Husband, love your wife as Christ loved the church." However though, while these words were echoing in their minds, they dare not speak them because if they did, they probably thought they would be sinning.

At the end of the day, the frontier wife would listen to the complaints of her husband. He would talk about his mules, cows, hogs, the things of the farm. She would usually sit silently during these times because she was probably thinking about her children. Even sometimes thinking about herself.

Isabella was seven months' pregnant, and this had been the worst pregnant of all. She felt sick most of the time. She was a loyal, self-sacrificing wife. Her life didn't belong to her; her life belonged to her husband and her children. She was probably thinking as Bill was talking about his farm, "I hope and pray that Bill don't want me to do my wifely duty tonight. I'm so tired and sick too. I know a wife can't say no to her husband for that would be sinning."

The obituary of Isabella says about her being born 1849, died 1897. These women who sacrificed their live for others hold great meaning. Remembering that they were born and had died just isn't enough. The headstone reads Isabella, 1849-1897. What about the dash between birth and death? The generations that were borne through their wombs should remember more than a dash between life and death: "I don't want to die, don't want to leave my children." But death took them anyway. Exhausting labor of their own hard work and childbearing was so great that this literally took their lives. Sometimes the midwife couldn't stop the hemorrhaging. And at other times women didn't die right away during childbirth; they would have reoccurring fever and dysentery. Pneumonia would set in, and the young mothers would take longer to die, with high fever and coughing with blood-tinged phlegm, and difficulty breathing.

The labor pains came hard and strong on this early spring day in April of 1897 while Isabella and her eighteen-year-old daughter were sitting in their wooden chairs at the kitchen table peeling potatoes. The pain started in her lower back—the familiar pain of childbirth. "Julia, go tell your pa it's time." Pa was sitting on the front porch as usual in his wicker rocker, smoking his pipe with his hunting dog Blue lying near his feet. "Ma says it's time, Pa!" Pa immediately rushed to his wagon with his horse, which, luckily, was still attached. He rushed to get the midwife who lived about a mile down the road.

Returning back into the kitchen where her momma was standing stooped over in severe pain that only the birth of a child could induce, Julia gently put her arm around her hurting momma to assist her to her and Poppa's bedroom. With her arm around her momma, Julia took a brief look at her momma and was alarmed at what she saw. The distress and agony on her Momma's face was downright scary. An inner voice said to her so plainly, "Your ma is going to die." The young girl gasped and said out loud, "No, oh no, not Ma! Oh God no!"

Within a short time, Pa returned with Mrs. Laura Mae, a full-figured woman who was tender and tough at the same time, a woman who knew the value of being a midwife, didn't take it lightly, had felt the pain of childbirth more than once herself. The two live births and one stillborn through that experience taught her the seriousness of child labor. And under these circumstances of urgency, Mrs. Laura Mae's toughness was unmistakable. She was a woman who knew how and when to take control. She had prepared an emergency bag the same way a doctor's bag was prepared. She made sure she had the essentials—a sterile pair of scissors, extra towels because from experience she had learned that some poor families didn't always have clean towels, and her jar of balm, which was a mixture of honey, oil, and lemon balm for the pain. Jeremiah 51:8 says, "Take balm for her pain, if so she may be healed."

Julia had assisted her ma to bed. The pain was getting stronger. Julia perhaps felt so helpless seeing the agony and the perspiration beaming upon her ma's face as she was biting her lips trying to control the excruciating pain. It had to be terrible for the young girl to watch her ma having such unbearable pain.

When they heard Blue barking, they knew Pa was returning with Mrs. Laura Mae. Before the dust settled, Mrs. Laura Mae was off the wagon with urgency that her full figure couldn't slow her down. She knew life and death was hovering over women in labor.

The minute her eyes fell upon Isabella, she knew from experience that this was a serious problem. Her eyes didn't look right: *"The soul is in the eyes.*" Looking at Julia, she said, "Go, child, hurry and heat up some water."

The labor was long and very difficult. It lasted long into the night. The light from the two kerosene lamps, one on the dresser and one near the table at the foot of the bed where the midwife was sitting, flickered through the night, casting an eerie shadow in the room. The moaning and grunting from Isabella's labor pains would occasionally break the silence of the night. Mrs. Laura Mae held in her hands a damp, cool cloth, which she used as a swab that she gently wiped the beads of perspiration off Isabella's forehead through the night. Occasionally rubbing Isabella's stomach with the balm mixture and also at times putting a dab on her tongue, she would say, "Honey, it's going to be all right. God is going to pull you through." Isabella could only give her head a tiny tilt in agreement. She was so tired.

The house was unusually quiet. Only Julia, Mrs. Laura Mae, and of course, Isabella was there. During these times when women gave birth at home, the husband would leave the house, taking the children with him because giving birth was a woman's job. Julia stayed as a type of nursing assistant, obeying the fervent request of Mrs. Laura Mae. "More hot water, another glass of water, more towels."

Finally it was time. The water has broken. "Push, honey, push!" The full-figured woman was sitting at the foot of the bed in a chair while Isabella's legs were spread open so that the midwife could have full access and an unobstructed view of the birth.

"There, honey! There, the head is coming! Push, darling, push, your baby has a full head of beautiful black hair." Isabella might have thought she was going to pass out. Her womb felt like it was being ripped apart. During labor, the whole body is engulfed in horrific pain: "For I have a voice as of a woman in travail, and the anguish as or her who brings forth her first child" (Jeremiah 4:31).

In 1882, Eugenia entered the world a beautiful baby girl. After cutting the umbilical cord, Mrs. Laura Mae, with the pan of warm water, bathed the infant and gave the newborn to her very tired momma.

However, there was a problem—the bleeding wouldn't stop. Panic set in, and it showed in Mrs. Laura Mae's eyes. But she prayed that it didn't show in her voice. As calm as she could fake it, she said, "Julia, bring me more towels and hurry, dear." Julia, being a good nurse assistant, was sitting right outside her ma's bedroom door, waiting for the next call for help. After returning with an armful of clean towels and mostly clean rags, she entered the room. Handing the midwife the towels and rags with fear and alarm on her pretty young face, she saw so much blood that she remembered the voice: *"Your ma is going to die."*

"Ma is dying, ain't she?"

"Oh no, honey, your ma is going to be fine. This kind of stuff happens sometimes."

Finally the hemorrhaging slowed to normal bleeding. "Oh Lord, thank God for your mercy." Mrs. Laura Mae from experience knew something still wasn't right with Isabella. She gently laid her hand on the new mother's forehead. Just as she thought—the patient had a high fever. While Julia had returned to her seat outside the bedroom door, Mrs. Laura Mae said, "Honey, bring me some cool water."

"Yes-sum." The young helper rushed into the kitchen and grabbed a clean pan off the top of the wrought-iron stove in the kitchen, hurried up, and went outside on the back porch where her ma kept barrels of rainwater with a lid to keep the insects and Pa's dog out. Before indoor plumbing, barrels were placed on the ground very close to the house to catch the rainwater as it ran off the roof of the house. Water was very precious because when we preserved rainwater, we didn't have to always draw water from the well for washing, cooking, and bathing.

With the pan of cool water, Julia hastily went back into the bedroom and gave the water to the midwife. Julia knew her ma wasn't going to make it: *"Your ma is going to die."*

As Isabella was lying, looking very feverish and weak with her newborn lying on her breast, Mrs. Laura Mae asked her, "What are you going to name her?"

"Eugenia." In an almost inaudible whisper, Isabella said, "Her name will be Eugenia." And so it was.

They heard Blue barking, which announced the return of Pa, probably after he and his six children spent the night with Deacon Jones, returning to check on his wife. He was alone because he had left the children with Deacon Jones and his family. Deacon Jones had done the same when his wife gave birth; his family had waited out the delivery at Pa's house.

Pa wanted to know if the coast was clear, so to speak, before he brought their children home.

Julia met her pa at the front door, even holding the screen door open for him. "Morning, Pa. Ma ain't doing so good. She's going to die."

"Hush, child, don't talk like that, and close the door. You're letting flies in. Your ma got a lots of years left in her yet." Julia followed Pa to his and Ma's bedroom. Pa slowly pushed the door open, removing his hat. With hat in his hand, he walked softly into the room the way that most people enter a mortuary. The room was filled with the stillness of death. Julia's words echoed in his mind. *My wife is dying*. He might have thought of Susie, who was to be his next wife. Mrs. Laura Mae stood as the dark man entered the room.

Pa's fear was obvious in this early morning stillness. Isabella looked at him, knowing what she and Julia and the midwife knew. She was dying. A dry and deep cough struggled out of her mouth. Her fever had gone up even more. She had taken one sip of the warm leftover vegetable soup broth that Julia had given, and she had thrown it back up. The boiled ginger that Mrs. Laura Mae had told Julia to make for her gave her little comfort. But as soon as she finished sipping it, the chills and headaches returned. The balm mixture didn't help either.

Isabella's husband looked down on her as though she was already in a coffin. The angel of death filled the room as though waiting for Isabella's last breath. Its presence was palpable; on her eyelids was the shadow of death. She knew her husband well enough to know that he might be thinking about Susie as he had been looking at her. Pneumonia had set in during her weakened condition from a difficult delivery.

It was time for Mrs. Laura Mae to go home. She was exhausted, probably wondering how long she can continue doing this. Looking down at this young lady was almost too much for her. At fifty, she felt old being a midwife because it was so often draining. Every time she has a delivery, she labored with the mothers. Her grandmomma, her own momma were all midwives. They passed the trade down to her. "Lord, I just don't know."

Isabella's family was back into their routine. The children were usually running through the house. Julia and Isabella's oldest son Willie was in charge when their Pa wasn't home. Since Isabella got sick, Bill was gone most of the time. It seems like sometimes men think they can run from death, couldn't bear to face it head-on. Perhaps that was Bill's problem. Always had a reason not to be around the shadow of death encamped in his house, lurking in their bedroom.

Little Eugenia was two weeks old now, and Isabella's pneumonia had gotten worse. The coughing, the mucus tinged with blood, chills, and fever would not go away.

How could she not hear her infant crying? How great must have been her sorrow knowing that she was dying and leaving her newborn. Probably as she lay dying in their wrought-iron bed on top of the straw mattress that was like a very large ripped pillowcase that was stuffed with the same haylike straws that her husband Bill used to feed his farm animals. Isabella was lying underneath the two quilts that she had stitched from her family's old clothes. It seemed as though her whole life was knitted together into the colorful bright quilt while she lay beneath it. The long hours that she lay there, she would look at each patch and recall the images in her mind like a movie playing in her head or like flipping through a family photo album.

Each patch told a story. The black striped patch was from the shirt her son Willie wore who was ten at the time. He loved to play ball, and while he was chasing the ball that his twelve-year-old brother Henry threw, he tripped and fell and had a banged-up knee. The blue-and-white floral patch was from the dress, Isabella remember so very clearly, she made for Kizzie when she was six years old, the only dress she wore on Sunday to church. As she continued to stare and gaze upon her quilt, the intense coughing would start and intensify. Once Isabella started coughing, it seemed that she wouldn't be able to stop. The coughing and thick mucus would interrupt her gazing. Julia was sitting near the bed, and she would lift the bucket that was filled with ashes for her momma to lean over so that she could spit the thick mucus that was tinged with blood into the bucket.

And what seemed like forever, the coughing would finally stop then Julia would lift her weak, feverish Momma's upper body and prop her back comfortably upon the two duck-feather-filled pillows. Her oldest eighteen-year-old daughter Julia would continue to sit by her dying Mamma's bed, caring for her, knowing that death was near. All throughout Julia's childhood, she was the child that her momma could and did count on. She was considered Momma's little helper. She was a lot like her momma. They both had long silky black hair and copper-tone skin. She had inherited her looks from her momma who was part Indian. Everyone had told her how pretty she was. Unlike her Poppa who felt uncomfortable around his dying wife, who was not sure what to say or do when he came into the room that had the smell of death. He couldn't bear to stay long. Julia felt the complete opposite; she didn't want to leave her momma alone.

As Isabella lay dying, the leaves had begun to turn yellow with a touch of fall in the air. Her husband Bill's hound dog Blue that was lying outside on the ground right underneath her bedroom window was howling more and more now that she was dying. People in the South knew that dogs howl more when death is coming to their master's house. Dogs just know these things, know that she was not going to recover, that she was actually dying this time, which was probably used to reflect upon her life and on all eight of her children.

Julia, Fannie, Mary, Kizzie, Elizabeth, Willie, Henry, and Eugenia were all born between 1861 and 1882. Knowing that Eugenia would be her last, she was hoping that her husband Bill would choose a good stepmomma for her children, for she had probably seen him looking at Susie, a young girl who lived down the road, while they were at church because a wife never misses the eyes of her husband. Mississippi Vital Records don't tell us much about these women whose lives were sacrificed to give life to their babies and a gift to their sometimes abusive husbands. Despite the odds, some women lived to be quite old.

When the chills and the coughing started, Julia would add another layer of quilt on top of the several layers that was covering her Ma. As she pulled the covers up to her Ma's chin, she gently lifted Ma's arms and hands and crossed them, forming an X. With the pneumonia taking all the strength from her hands, her ma's hand dropped down like a wet dishrag. For the first time, Julia paid close attention to her ma's hands. How weak and fragile they were, the scars from the years of her momma stooping over the corrugated tin washing board and scrubbing from the tin tub full of her family's dirty clothes still visible as her hand would occasionally scrap against the tin washing board. Once when her little brother Henry was about four years old, Ma was churning milk to form butter and was sitting not too far from the stove where she had some chicken frying in her big old cast-iron skillet. Her little brother had reached for the handle of that skillet full of hot grease, and by the grace of God, Ma was facing the stove. She leaped out of the chair, knocking the chair over where she was churning milk, almost knocking the speckled stoneware milk jar over too. Ma pushed Henry aside, knocking his little hand off before he placed his hand on the hot skillet handle. When Ma pushed his hand, she accidentally hit the skillet handle, and some hot grease splashed on her right hand. As she lay dying, the scar was still there.

Jesus said, "*See these scars on my hands? I did it for you.*"

Julia had a heart that was responsive and sensitive to her Ma's needs, perhaps feeling that she could take Ma's place. She knew how to do things Ma did—the cooking, ironing, scrubbing the clothes on the washing board, even listening to her younger sisters and brothers pray the way Ma taught them: "*Now I lay me down to sleep, bless Pa, bless Ma . . .*" This made her think of her dying Ma, that she couldn't bless Ma anymore when she died. Would she be able to bless their new Ma when their Pa married again? "Lord have mercy."

She continued to look at her Ma's hands, and she gently put her hand over her Ma's fragile and scarred hands and bowed her head down on top of their hands and wept. "Oh, Ma, I love you so. Lord, why do you have to take her?"

Julia knew she couldn't fill her ma's shoes, couldn't be a wife to her Pa. A man needs a wife.

And as she continued with her head lying on top of their hands, she noticed that her ma hadn't coughed and was lying very still. Blue was howling. Julia slowly raised her head up. Her ma's mouth and eyes were open, and she wasn't breathing. "Oh, Ma, Ma, God, you have taken my ma." Sobbing and weeping, she said, "Ma, Ma is gone."

Again, there was little known about Grandpa Bill's next wife, Susie Collins. Born 1857, she gave birth to three children before dying. And his last wife, Sallie, born in 1855, died at the age of twenty-five after giving birth to three sons.

Grandpa John and Grandpa Wesley each had three wives, all dying young. The story of Grandpa Bill is repeated here. Grandpa John married young Mollie, born April 1880, giving birth to five sons before death tore her away from her sons.

It's hard to imagine the life of these women who lived through these times. History has a way of drawing the curtain on women's lives or barely touching the surface of their lives. However, to disregard the huge sacrifice many women like Isabella have made from this silence. But if we follow the thread to the past, the hardworking farmwomen served their men and their children where everything was done by hands— laundry, a tub, a washing board, dirty clothes were soaped in the tub before a woman would rub each piece of cloth against the tin corrugated metallic surface on which clothes are rubbed in the process of washing and hanging each piece on a clothesline out to dry.

A wedge-shaped metal iron heated by the fire or on top of the stove was used for ironing. The woman would use a board supported by two chairs. The clothes she hung out to dry, the woman usually used her hands as a sprinkler. Dipping her hands in a bowl of water, she would sprinkle piece and ball each sprinkled piece into a tight ball to keep them damp before ironing, which made the ironing easier. She then placed them in a large basket. She would pull a chair up to the ironing board near where the iron was being heated so she wouldn't have to get up and down to reheat the iron because it didn't take the iron long to cool down. She would then have to reheat the iron. Obvious this was a long, slow, time-consuming process.

Preparing the family meal was going to the garden with a basket to pick the fresh vegetables, washing and trimming the stems and separating the ones that the insects had eaten off, making sure that there was no dirt or sand left on them before cooking them with their favorite meat, usually some parts of a hog.

The lady of the house has long prepared covering to keep her family warm. The cotton that her husband has gotten from the gin was removed with the seeds, leaving the pure white pure lint. She would pull a handful of pure white cotton and stretch it as much as possible and spread it up on a sheet that was to be used for the underside of the quilt. This sheet was mounted on two frames, one on each end of the sheet with legs that she had secured with small nails to keep it in place. This mounted frame is high enough that she could easily place her chair, sort of like a table, beneath it. This way, she could stitch the quilt together comfortably. She would lay the cotton as thick as she wanted the quilt to be for the cold winter months. The long hours of patchwork from her family's old worn-out clothes would be the top layer of the quilt. She would then sandwich them, and with needle and thread, stitch all of this together which would complete the process.

Sometimes ladies across the pasture or ladies from the church would come and pull up a chair and join her. Like in a tea party, they would talk about their children and their men.

# 12

## *The Picture*

Our poppa's dad, Grandpa Wesley, married our poppa's mother Cynthia and gave birth to his sister Mary. After giving birth to him, she died when our poppa was six months old.

Our poppa talked about not knowing his mother. "I never knew my mother. She died when I was six months old. I didn't see a picture of her until I was forty-three, the year was 1951. My sister Mary, although she had married and was living with her husband across the pasture from our poppa's house, would often go by there to get some of her belongings that were still there. And early this Sunday morning, she remembered a hat that she had left there, so she walked across the pasture to see if she could find the black hat that she wanted to wear to church.

"When she reached the house, no one was there, which wasn't unusual. Our poppa and our stepmomma was probably out back doing what needed to be doing—feeding the chickens, checking on the farm animals.

"Mary said she went and got the three-legged stepping stool that was in the corner of the living room. A stool that brought back so many memories. When she was six or seven, she used to stand on that stool and wash dishes from their dishwashing pan. Anyway, she got this stool to stand on so she could look in the top shelf of the closet for the black hat that she wanted to wear to church, and as her hand was searching for the hat, her hand rubbed against a book. She picked up the book that had been coverless long ago and which pages had begun to turn yellow, and she stepped off the stool and went to the wooden kitchen table and sat on a wooden chair because my sister never saw a book that she wouldn't scan through just to see what the book was about. She started flipping through the book. And as she opened the book, the picture was like a bookmarker, and it opened to where the small picture was stuck between the pages that held the picture."

When Mary opened the book, the book fell open to where the picture was, and there was the three by four inches in black and white picture staring back at her. Poppa said his sister knew instantly it was their momma. Mary said tears started welling up her eyes. She exclaimed, "Oh my God, that's our momma!" With trembling hands, she continued to stare and pay close attention to every detail of the first image that she was seeing of her momma's face—her hair, her eyes, her nose and lips that looked like her own. And as she continued to hold the picture, she thought about her brother.

By it being Sunday, Mary knew Sam was at church. And she had to pull herself together and finish getting ready for church herself. She and her brother went to the same church, and she knew she would see him there. Poppa said that his sister knew that upon seeing the first image of his mother that he had ever seen, this would stir up strong emotions in him. As Mary and her husband Clay walked into church, her brother was dressed in a dark suit and was sitting in one of the pastor's chairs on the platform with two other young ministers. She greeted him with a small smile; he gave a slight bow of his head in acknowledgment. Her sister-in-law Beatrice was sitting where the ushers sit, looking shy and very pretty in her blue floral dress and blue hat. Mary was an usher, and her husband Clay was a deacon. Mary sat near her sister-in-law, and Clay went and sat with the deacons.

After the amen and halleluiahs and the choirs had sung their last song "God Shall Wipe All Tears Away," Poppa said he came down from the platform to join his sister and his wife. Momma and Mary stood up to greet him. Poppa, as usual, gave his sister a hug. As Poppa was hugging her, Mary whispered in his ear, "I have something to show you. Come here and sit down." They sat down near Beatrice. Mary reached into her purse and pulled out the small picture that she had gently wrapped in her white handkerchief.

As her brother was sitting next to her on the pew, she gave him the handkerchief. Poppa slowly unwrapped the handkerchief, and the first image of his momma stared back at him. He gasped out the words, "Momma, our Momma?" He could only weep. "Momma. Mary, where did you get this? Oh my God," he said while still gazing at his momma. "Why, Cozetta favors her" (Cozetta was Poppa's fourth child).

However, as time passed with the midwives being replaced by hospitals, the longevity of lives for women surpassed those of their husbands. The days of husbands burying their young wives were practically over as the role had been reversed. Men started having heart attacks, triple bypasses, high blood pressure, strokes, Parkinson's disease. Their wives lived long lives after burying their husbands.

Grandpa Bill was the strong link that connected the Gathing men that followed him. Poppa's grandpa John was a furniture maker. He built a wooden chest in the late 1800s that was passed down to his poppa Wesley, and his poppa gave it to him that our family kept as a family heirloom. Poppa said his grandpa John enjoyed weaving straw baskets, said often to "never owe a white man nothing because if you do, you will never be free. The bondage of debt will always be with you. Never owe those 'dogs nothing' because they will keep changing the numbers on you. And there is nothing a Negro could do about it."

# 13

## They Didn't Rebel

Roberta said, "To my knowledge, never did any of the men in our poppa's family history rebel against the injustice of the Jim Crow laws. Although at the family gathering these laws were the topic of discussion, knowing that the ruling class was against their interest, they knew better than to step beyond the fixed limit into forbidden territory, a willful transgression or overstepping of limitations which the Jim Crow laws had set. To violate these limits would cause severe consequences, including lynching. These Negro men had seen enough in their lifetime living under this system to know that when Jim Crow spoke, he wasn't bluffing. Men they personally knew who had rebelled were left hanging from the limb of a tree with a rope tied around their necks."

### Chopping Cotton

The winter months were long and uneventful; however, on the farm there's always work to be done—mending fences, spreading manure to enrich the soil, knocking down the old cotton and cornstalks, and breaking the soil of the fields to be planted.

In 1950, Poppa was saving money for a tractor, but for now, his two mules assisted him and his five boys to do the work that was too difficult for them to do alone and which the human body didn't have the capacity to do, like plowing, riding, hauling.

After Poppa's boys had cleared the cotton field of all the dead cotton stalks from the previous year by knocking them down, pulling them up, cutting, or by any means necessary, this of course was a major job because some of these fields were ten acres or more. When the field was finally cleared, it was now time for breaking the soil of the fields to be planted.

Ulrich B. Phillips writes in *American Negro Slavery*:

> The farmer "listed" the field by first running a furrow with a shovel plow where each field cotton row was to be and filling it with a single furrow of a turn plow from either side; than when planting time approached they would break out the remaining balks with plows, turning the soil to the lists and broadening them into plows, turn the soil to lists and broadening them into rounded plant beds. This latter plan was advocated as giving affirm seed bed while making the field clean of all grass at planting. The spacing of the cotton rows varied from three to five feet according to the richness of the soil.

Once our brothers had taken care of the soil, planting begins in April. And our dreg alone with their planting because we know our poppa will be sharpening our hoes soon. Poppa would walk across the pasture to the field daily, looking at the soil and knowing that the cottonseeds that were planted should be popping up their head through the soil within two or three weeks.

When it's time to what we called chop the cotton early in the morning just after sunrise, we were all in bed and we could hear the file sliding against the hoe as our poppa filed our hoes. Meanwhile, school has been out for two weeks or more, and that gave Poppa's girls the opportunity to sleep past 7:00 a.m.

The boys didn't ever get that privilege because farm animals demanded that their routine wasn't broken—the cows would moo, horses hew-hawed, pigs squealed and oinked, chickens clucked and chatter. Cows had to be milked, animals had to be fed. Besides, Poppa could put up with a little laziness in his girls, but he couldn't tolerate it in his boys. "The Bible says if a man don't work, a man don't eat. Lord, there's nothing I hate more than a lazy man," Poppa would continue. "How can a man feed his family if he don't work?" And as an afterthought, he would say, "A woman should learn to cook so she can feed her family."

Momma, as usual, was in the kitchen standing near the cast-iron four-burner stove that has a twelve-gallon hot water preserver on the right side of the stove. This water was used for washing dishes, clothes, and for taking baths. Cozetta was standing near Momma, frying the bacon while Momma was scrambling the eggs. Cozetta would open the oven's door to check the large baking tray of golden brown biscuits that she had made from scratch. The bacon, eggs, rice, and biscuits smelled so good. We were so anxious to eat. Meanwhile Roberta and Shug were already in the kitchen setting the table with Cozetta helping Momma.

Cozetta, Ruth, and Christine were home from BI (Baptist Industrial Academy), a Negro private school in Hernando, Mississippi, for the summer. Before 1958, there were no public high schools that went beyond the eighth grade for Negroes in Mississippi; I will discuss this in more detail in a later chapter. Consequently, Poppa sent his children who had finished the eighth grade to BI.

Momma told Roberta to go and wake up the "other sleepyheads." Roberta opened the girls' bedroom door. Christine and Ruth were in one bed. Alberta, Betty Joe, and Peggy were in the other doubled bed, buried beneath several layers of quilts. She said in a loud voice, "Momma told me to tell you all to get up! If you don't, Poppa is coming in here and I know y'all don't want that!" Hearing Poppa's name, they would all begin to stir, very slowly, sluggishly dragging themselves out of bed.

Poppa's boys had responsibilities before the break of dawn, even before the rooster crowed. They were responsible for milking the cows and pitching hay to feed the farm animals. Making sure the woodpile was high, Poppa would say with great authority, "Whose turn is it to cut the wood?" Lloyd would look at his buddy Fred and try to stifle a laugh, knowing that Fred was the guilty one. "Fred, go and cut some wood, you see that woodpile is low! What's the matter with you, boys? I shouldn't have to tell you all that, you can see as well as me."

Once Poppa has finished filing a hoe, he would carefully touch the sharpened hoe to make sure it is sharpened to his liking, knowing that his children would be using it all day while working in the field.

When the filing of the hoes were silent, Lloyd and Fred knew that Poppa was going in for breakfast. This was a signal that they could come indoors with their milk pails full of milk. No way would they walk past Poppa and he was still working and they were not working also.

Poppa would line all nine of the sharpened hoes in a row on the end of the back porch. "Morning, Poppa," they would say in unison. Poppa didn't respond with "good morning." He really wasn't interested in how good their morning were. "You boys through?" "Yes-sum, Poppa."

As Poppa led the way, they followed him up the back porch steps. Fido, one of the boys' hunting dogs, is hungry too, so the dog trails them up the back step into the kitchen. Poppa saw that the dog had gotten into the kitchen with them. Poppa raised his voice. "Boy, you know better than letting the dog into the house!" Fred kicked the dog out the back door. Momma said, "Don't kick the dog, that's mean." Poppa said, "One thing for sure, dogs should not be in anyone's house. They have fleas, ticks, and they eat all kinds of dead things that other animals ignore as they roam outside." Poppa continued. "It's amazing to me when I see white folks letting their dogs lick them in the mouth. All I can say they haven't seen the things I have seen dogs do."

The smell of bacon, eggs, homemade biscuits, and rice greeted their hungry stomachs as Poppa, Fred, and Lloyd joined the crowd waiting for them in the kitchen.

Poppa's family has congregated in the kitchen, waiting for him to sit at the table before them. We were all standing behind our chairs where we were going to sit. Momma fixed Poppa's plate once we were all seated. A small portion of rice, eggs, two strips of bacon, and one biscuit— Poppa was a light eater. And usually when he sees nothing sweet on his plate, he would say, "Bracey, you don't have something sweet'?" Momma would rise and go to the kitchen cabinet and get a jar of her homemade preserve and put maybe two tablespoons on her husband's plate.

Lloyd and Fred were staring at the table, eyeballing the food, probably thinking of how their plates were going to look once it was full. Once Poppa was seated, you could hear the hasty dragging of the chairs on the wooden floor as everyone hurriedly pulled their chairs out before sitting. Once seated, everyone bowed their heads for prayer. Poppa led by bowing his head in prayer: "Graces, Lord, thank You for this food we're 'bout to receive . . ." Momma would say her blessing next: "Lord, have mercy." One by one, all their children would say their Bible verses.

Fred and Lloyd would both race for the bacon as though they there might not be any left if they don't get theirs first. Poppa would say, "Don't take all the bacon from the rest of the children! Why, your momma hasn't gotten hers yet!" All of us would giggle at that.

Once everyone had finished reaching and grabbing, their plates were full and they began to eat. Poppa said, "I've got a story for you." We all listened closely. "A man found a frozen snake. He brought the frozen snake into the house and set it by the fireplace. When the snake thawed out, the snake bit the man. The man said to the snake, 'I felt sorry for you and brought you into the house so you wouldn't die and you bit me.' The snake said, 'You knew I was a snake before you brought me into your house.'"

Everyone laughed. Momma giggled and said, "Be careful what and who you bring into your house. Mr. Lee felt sorry for this hobo that was walking on the side of the road, stopped his truck, picked him up, brought the man in his house, fed him, and when the man finished eating, the man robbed him." Alberta said, "That man was a snake."

After breakfast, we began our first day in the field. Most of Poppa's children had on long-sleeved loose-fitting clothes that can help protect us from the sun and insect bites. The girls usually took gloves with them to cushion their hand from gripping the hoe handle; this would help protect their hands from calluses that form while gripping the wooden hoe handle all day.

The boys didn't wear gloves. They would view this as being a "sissy." They took pride in their big working-man hands. They didn't whine about the calluses, scratches, cuts, bruises, dirty fingernails; these were the signs of a real man. Cuts that didn't require stitches were ignored. Lloyd said, "When I shake hands with a man with soft hands and manicured fingernails, this gives me a creepy feeling. A man's hands should feel like he is a working man and not like a woman's hands. That he has held a hammer, held a shovel, dug a ditch." Fred said, "Lloyd, man, you're right. Once I shook hands with a preacher, you know I am still not over the soft mushy feeling of his hands."

We were all laughing and talking. Now that we were all together, the mood is upbeat. Chopping cotton, here we come! Sometimes the field that we would be working in is right across the pasture, and we would walk instead of our poppa taking us in his pickup truck. On this spring day in April 1954, Momma and Poppa's children are practically walking by twos, walking on the very familiar footpath across our poppa's 150-acre farm, a path that had been trampled out by our poppa's livestock and his family too. This path was as visible as city sidewalks snaking through tall weeds, wild flowers, bushes, and trees. With their sharpened hoes lying across one of their shoulders like a hobo carrying his belongings at the end of a long stick, the followers kept their distance so the hoe in front of them won't hit them in the face. Fred and Lloyd led the way with Fido walking near Lloyd, with Ruth and Cozetta following, then Shug and Roberta, Alberta, Christine, and James. Six-year-old Betty Joe and our nephew six-year-old Henry trailed behind.

Fido saw movement in the weeds nearby and took off running toward the weeds that were in motion. Lloyd chased his favorite hunting dog. "Fido, Fido, here, boy!" Fido ignored him and kept on running. "You stupid dog, come back here!" Now we were all laughing, seeing how funny this scene was. Fido stopped and very slowly followed the moving weeds, and with one quick motion, his head was buried in the weeds. Fido then started rapidly shaking his head from side to side.

Cozetta screamed, "Oh my God, Fido has a snake in his mouth!" This stopped Lloyd in his tracks. Lloyd knew that there was nothing he could do now but wait until the killing was over. Once the snake was broken from the violent force of Fido's shaking, the dog knew he has won. Fido went to Lloyd for approval. Lloyd bent down and patted his dog on the head while Fido wagged his tail. "Good dog, good dog Fido."

And that was the way the announcement was made that the snakes had come out of their long winter hibernation. Once we saw one, we were on the lookout for many more; we knew the snake season had begun. From then on forward, when picking blackberries for our favorite cobbler or picking wild plums, we would often see snakes slithering beneath the bush trying to get away from us. We would quickly jump back from them. "Oh my, there is a snake! Be careful." Once the snake was out of sight, we would keep on picking berries that our momma was expecting for the pie she was going to make for her family.

Poppa had gone to Holly Springs as usual to take care of what he called "taking care of some business"; meanwhile, his children were at the ten-acre field looking out at the long rows of young cotton plants.

A cool breeze was blowing from the south. The weather was perfect for chopping cotton, not too cool and not too hot. Without giving it any thought, we all walked with our buddies to the large field. When we were finished with this field, we would be going to the next field. Poppa had an expected time for us to finish this ten-acre field, maybe two weeks or less before moving to the next field. Any delays could cause serious problems.

Ulrich B. Phillips writes,

> The cotton plants in the earlier stages were very delicate. Rough stirring of the clods would kill them; excess of rain or drought would be likewise fatal; and a choking of grass would altogether devastate the field. The plants, furthermore, were liable to many diseases and insect ravages. In infancy cut-worms might sever the stalks at the base, and lice might sap the vitality; in the full flush of blooming luxuriance, wilt and rust, the latter particularly on older lands, might blight the leaves, or caterpillars in huge armies reduce them to skeletons and blast the prospect; and even when the fruit was formed, boll-worms might consume the substance within, or dry-rot prevent the top crop from ripening.

Lloyd and Fred had chosen their rows and so did Cozetta and Ruth, Roberta, Shug and Alberta, Christine and James. Young Betty Joe and Henry went under the shade tree and were playing tag or any game to stay busy until we called for them to bring us water. When someone hollered "Water!" they would fetch the pail of water with a long handle metal dipper and start running toward the thirsty worker. The children reached Fred first. Fred took the pail from the small children's hands, and using the dipper, he leaned over the bucket, scooping the water into the dipper with water overflowing out of the sides of his mouth while he slurped water from the dipper. Water is dripped down his chin back into the water bucket.

Cozetta raised her voice while looking at Fred, "Stop doing that! Your old spit is running back into our drinking water." Fred replied, "You think I'm poison or something?" We were all standing around Fred waiting our turn.

Lloyd snatched the dipper from Fred's hand. "Hey, man, save us some water!" When Lloyd snatched the dipper, Fred dropped the water pail. We all started grumbling and murmured in disbelief as we watched the dry earth drink our only source of water and turn to mud.

"Now look what you have done! What's the matter with you, always doing something stupid!"

Fred replied in anger, "Who are you to call me stupid!"

"Man, I can't believe you." Lloyd walked over and stood so close to Fred, Fred could smell his breath. Fred pushed Lloyd out of his face. Lloyd struggled back, almost falling. Lloyd looked at his brother and started laughing.

Shug looked at the puddle of water from the empty water pail. "I don't see nothing funny about this. This is no joke, no one had a drink but Fred. Now, if someone has to walk all the way back to the house to get some water, it should be Fred. Or he can go over to Mr. Matthew's place where he can get some fresh springwater. There's always lots of water seeping out of that spring.

Fred said, "Y'all must be nuts or something. I ain't walking all the way over there, that's three miles away." We were all in agreement with Shug as our eyes rested on the empty water pail. Lloyd replied, "That's what's so funny, he is the only one that's not thirsty. Besides, Poppa will be here soon because it's almost noon."

Once we had started chopping cotton, the rhythm of the season has begun. Practically when the first hoe hit the ground, the singing would start. Lloyd was the number one singer, and without warning, he would start singing, *"There is a dream that I dreamt about, a heavenly home, I know I'm going someday, it may be morning, noon or night—that's why I'm sending up my timbre every day. There is a mansion my God have for me that's why I'm sending up my timbre every day."*

At the sound of Lloyd's singing, we would stop chopping cotton and started clapping our hands and singing along with Lloyd. Cozetta said in a loud voice, "Y'all better put your hands back on y'all hoes. When Poppa gets here with our lunch, he's going to be mad at us if we haven't chopped enough cotton. We've got less than two weeks to finish this field."

When Cozetta reminded us of the task at hand, Ruth said, "The last one at the end of this row is a dead duck." When Ruth said that, the children who loved to compete and couldn't resist the challenge to be competitive started chopping with accelerated speed, with Lloyd and Fred leading the way. Cozetta, Ruth, Shug, and Roberta followed close behind. Christine, Alberta, and James could care less. They still chopped at their regular pace.

Lloyd hollered without skipping a beat, "Y'all be careful now, don't chop too much cotton down." We knew how important it was to take extra care while thinning the cotton and eliminating the weeds that grew at the same rate of the cotton, chopping cotton and leaving only two plants to grow with gaps between the next two plants. The competition ended with Lloyd winning and Fred coming in second.

Looking at our shadows that we used as a sundial that indicated the time of day by the position of our shadows as cast by the position of the sun, we knew it was almost noon and our Poppa would be returning with our lunch of bologna, liver cheese and crackers, delicious moon pies for dessert, and soda pop.

We heard the pickup before we saw Poppa's truck trailing a cloud of dust. Someone hollered, "Here comes Poppa!" We all dropped our hoes on the spot and started rushing toward the large weeping willow tree that supplied us with abundant shade and cool breezes too.

Before Poppa parked his truck, we all started walking toward the truck to greet him and get our lunch. Two large Kroger's grocery store brown shopping bags were sitting on the front seat next to Poppa. Lloyd and Fred grabbed one bag each and headed to the shade tree with the gang of us following them.

As soon as they set the bags on the ground, all hands were reaching in to make sure they get their favorite soda pop. Poppa interrupted the haste by saying, "Will y'all please wait?" He looked at Cozetta. "Will you divide the food? I don't want Fred and Lloyd taking too much and not leaving the rest of you all any."

As we were eating lunch under the large weeping willow tree, our poppa walked the field, looking at the young cotton plants, praying and hoping that the insects and the weather would be merciful this year. For he could never forget the year of 1946, the year the rain and heat created a breeding ground for diseases and an invading army of insects that ravaged and devastated his crop—and he wasn't alone in Mississippi that horrible year. "The Bible says it rains on the just and the unjust alike," Poppa said. "One thing about Mother Nature, she doesn't discriminate."

At the end of cultivation in July, the crop at this stage looks healthy; however, our poppa's prayers for a successful crop won't end until the last boll of cotton was picked in October.

Being freed from chopping cotton, we entered the hot and sultry days of summer with the younger children contented with playing games. The older children who had outgrown the fun of games and nursery rhymes would have to tolerate the heat while fanning the onslaught of flies, at times suffering from boredom. Momma and Poppa's older children would watch their younger siblings play the same nursery rhymes our parents shared with us and were still portrayed through our younger sisters and brothers that the older children once played also:

*"Here we go around the mulberry bush . . ."*

Living miles from outside activities like movies, which our poppa wouldn't have given his permission even if we had lived closer because he saw those things as worldly, things that "God frowns upon." Subsequently, these idle months were especially difficult for his teenage girls. A since of boredom and restlessness would slowly creep into our spirit.

Momma was where we brought all our complaints. Her children pains, dissatisfaction, and problems were laid in her lap as her plump body sat comfortably in her favorite chair. Did we remember somewhere deep in our subconscious how she comforted us as infants and small children and see her gently ways of caring for our younger sisters and brothers? Always making our grief and distresses seem lighter.

"Momma, why won't Poppa let us girls do nothing? He let his boys do whatever they want to as long as their work is done." Momma said, "Men just don't look at their boys the same way they look at their girls. They are more protective with their girls, it's always been that way and it probably will stay that way."

"Well, that's just not fair. It's like we are held captive or something," Roberta said as she was brushing her momma's long soft hair.

Although Poppa's children had a long-awaited break between chopping and picking cotton, Poppa did not have the privilege of being freed from worry. The unpredictable weather would greatly threaten their livelihood. And this was the upmost of Poppa's concern—his family's livelihood depended upon it. Knowing the weather can be a blessing or a curse, he always prayed for a normal rain fall.

Therefore, our poppa was greatly aware of the activities of his surrounding when he was outdoors, mentally eyeballing everything within view. Were all the animals where they were supposed to be? In their own neighborhoods—cattle in the barnyard, hogs in the pigsty, chickens in the chicken coop. All animals accounted for, all gates secured and locked.

Before going indoors for the night, he would look up into the late evening sky because he couldn't afford to ignore the signs of the sky and the weather. Wind's blowing coming from the east, a storm is coming, and that's driven by a few dark clouds. Our poppa would come indoors and say to no one in particular, "Lord, I think it's going to rain. Lord have mercy, we don't need more rain. If it continues to rain, my cotton crop will be devastated. Last year I prayed for rain, that was an awful year for an expanded drought. Praise God it rained before my crop were lost. I was afraid the young cotton plants wasn't going to survive the long drought that was almost fatal before the rainfall."

Despite hearing our poppa's prayers, his children prayed that rain would interrupt our work in the field. We therefore, like other children, didn't enjoy going to the fields to work, so the rain made us happy knowing that it would be too wet to work in the field the next day.

These traditional framed houses were cold in the winter with maybe one wood-burning fireplace. The desire to keep her family warm kept our mother and other mothers of that area very busy making quilts from old cloths by cutting out small pieces of fabric from them and stitching them by hand together. When this work was finished, it would form a beautiful tapestry work of art.

Sometimes women would get together to make quilts. They laughed and talked like women do today about their men and children.

When the weather turned warm, everyone was anxious to get outside and out of the heat indoors. Poppa and Momma would sit in their favorite chair on the front porch as they watched their children play barefoot in the dust, singing nursery rhymes.

Maybe four or five of their daughters would make a large circle as they held hands while one of the girls would be squatting in the center. Round and round they would go as they sang to the squatting girl with dust flying as the girls' bare feet hit the earth.

*Little Sally Walker*
*Sitting in a saucer*
*Rise, Sally Rise—*
*Put your hands on your hips and let your back bone slip.*
*Shake it to the east,*
*Shake it to the west,*
*Shake it to the one that you love the best.*
*Your Momma said so*
*Your Poppa said so*
*That's the way to shake it if you want to catch your Bow.*

The girls had their street rhymes, and the boys had theirs also. "Hambone" was one of the boys' favorite. The boy would lean forward as he sits on a chair with one hand hitting his lower thigh. While still leaning, he would hit his lips with a popping sound while singing,

*Hambone, Hambone, where you been?*
*Round the world and back again*
*Hambone, Hambone, where's your wife?*
*She's in the kitchen cooking rice.*
*Hambone, Hambone, have you heard?*
*Poppa gonna buy me a mockingbird.*
*If that mockingbird don't sing,*
*Poppa gonna buy me a diamond ring.*
*If that diamond ring turns brass*
*Poppa gonna buy me a looking glass.*
*If that looking glass gets broke*
*Poppa gonna buy me a billy goat.*
*Hambone, Hambone!*

Jump rope, hide and go seek, checkers, jack rocks, and there were other games. Poppa's children played many games.

Our Poppa didn't get his first television until the early fifties, and even after getting it, TV only had three channels and it wasn't aired all night. Their children, especially the younger ones, had a lot of leisure time and used it for fun and games.

Poppa and Momma's children had lots of play time. We played cowboys and Indians; BB guns and cap pistols were considered toys to play with. The girls played in a homemade playhouse outside where we had tea parties with the tea set we got for Christmas. These were the days of the Lone Ranger, Hop-Along Cassidy, Roy Rogers, and Dale Evans. The games we played were influenced by these TV programs.

At night, because we were many miles from the city lights, we got the full effect of the nights. As we played outside, from the lights of the moon alone we could see our shadows and many falling stars. We would look up the night's sky, which was a huge playground for our imagination. That angels lived there and that if we obey God, we will live there too. We were captivated by them, lost in the stars in our little galaxy, unaware of the billions of other galaxies that control and support our galaxy. We didn't know the proper name of what we saw. We only saw its profound glorious, spectacular, radiant beauty. Later as we got older, we learned words like *astronomy, astrophysics,* or *meteor showers.* But for now, falling stars will do.

Is it any wonder the galaxies that captivated James and Lloyd as children in Mississippi still hold their interest as senior citizens? James spends hundreds of dollars on telescopes so he can stargaze as a hobby.

# 14

## *Making Preparations*

Poppa mostly cultivated cotton, corn, garden vegetables, and other kinds of root vegetables. All hands were required in the fields. Our lives revolved around the cycle of plowing, planting, and harvesting.

Mississippi was known as the king of cotton where we grew up. Almost everyone we knew picked cotton. And almost everyone we knew hated the laborious, tiresome labor.

Planting, harvesting, and reaping there takes great preparation and much hard work that all family members had an assigned task.

On the farm, boys and girls had clearly defined responsibilities: Boys milked cows, pitched hay, fed the farm animals, plowed, cut wood. Girls cooked, sewed and mended clothes, churned milk for butter, picked and washed fresh vegetables for our meals. They also washed clothes by hand in a tin tub, scrubbing them with a tin scrubbing board, hanging them on a clothesline outdoors. We pressed clothes with a wedge iron heated on the heater.

Before the rooster crowed at the break of dawn, Momma and Poppa were already making preparations for their children's sunup-to-sundown workday in the cotton fields. Momma and Poppa were the first to rise while their children were still tucked underneath their covers dreading the long workday ahead. The house was silent with the low voices of our momma and poppa occasionally breaking the silence. Their girls were in the girls' room, a room with two double beds and the cramped space of three girls to a bed. The five boys shared the same type of sleeping quarters like a military barrack. Consequently, these cramped living quarters even made us share the same pillow, sometimes facing each other, breathing in their exhale and they breathing in ours, breathing droplets of each other's coughs and sneezes, especially in the damp winter months, which added to the cacophony of hacking coughs, flu, fever, chills.

Momma and Poppa, like the generations before them, were born into an environment of home remedies. Momma would check her kitchen cabinet where she stored the medicines she knew she would need with the approaching winter—Epsom salt for upset stomach, Vick's Vapor Rub for stuffy nose. Sometimes she would even have Bayer aspirins for fever.

With the aroma of coffee and Momma's frying sausages or pork fatback, scrambled eggs, rice, and biscuits made from scratch, which was a typical southern breakfast, we knew Momma would be calling us to breakfast. "Breakfast!"

We children would throw the covers off them immediately because we knew our Poppa had zero tolerance for not being on time for meals. Our bare feet hit the cold floor. With great haste, we rushed to put on the dirty clothes that were thrown in the corner of the room on the floor that we wore the day before. The worn dirty shoes are somewhere beneath our pile of clothes. These old shoes were fine for the day's work in the cotton field. We all had Sunday shoes for church.

At mealtime, Poppa sat at the head of the table, and before sitting on the right of Poppa, Momma fixed Poppa's plate with great care, serving him the exact portion that he wants—one biscuit, small portion of scrambled eggs, a little rice, and a dab of jelly. Poppa supplied the food. Momma cooked the food and put it on her husband's plate. When everyone was seated, our poppa blessed the food. Momma, with head bowed, said, "Lord have mercy." Their children's minds were on the large platter of scrambled eggs with stacks of bacon on the same platter and a heaping platter of biscuits near the big bowl of rice. Poppa knew that all hands would be reaching at the same time, trying to be the first to fill their plates; his boys were the biggest aggressors. One by one, each child repeated a Bible verse, and after the amen, Lloyd grabbed three biscuits in one hand. Fred grabbed several strips of bacon. Poppa, as the supervisor, said, "Lloyd, don't take all the biscuits, you and Fred know the other children has to eat too."

After blessing the food and we started to eat, Poppa would say, "I've got a riddle for you." Momma would start giggling before he told the riddle. "Bracey, don't laugh before I tell the joke." Subsequently, this would get the full attention of Poppa's children. Some of Poppa's children would laugh because Momma had laugh. "Can't y'all wait until I finish? Okay, here is the riddle. *A man rode across the bridge but yet he walked.* How did he do it?"

One by one, Poppa's children would try and get the answer. Lloyd, the fourth boy, said, "The man rode across and walked back."

"Naw, that's not it." Everyone tried to get it. Everyone failed. Poppa looked at Momma who was still giggling. "Bracey, don't tell them." Then Poppa would ask, "Y'all give up?"

"Yes, Poppa, what is it?" we all asked in unison.

"Well, the man rode across on his horse and he had a dog named Yet and Yet walked." We erupted into laughter. And that was the way Poppa and Momma's children would start their day.

After breakfast and a full stomach, we would start making preparations for the long, hot day in the cotton field. Poppa had gone to Holly Springs and bought his children wide straw hats that shaded our face from the sun's harmful rays. Each hat had different-colored hatbands, which, once we chose a color, we could judge who it belonged to. We were also issued six—to seven-feet new cotton sacks for picking cotton, the straps wrapped across the shoulder like a woman's purse and the cotton sack dragged along the ground as we picked cotton.

We prepared for the day in the field the same way a camper prepares for a camping trip. We made sure we had on loose-fitting clothes with long-sleeved oversize shirts and plenty of drinking water. All ten of us would climb into Poppa's 1958 Ford pickup truck.

Momma was alone now on this warm October day. She had dried her hands on her apron. She was standing in the front door as her children were laughing and talking as they climbed into the back of the truck. Ruth and Cozetta got in front with Poppa. Ruth sat next to Poppa because she enjoyed being near him. Poppa would discuss church business with her. Ruth wanted as much information as possible so she could write better speeches for him when her Poppa needed her. Cynthia, Cozetta, and Ruth were best friends. Momma and Poppa noticed that most of their children had their favorite sisters or brothers. Shug and Roberta were close although it was hard to see why. Shug could have a mean streak at times, wanting always to control. Even though Shug had some rough edges, she also had a sense of humor. I guess Roberta probably appreciated that. Roberta was lighthearted, laughing a lot. Even with her and Shug's differences, they were close. Alberta and Roberta, although twins, weren't that close. It was obvious though that they really cared for each other. Alberta was serious-minded, which clashed with Roberta's lightheartedness. Christine was a loner, very pretty, spent more time in the mirror than any of the girls.

Momma and Poppa's five boys had their buddies too. Their two oldest boys, Plaite and Junior, were close in age and friendship. As they experienced racist hostilities and threats from the environment in which they lived, they lost trust in the God of their father. To repeat what I've said before, they didn't trust the "white Jesus." Subsequently, they both grew more and more militant as they got older.

Fred and Lloyd were buddies and also close in age. Usually when you saw one, you saw the other. They shared most of the same interests. Both loved to joke, horseplay, and just have fun. Unlike their two older brothers, neither one of them turned militant; they just didn't take life that seriously.

Their younger son James was a loner. Maybe with the pairing off of his older brothers, there was no one left for him. Junior and Plaite, Fred and Lloyd, and then there was James.

James always had problems living in the world as it is, thinking it to be not the way it should be. His hate against violence was embedded in all his thinking. His service in Vietnam in 1968 changed him. After coming home from Vietnam, he wasn't the same. The world living under Jim Crow didn't make sense, and after Vietnam, the chaos was more visible, more real. James was like a champion chess player always trying to put the world in order, thinking there has to be a way to eliminate social evil. His way of thinking continues to this day. The killing of Vietcong, the Jim Crow laws, the killing of women and children in Vietnam villages and in their homes—he was confused and angry. Even growing up, unlike his brothers, he never enjoyed hunting, didn't enjoy killing. "How can anyone kill an innocent animal?" James would ask.

James shared an interesting story with his family. He said he was in a military barrack lying in his bunk bed during the monsoon (rainy season) on a warm night in Vietnam. Vietnam is known for a large variety of snakes, spiders, scorpions, and lizards. As he was lying there in the silence of the night listening to the rain, thinking of home and about Momma, he saw a large long black snake crawling on the floor near his bunk bed, probably looking for food. The snake lifted its head off the ground and looked him dead in his face. James said, "I looked at the snake and the snake looked at me, and the most amazing thing happened to me. Total peace flooded my body, and I turned over and went to sleep with the snake still looking at me. That night in 1970 was the most peaceful sleep I had ever had while in Vietnam. Over forty years has passed, and I often think of that amazing peace that flooded through me, creating such calm and tranquility."

The children were crammed into the truck bed as Momma continued to stand in the doorway. She saw Lloyd and Fred horse playing in the crowded truck's bed. "I pray God that none would fall off the truck." Seeing them playing that way may have made her recall the time that Shug was ten or eleven and she fell off the back of the truck while the truck was in motion. Would have been killed, thank God, who saved her with only a broken arm. Her broken right arm never was quite the same. Shug would say, "With my right arm, I can't touch my shoulder." When she said that, her sisters would say, "Shug can't touch her shoulder." And they would laugh, and Momma would say, "Stop laughing at your sister, that's not funny."

Momma would continue standing in the doorway until her husband's truck trailed clouds of dust, slowly fading from sight as he sped down the gravel road. She was probably hoping that when he drops his children off at the cotton field and go to Holly Spring, he wouldn't forget the things she told him to bring back—coffee, baking soda, flour, and sugar—for she had promised the children she was going to bake them some tea cakes.

With her family gone, the house was unusually quiet. Just her and her baby girl, four-year-old Peggy, and Peggy's golden pet cat Thomasine.

# *Momma*

At age forty-three, Momma gave birth to her fifteenth baby, a baby girl she named Peggy, which would be her last. She didn't plan it that way; in fact, she thought that God would give her more children.

Cozetta said, "I was home with Momma and she was in her and Poppa's bedroom in the middle of the day. I knew something was wrong because Momma would never be in their bedroom with the door closed and Poppa not with her. I knocked softly on their door, asked, 'Momma, are you all right?' She didn't answer. With alarm, I gently turned the doorknob and pushed the door open. There was my momma lying on top of their bloody bed covering with bloody towels between her legs. Momma! Oh my God, Momma! I rushed and kneeled and kissed her. Oh my God! My momma is dying! 'Momma, why are you bleeding like this?' She said in an almost inaudible voice just above a whisper, 'I tried to make it stop but it won't stop.' 'Momma, am going to get Poppa! I will be right back.' With the blessing of God, Poppa was coming in from the barnyard. I ran to meet him. 'Poppa, hurry! Something is wrong with Momma, she is bleeding to death!'"

Poppa didn't say a word; he just took off running to his bleeding wife. Cozetta said she followed in close pursuit. Poppa rushed into their bedroom and scooped his bleeding wife up like she was a small child. "Lord have mercy" were the only words he spoke as he held his bleeding wife in his arms, rushing out the front door to his car and gently laid her on the backseat. Cozetta thought about her sisters and brothers working in the fields, so she hastily grabbed a sheet of paper from the note tablet that was lying on Momma's dress and grabbed a yellow pencil from the cup of pencils that was near the note tablet. With trembling hands, she frantically scrambled out a note: "*Momma very sick! Me and Poppa gone to hospital.*" She taped the note on the kitchen door because she knew that would be the door they always used when they came from the fields. Cozetta then rushed to the closet and grabbed more clean towels and hurriedly got in the backseat and lifted her momma's head and placed her momma's head with great care upon her lap. As Poppa drove speedily down the gravel road, the only sound they heard was the sound of the gravel hitting the bottom of his car. About a mile down the road near the country store were bored men congregated to play checkers, telling jokes and sharing a pint of whiskey. When they saw Poppa speeding and passing them, they recognized the car, and they knew something was terribly wrong by the way he was speeding.

Cozetta, from where she was sitting in the back, looked at the way Poppa was driving. She had never seen him drive that way—bent just a little with both hands gripping the steering wheel and staring straight ahead.

The ten miles' drive to Holly Springs Memorial Hospital seemed to take longer than it should have. When they arrived at the emergency room, Poppa opened the back car door and lifted his wife out of the car the same way he lifted her in, like a small child. When he walked through the emergency door, the nurse saw the urgency right away. She called "code trauma" then rushed for a stretcher. Poppa laid his bloody wife on the stretcher, and after the nurse gently covered her with a sheet, all eyes were on Momma. After the trauma assessment, they asked Cozetta and Poppa a few questions and admitted Momma for her first experience in a hospital.

Poppa and Cozetta were now in the emergency waiting room. As they were silently sitting, waiting for the doctor's diagnosis, they were both fighting the fear of what-ifs. Poppa had a deeply intense look upon his face. Cozetta said that she could sense the prayers and the hope that everything will turn out for the best.

Finally, after about an hour, the young doctor walked into the emergency room. They both anxiously stood up. He said, "I got good news and bad news. Your wife is going to be all right; however, she needs surgery right away. Her problem is a ruptured fibroid tumor, and she needs a hysterectomy right away and this means she has had her last child and she has lost so much blood she is going to need a blood transfusion before surgery. You can go in and see her now. She's in room 112." Poppa said, "Thank you, Doctor, and praise God." Cozetta said, "Thank you, Jesus!" As he was getting ready to leave, the doctor said, "By the way, she don't know yet that she won't have any more children. I thought it's best that you tell her."

Poppa walked into the room with Cozetta right behind him. Momma was lying in the raised hospital bed to support her back, looking pale but comfortable in her white hospital gown. Poppa walked over to the bed and held her hands. "Bracey, how do you feel?" he said.

"I'm sorry I put y'all through this," Momma said.

Cozetta said, "Momma, don't say that, you just got sick, that's all."

Momma asked, "What's wrong with me? Where did all that blood come from?" Poppa told her what the doctor said about what caused all the bleeding and that she has to have surgery. He didn't know how to tell her the rest, about not having any more children. He looked at Cozetta for help.

Poppa stepped back, and Cozetta stood where he was standing and held her momma's hands. "Momma, you have to have a hysterectomy, and when that happens, you can't have any more babies."

Right away, tears started rolling down her cheeks. "No more babies. You mean I can never have another baby? Peggy is my last baby?" She continued to cry. Poppa felt like crying himself, so he quietly left Cozetta and Momma alone.

Poppa's family had all come in from the fields. Junior, as usual, led the children; and as he opened the back door, he was the first to see and read the note. "Oh my God, Momma is in the hospital! What-what happened?" Surprise and confusion erupted among the children. This surprising news went right inside the most inside part of their hearts, bringing with it shock waves of sadness and fear. Four-year-old Peggy began to cry. "I want my momma." Ruth reached for Peggy to comfort her. And as she squatted to eye level with Peggy, she said, "Peggy, Momma is going to be all right because Poppa is not going to let nothing bad happen to her." Everyone was afraid because nothing like this had ever happened before.

Roberta and Alberta walked into Momma and Poppa's bedroom and saw the bloody sheets on their bed. They both gasped, putting their hands over their mouth, seeing the bloody sheets. They both begin to weep. "Oh, Momma, oh, Momma! What happened to our momma?"

Roberta closed the door because she didn't want the other children to see their momma's blood. She turned to comfort Alberta, to try and quiet her down. "Shhh, be quiet, we don't want our brothers to see this." Alberta, weak at the knees, fell on the bed. Roberta said in a whisper, "Get ahold of yourself, Alberta, we have got to clean the bed up before anyone else see this." Tears was rolling down Roberta's cheeks. She reached into her parents' closet and got clean beddings and replaced the bloody covering. Roberta said to her sister, "So this is why Momma insisted that Peggy go to the field even though she was crying to stay home with Momma. I knew that was odd at the time. Momma wasn't feeling well even then."

Roberta closed their parents' bedroom door, and she and Alberta walked back into the living room. No one paid attention to them because they were wrapped up in their own personal worries about their momma.

They all heard the car coming down the gravel road on this warm October day in 1955. There was a touch of fall in the air. Leaves on the Mississippi magnolia trees had begun to turn yellow. They all rushed to the front yard, anxious to find out what happened. Poppa's car was instantly surrounded by his worried children almost before he finished parking it.

Poppa and Cozetta were flooded with questions about our momma. "Your momma is going to be all right. I will tell you all, but let me get into the house first." Once inside, Poppa flopped down in his green leather chair, obviously from exhaustion. He told his children the whole story from beginning to the end.

When Poppa got to the part about the blood transfusion and that Momma needed blood, all hands went up. Junior stepped forward with authority. "Poppa, I'm the oldest, I'm going to give Momma my blood." Poppa's eyes quickly scanned and crossed his children and he said, "Junior will do it."

I've stated this before, and I think it bears repeating here. During the time of the Jim Crow laws, a land fraught with difficulties and danger for parents and their children, who were on a daily basis fed negative mental stimulus from their Jim Crow surroundings, Momma and Poppa had many worries and fears for their children. They knew too that we were all influenced by our surroundings and how easily it would be for one of their children to cross the forbidden line drawn by Jim Crow.

Blacks and whites in the South were forced into separation. Separate school, separate neighborhoods, separate public eating. Whites had school buses. Negro kids in the 1950s didn't have school buses in Mississippi. Our books were leftover, used books that the white schools didn't want anymore.

Momma's children would rush home from school with the smell of a pot of pinto beans and ham hocks cooking or maybe cabbage and cornbread waiting for their hungry stomach with homemade tea cakes or fried apple pies and tell her about the insults they encountered from the white children as the busload of white kids passed them while they were walking home from school.

"Hey, you stupid nigger!" "The nigger kids has to walk!" Sometimes some of the white kids leaning with heads sticking through the bus window with sneering, contemptuous facial express would spit on us.

And as the big yellow school bus passed us with the Mississippi red dust from the gravel road covering us, we could hear laughter from the white children. "Ha ha ha ha!"

I can only imagine how my mother felt listening to her children telling her about the insults they encounter daily. How can she fight against a system that was designed to bully her children? How can she prevent them from turning bitter?

Earlier that day, Momma had gone to her vegetable garden and picked fresh vegetables for her family, and during midsummer, there would be an abundant supply. This time of the year, Momma's garden was overflowing with ripe fruits and vegetables. Our mother and her older daughters assisted her in canning part of the surplus vegetable for future use. Poppa and his older boys, likewise, would slaughter a hog; and Momma would, after making sausages, preserve some of these in glass jars also.

Momma was in her kitchen where the old wooden kitchen cabinet had many fingerprints as a reminder of the trips that her children had left there as they opened the doors, looking for food or to get a tin cup that once held a can of peaches or some store-bought preserve once her homemade preserve has run out and Momma would then buy some because Poppa always wanted some sweet. On the kitchen counter was the large tin can that was once used for Maxwell house coffee but was now being used for her homemade tea cakes that were eaten almost before she has finished putting them into the can. On the counter was a large tin pan that was used for washing dishes. The used dishwater was dumped into the knee-high bucket near where the dishwasher was standing so Momma can easily dump the water when through washing dishes. We called the bucket "slop bucket" to put the scraps in that was left from the dirty dishes. All of our table scraps would also be dumped into the slop bucket. The waste from this bucket would be fed to Poppa's hogs. Hogs were our garbage disposal.

The hog pen was a stone throw away from our house. There was a long trough that was inside the fenced-in pigpen that was used for feeding the hogs. Sometimes Poppa would have six to eight hogs in there. And when the hogs saw one of Poppa's boys coming with the bucket of slop, they would respond wildly with oinks, grunts, and squeals while standing on their back legs with the two front feet pressing against the fence, clamoring for food. Watching hogs eat, you can see why they earned the names gluttonous, greedy, selfish, and fat. Once the slop bucket has been emptied into the trough, the hogs squeezed tightly and forcibly together, trying to be the first to eat.

In the summer, the warm weather brought in many varieties of insects of all kinds. The houseflies were the worst to keep out of the house. "Will you shut the door? You are letting flies in my kitchen," Momma said. This was a losing battle. These terrible pests knew exactly what they were looking for—food! They would land on our food. We would get a rag, sometimes the dishrag, to whip them through the door. Throughout the warm months, "Shoo, fly, don't bother me" were said repeatedly.

Momma looked at her children as she stood at her cast-iron wood-burning stove, refilling the empty bowl with pinto beans and ham hocks from the large cast-iron pot on top of the stove. Thomasine the cat was rubbing against Momma's calf for attention, hoping that Momma would drop a small piece of food on the floor for her; the aroma in the kitchen had stirred the cat's appetite as the children were eating while sitting around the large round table. In the late 1950s home economics had slipped into our schools. We were taught the proper way to do things.

We became aware of things we didn't know before—how to set a table; how to use a fork; how to drink water from a glass without slurping it; even how to chew our food with our mouth closed, "Your food should be chewed thirty-two times before swallowing"; never to put your elbow on the table. Even with this new teaching, some still preferred using their old customary way of eating using their fingers instead of the forks and spoons that Momma had placed on the table. "Food just tastes better when using your fingers rather than a fork or spoon," Alberta said.

"Y'all just plain old country, that's all. I hope y'all don't let no white folks see y'all eating that way when we go to town," Roberta said.

"No matter what we do or say, they are still going to call us niggers. Once a nigger, always a nigger."

As Momma placed the full bowl of pinto beans on the table, she continued to pay close attention to her children. They looked the same— no frowns on their faces, except maybe they weren't smiling as much. You know how children are; they always seem to shake everything off so easily.

As she watched them eat, she said a silent prayer for her children that that incident of extreme verbal hatred thrown at her children almost on a daily bases as they walked to school wouldn't destroy their spirit; for everyone had heard about that Till boy. Emmett Till was his name.

Momma said, "Why, they killed that boy. The KKK did it, all right. I heard somewhere that that his mother had put that poor fourteen-year-old boy on the bus leaving Chicago to see him off to spend two weeks' vacation with his relatives in Mississippi Delta. His mother did the same thing me and Sam always did down here in Mississippi. We tell our children how to act and talk around them white folks. There are rules down here that we colored folks have to live by because if you don't, you'll die.

"Mommas and poppas all throughout the South teach their kids on a daily basis what they must do: (1) always say, 'Yes sir and no sir' and (2) never look them in the eyes because they'll think you are an uppity nigger. White folks don't like uppity niggers. They have been known to be lynched. We also tell our children especially our boys if they tell you to get down on your knees, do it because, child, whites has no law or rules that they have to obey regarding Negroes. But we have to obey them as they make or change their minds about Negroes.

"You know, that Till boy made headline news when they lynched that boy for looking at that white girl. But no one is talking about

Brother Franklin's son, that deacon in our church. The dogs found his boy near the river. They found him dead with his face down in the mud."

"Lord have mercy," was our momma's daily prayer. In Sunday school, we teach our children to love one another.

"Lord," Momma may have been thinking to herself, "how can I, Lord, teach my kids to love these evil white folks? Lord Jesus, I know there's some good whites. But down here in Mississippi, they are so mean. Lord, only you Jesus know the reason they are the way they are. This was the prayers of the faithful who had never ceased, both day and night, to cry out for deliverance." Momma and Poppa read in their Bible that they would be delivered out of this horrible fear of raising their kids here, how long before one of her five boys would react in response to their hostile environment.

That was the way Momma felt a few years later in 1968 when her youngest son James went to Vietnam. She had heard about the hand grenades, mine fields, all that shooting, danger all around. Her baby boy was in the midst of it all. It was awful.

As we heard Momma praying, sometimes we would walk past Momma and Poppa's old wooden cracked bedroom door. A door that had many little hands and fingerprints from her small children pushing and pulling the door to close or open, saying, "Momma, can I?" Or "Momma, make him or her stop." There was a KJV Bible on top of her pillow that she would always read before going to bed. We could get a glimpse of Momma in her long-sleeve pink flannel nightgown kneeling on the hardwood floor with her head leaning on the side of her and Poppa's bed in prayer, the bed that always reminded their children of the fairy tale "The Three Little Bears." Even the colorful quilt that she had made looked the part that was portrayed in the story. One child would say to another, "I smell apples." The other child would say, "I do too!" We knew that that meant. Christmas is near. Santa Claus is coming soon. Wow! Anticipation and excitement would start to build.

Like other small children, Poppa's children did not know that their poppa was also their Santa. They did not know yet that once a year, Poppa bought them the big red delicious apples, oranges, and big bags of candy that make you know it's Christmas and hid our Christmas goodies in his old wooden padlocked chest that he kept hidden in his bedroom closet.

A chest it seems like it's been around since the beginning of time. Sometimes, when Poppa and Momma wasn't around, some of his children would sneak into their parents' bedroom, open the closet, and stare at this old chest, a chest that held so many secrets. Poppa's children would wonder what they were. There was a mystery about this old chest. As Poppa's children grew older, they learned that Poppa was their "Santa." Everything that was important to Poppa was kept there. Aware of children's curious, prying, impatient ways, Poppa always kept this chest under lock and key.

Poppa said that his grandpa John made this chest in the late 1800s, gave it to his dad, Grandpa Wesley, and Grandpa Wesley gave it to him.

Poppa's children, like children today, made their Christmas list. But our lists consisted of one gift each. And we were filled with joy with that one gift. One child wanted a comb, brush, and mirror set, she would get it. Another wanted a tea set, she would get it.

A doll, she got it. One of the boys wanted a BB gun, another boy wanted a cap pistol. With these gifts, we were as happy as the children today who got many gifts at Christmas.

Sometimes when Poppa and Momma had gone to town or were away from the house, some of their small children could not resist the temptation to sneak into their parents' bedroom. On their bedroom wall hung generations of old black-and-white pictures, ancient pictures of our grandparents, our great-uncles and aunts, some having cracked lines from age. Our eyes swept across these pictures that had round black eyes that stared back at us. These eyes seemed so alive, even following us, and they seemed to speak to us, saying, "We are watching you." We trembled from cold fear and would run out of the room.

Momma had fear and dread whenever her boys were out, especially at night. When her youngest boy was in Vietnam in the late '60s, this familiar fear intensified. While James was in Vietnam, our Momma started complaining about headaches. "I can't get rid of this headache."

Never before in American history had live images on television abundantly illustrated the reality of this horror of war that was brought into American homes. As our young soldiers were being blown to pieces, there were cameramen lying on the ground in the war zone capturing these dreadful live images of our young boys and sending these bloody images back to American for their loved ones to see. "James, James, was that James?" Momma asked as she watched in total fear, terrified that it might be her son's body that wounded soldier who was being dragged by his buddy to a safer place. One of Momma's children would rush and cut the television set off and then try to calm their frightened, confused, crying momma.

She probably felt that way, not quite as bad, but sort of that way when one of her boys left the house at night, praying they would follow the rules set for the Negroes.

She could see the times were changing. Negroes in the South were stirring up lots of trouble listening to Dr. King, Malcolm X, the Black Panther. Momma said, "These men are going to get my boys killed."

Once Momma's family was safe in her home, none of her boys out in the night where the threat of impending danger or harm was a real menace, there was laughter. Momma's children would keep her laughing. We used to love to touch her on her sides. With a light touch, our mother would jump. We knew she was so ticklish.

Not sparing the rod, our home was filled with laughter. When Momma whipped us with a belt or a switch, she sometimes would tell us to go and get a switch from that elm tree out back. Now that was hard to do—to pick out a long twig from this tree. Momma would choose between the switch from the tree and a belt. This may sound strange, but as soon as the pain from the whipping had stopped, in a little while, we were playful again.

Momma's children knew that the Bible said to "spare the rod, ruin the child." "And besides, a whipping seem to be the only thing they understood," Momma said.

"What am I going to cook today," Momma said. "I'm so tired of cooking." Three times a day, Momma cooked. Breakfast, dinner, and supper, Momma never took a vacation. Disciplining, nursing, and teaching.

But she saw that her life was changing. Her children had started feeling that maybe these white folks were right about them—ugly nappy-headed nigger kids, black and ugly. Dumb, stupid nigger kids. Why, now Momma heard her children calling themselves those horrible names. One of her children would say to the other, "You got nigger hair and you are black and ugly." She and their poppa couldn't protect them from their surroundings. The negative influence was devastating on her family. Momma would say, "My children ain't ugly."

The large batteries-operated Philco radio that was the center of entertainment before Poppa got his first television in 1954 connected us to the outside world. Poppa would tell his children as he was sitting in his old wooden rocking chair near the cast-iron heater with his head leaning close to the radio, to the voice of the news anchorman Douglas Edwards coming through the radio with the five-minute evening news. He had a serious intense look upon his face because our poppa took the events of the world very seriously. "Be quiet, I'm listening to the news."

Subsequently, on this late Friday evening when President Harry S. Truman's weekly five minutes' *Fireside Chat* came on the radio, you could hear a pin drop with Poppa's ears still glued to the radio. Poppa's interest intensified when President Truman spoke on civil rights, the voting rights, and fair employment practices. As our poppa continued to listen to the president, he heard the president say, "But my very stomach turned over when I had learned that Negro soldiers, just back from overseas, were being dumped out of army trucks in Mississippi and beaten."

Poppa erupted in total joy! "Did y'all hear what the president just said? President Truman just said how horrible these white folks are down here. Lord, thank You, Jesus! There's a change coming. When the president of the United States speaks, the world listens."

Through the radio we enjoyed the broadcast of live drama, comedy, music, and news. Comedies like that of Bob Hope, Groucho Marx, Amos and Andy. Radio featured daytime soap operas. Although we couldn't see our favorite radio character, that didn't stop us from creating what we thought they looked like in our minds. Consequently, you can imagine how shocked we were to learn after years of mentally picturing Amos and Andy as black men and finding out they were very, very white. Amos and Andy sounded very black on the radio when in reality they were voices of two white men. However, when Poppa bought his first television set in the mid '50s and we were introduced to the black characters of Amos and Andy, we quickly forgot that they were once white men on the radio.

In 1948, WDIA was the first black radio station coming through the airways from Memphis, Tennessee. And as time passed, we were introduced to a world of a variety of joyful unknown spiritual songs. We clapped our hands and stomped our feet to the beautiful voice of Mahalia Jackson, the Staple Singers, the Five Blind Boys, who were popular. And when Poppa wasn't home, we listened to the very popular black DJ Rufus Thomas. We continued to clap our hands and stomp our feet, but to a different tune of "worldly music." Bobby Bland, B. B. King was a few of our favorites. This music had an early influence on the young people during this time.

When Poppa wasn't home, Momma showed a little more tolerance for our youthfulness. "Can't y'all turn that off? You know your poppa don't want you all listening to that stuff."

"Oh, Momma, we are just having fun."

"Well, at least turn the volume down," Momma would say.

Then one day, it seemed without a warning, Roberta called to Momma. "Momma, hurry, come in here for a minute." Momma quickly came out of the kitchen where she was peeling potatoes for her vegetable soup. Roberta turned the volume up real loud when Momma entered the living room. "I am black and I am proud. Black is beautiful." Roberta studied her momma's face as the song was being played; a sense of surprise, disbelief, and amazement showed on Momma's face. This was the very first time Momma had heard that black was something to be proud of. And how can black be beautiful? She and Poppa owned some black cows. They were pretty, come to think about it. We have all seen blackbirds; they were pretty too. But black people being pretty? This way of thinking was unknown to her.

However, the more she listened and looked at the excitement in Roberta's face, she probably felt that this newfound reality was filled with truth and hope. Then Momma said as an afterthought, "I don't know about all this black stuff." She stifled a giggle. "All I know and I see it all the time, like after revival service at church last night. I was walking behind Joe Ann, this peach-colored girl with long, wavy black hair that hung below her shoulders. When she left the sanctuary and went outside, there were three young colored men talking to Rosa, a dark-complexioned young girl about eighteen with short hair. When Joe Ann walked past them, two of the young men immediately deserted Rosa, as though talking to her was a waste of time, and followed Joe Ann. And eyes of the one man that stayed standing near Rosa were no longer on her but were on Joe Ann."

Even with Momma's doubts, this did not stop her children from singing a new song; they had the backbone of a new attitude. However, Momma had doubts that words in songs could change old attitudes. She and their father had told their children not to listen to worldly music, evil music. But this music was different. It seemed like it was coming not from the world but were from God. This worldly man James Brown was singing, "I'm black and am proud, it's time for the big payback!" Lord have mercy. Even with her doubts, her "wait and see" hope were mixed with her perplexities. She was hoping now that her children may start to believe her that maybe, just maybe, they're not ugly after all. Our Momma had common sense that was built on strong logic.

On this warm day in September with her family away working in the field, Momma would enjoy this quiet time with just her and her baby girl, three-year-old Peggy. Peggy loved this time alone with her momma. Everywhere Momma went, Peggy wanted to be with her. As a small child, she had a strong emotional attachment to Momma that continues to this day, even at times suffering from separation anxiety.

Momma didn't work in the field because Poppa didn't allow it. What would people think if they saw the preacher's wife working in the field? Her own children would have been outraged. Our momma working in the field, no way! She was treated as the "first lady." Once her family had left to go and work in the field, Momma probably started thinking ahead on what she was going to cook for dinner.

Momma would go to her vegetable garden with a large basket that she used to put fresh vegetables in where there was an abundance of fresh tomatoes, green beans, turnips, potatoes, and other kinds of fresh fruits and vegetable. The vegetables that her family loved, the insects loved them too. Momma, when working with Peggy by her side, would usually hum, and every now and then she would sing a couple of words to the song "Lord Don't Move the Mountain." Momma would say the next few words with her mouth closed "Just give me the strength to climb," and as she was picking greens, worms were on them. This did not disturb her spiritual mood; she thought nothing about them. When she saw them on a leaf, she would just shake them off and keep on humming and singing. No big deal.

She was unlike some of her girls who had serious problems dealing with worms. Roberta, Betty Joe, and Peggy didn't want to go near them unless they were forced to, like when they were picking cotton.

Momma has now picked her basket full of fresh vegetables as she and Peggy were leaving the garden. They walked the narrow path that was fenced in by tall weeds on both sides leading back to the house. Her hands were not free to hold her little girl's hand. As Momma looked down on Peggy, knowing that her little girl didn't have enough confidence to walk without the security of her momma's touch and Momma probably needed that connection more than little Peggy, she said, "Baby, hold on to the hem of my garment." Once Momma felt Peggy's little hand grip the hem of her garment, they both most likely felt more secure at not being separated from each other.

As Momma and Peggy walked the short distance to the house, entering the clearing, they came to our poppa's orchard of pears, apples, and peach trees. Because of the windy night before, quite a few had fallen to the ground, which was a delightful attraction for wildlife. There were two fat raccoons and several squirrels enjoying the gift of a meal without labor. The wonderful aroma from the fruit trees probably made Momma think of fried apple pies, and she came back out later to pick some to make pies that her family loved so much.

All vegetation reaches its peak during harvest time in October, ripe and ready for picking. Children that lived on a farm spent more time outdoors than indoors, especially when the weather turned warm. We all were rewarded from the harvest of our poppa's land. A fresh nature-grown snack was available at every turn. We didn't stop playing and went inside for a snack, playing cowboys and Indians in the open pasture with the cap pistols our poppa had given his boys for Christmas the year before. At the first signal our stomach gave us of hunger, we would go to our poppa's watermelon patch nearby, pick up a ripe melon or cantaloupe, crack it by gently bumping it on the ground once, and open, displaying the delicious, sweet red meat inside. The delicious aroma got the attention of wildlife secretly prowling in the tall grass, lurking in trees anxiously waiting for our leftovers.

The summer fruits of a variety of berries were plucked off the bush as is, no washing before eating. The insects that shared the berries and fed sweetly upon them with us would still be there, and their droppings and whatever these things left behind clung to the sweetness of the berries and their leaves and vines.

Our poppa gave his children signs to look out for on what to eat in the wild and what not to eat. "If birds and insect don't eat the wild berries and fruits, God gave us a warning we shouldn't eat them neither. If apple has a small pinhole in it, that's a good possibility that a fat worm has lodged there and you surely don't want to bite into it."

# 16

## Picking Cotton

Children started going to the fields at the young age of six or seven years old. This was the beginning of their life as a worker, and they have been working ever since. The task of the children that were too small to pick cotton was to tote water for the cotton pickers. Six-year-old Betty Joe and our six-year-old nephew Henry would be playing barefooted under a nearby shade tree with our water bucket close by. When one of the cotton pickers says in a loud voice, "Water!" Betty Joe and Henry would leap up from the bare earth with one on each side of the bucket with the long handle metal dipper inside, the two of them carrying the bucket of water, taking short steps and swaying from side to side. Shug would holler in her authoritative voice, "You chaps, stop running before you drop the water!"

Poppa's young children were given a croker sack for the cotton they picked. The very young children would sit under the shade tree and play, picking cotton between playing. Betty Joe and Henry would get their small sacks when they got bored and run out into the field were their older sisters and brothers were picking cotton. The cotton plants were taller than they were. They would put their small fingers into a boll of cotton and, for the fun of it, pull the cotton out. Shug told them, "Y'all be careful now, there are worms on those plants. And they will sting you." With that being said, they both would run back under the shade tree. The small sacks were once used for corn seed.

However, though, the word *recycle* wasn't part of Poppa and Momma's vocabulary. They only saw what could be reused. In today's climate, recycling is encouraged to protect the environment. For Momma, it was to keep the cost of the running of her household down. With many mouths to feed, this was important.

When a cotton plant has reached maturity, it looks like a white rosebush in full bloom. Instead of flowers, there are pure white fluffy cotton bulging out from its hard pod shell that dries and splits open with pointed sharp spikes and attracts all kinds of insects—caterpillars in huge armies, boll weevil, bollworms; and to add to the enemies of the cotton and the pickers, some of these worms has a stinger running the full length of their two-inch back. The cotton is at the center of this boll begging to be picked. Often the cotton picker's hand is scrapped, punctured, pricked by these sharp spikes. Each picker has his own rhythm while he is stooping and bending over the cotton plant while picking cotton, and at the end of the twelve-hour day, many pickers could justify their aching back.

The really fast picker can talk or sing and not miss a beat. Having skillful, swift hands like a typist typing on a keyboard using both hands at once for each key, a picker would rapidly pull out the fluffy cotton from its boll and put the handful of cotton into the six—or seven-feet cotton sack that they are dragging along the ground; and when the sack is full, it will hold a hundred pounds if stuffed hard enough. Lloyd said he and Fred would compete, which spurred them to pick more. And at the end of the day, they would have sometimes picked three hundred pounds of cotton each. And the pride on our poppa's face was visible for all. He would reach deep down in his back pocket and pull out his old worn black billfold and give them three dollars each.

When Poppa encountered people he knew, he would brag to them about the cotton his boys picked.

Our Poppa and Momma insisted that they didn't play favorites, but when they needed something done, they knew what to expect from each of their children. Their two older
daughters Cynthia and Cozetta would take charge in assisting their momma, performing duties that the family needs. Ruth could be

counted on to write some of Poppa's speeches. Christine was one of the best bakers, could bake the best egg custard pie. Shug, when she wanted something done, made demands as though she was the lieutenant and the children she spoke to was her soldiers. Roberta could be counted on to ask more questions about the Bible and the world at large. Alberta had a very attentive ear, willing to pay close attention to the words our Poppa spoke. Betty Joe at her own convenience could move faster than anyone else, picking more cotton than any one of Poppa's girls. Peggy, Momma's last child, was very sensitive to our momma's wants and needs.

Poppa's older son Junior could be counted on to be the authority figure when Poppa wasn't present. Obadiah, whose nickname was Plaite, wanted to know as much about family history as Poppa had to tell. Poppa had high hopes in his son Alfred because he had the gift of an orator, very skilled at public speaking. However, his son's struggle with alcoholism robbed him of that gift. Lloyd was the provider. He loved hunting and fishing and has provided our family with many delicious meals.

# 17

## *They Came at Night*

I t was a crime that was so shameful, filled with repugnance and fear. On that moonlit night of 1947, Junior was in a discussion with some of his friends playing checkers on their homemade checkers board using a collection of soda pop caps for checkers, in which one of the player's caps would be facing down and the other caps would be facing up to distinguish the players. In the front yard of MJ and Johnny's faded wooden shotgun framed house, they sat on top of two upside-down five-gallon buckets with their checker boards on other buckets separating them, their hunting hound dog old Blue with long drooping ears lying comfortable nearby.

These young men had been in a debate far too long; MJ, tall, very dark, and slender and Johnny Lee, big and burly with his big behind hanging over the side of the bucket. "Man, why you keep worrying about things you can't do nothing about? White folks are white folks, and we are black folks and nothing can change that. My advice to you, Junior, you better be getting home it's almost dark." Even at fifteen, Junior had difficulty leaving a discussion until he had won his listeners. For the rest of Junior's life, he wished he had taken their advice. Junior talked to his friends until it was too dark to play checkers. They folded up their checkerboard and stood up without saying another word, turned their backs, and left Junior standing in the yard alone. Their dog old Blue followed them and lay on the porch as they closed the door.

The two miles home was a long distance for a colored boy to be walking home alone on an isolated Mississippi dirt road. Junior probably knew that he stayed too long. There was nothing on this road but darkness and fear. The walls of fear were all around him. A cloud was slowly moving and passing the full moon, and this made his walk more eerie, the sounds of the night more pronounced. He heard the howling of a wolf at a distance. He probably thought of Momma knowing the fear she felt when one of her boys were out at night. Then the headlights appeared, and he thought of running. But he was prideful, didn't want to show his fear by running, he said later. The old Ford truck was covered with dusk and mud; the cab of the truck had three white men in it. They pulled up right beside him and stopped. He had to control his pee. He was terrified. The driver got out first; the strap of his overalls was loose and hanging off one of his shoulders. He had on a red-and-blue padded shirt, the kind a lumberjack wears. The moonlight was so bright that Junior could see his face. He recognized this man, had seen him before, but in his fear he couldn't remember where. The other two he hadn't seen before. They smelled of beer and cigarette smoke. All three walked slowly toward Poppa's oldest son. Junior couldn't hold his pee any longer. His pants were now wet, and he heard them laugh. He felt the warm urine run down his leg as he trembled in shame. *"Big boys don't wet themselves,"* he heard his momma say from so long ago. This was the beginning of his perpetual shame that shall not ever be forgotten.

The smell of these men hovered over him. Junior's fifteen years old body tried to rid himself of their filth, and he started to vomit. The tempest of blackness covered him, and he found himself lying in his vomit and urine, their footsteps leaving him there, their laugher and nigger jokes slowly fading. Then came the sound of the cab of the truck closing. The speeding of their truck covered him in the Mississippi red dust. Lying there covered in shame, he struggled to stand.

Poppa and his family were gathered comfortably around the fireplace listening to *Amos 'n' Andy* on our battery-operated radio. Everyone is accounted for, they thought, then out of the blue, Poppa asked, "Where is Junior?" Everyone looked around as though Junior was standing there unnoticed. Looking at Plaite, he said, "Plaite, where is your brother?"

"Me and Junior was walking home, and when we got to MJ and Johnny Lee's house, Junior saw them out front playing checkers. He asked me to go with him to just visit them. Poppa, I told Junior I didn't have time because it was my turn to cut wood. And everybody knows that once Junior started talking, he doesn't know when to stop. I thought he was here already."

Poppa immediately stood up. Intense fear flooded him. Junior out at night alone. Momma walked into the room from the kitchen. "What's the matter, Sam?"

"Bracey, Junior is still out there . . . My God, Plaite, where is your brother?"

"Momma, I thought Junior was here already." Quietness and stillness covered the room. Poppa turned the radio off. The fear was palpable that everyone present felt it. Fido started barking. They all knew it was Junior. Poppa opened the front door, going out on the front porch, and his family followed. Their eyes followed Fido and his barking. They saw their son by the light of the full moon coming up the dusky road that led to their house. It was his son, all right, swaying, staggering, and stumbling down the dark, dusky road. As Poppa walked down the front stoop, he raised his right hand like a city cop directing traffic, a signal for his family to stay. "Y'all stay here." Everyone stood still.

Fido was the first to arrive. The dog leaped upon Junior, and in his weakened condition, Junior stumbled and fell. Fido started licking Junior's face as though trying to clean him of the shame and filth. Walking fast, almost running, Poppa met his son. Poppa didn't have to ask. He knew the horror, the poisonous venom that consumed his son; the smell was all over Junior. Our momma knew by instinct that she should take her family back into the house. Fourteen-year-old Plaite walked off the stoop without asking Momma's permission to join his brother and his Poppa a few feet down the road. Nearing his brother, Plaite started crying. The horror could be seen at a distance. Junior was lying on the ground in a fetus position, silent tears streaking his cheeks. Fido continued to lick his face, his hands. Poppa leaned over to lift his son and shoved Fido aside.

Plaite was now assisting our poppa with his brother. "Junior, what happened, man?"

"It's not time to ask questions, son. We'll talk later. Now, we are going to take Junior out back. Your momma and your sister shouldn't see him like this." They led Junior to the back of the house where there was a fresh barrel of rainwater that Poppa used to bath his son, taking the bar of homemade soap of lye and animal fat that was still on the washing board.

"Boy," Poppa spoke softly to Plaite. "Climb through y'all bedroom window and get your brother some clean clothes."

"Yes-sum, Poppa."

"And be real quiet now."

"Yes-sum."

Junior had on fresh clothes that couldn't cover his shame. Poppa talked softly to his boys, "We shall never talk about this evil because the one that hears it would put the shame on Junior and our family."

Consequently, this hideous crime was whispered about for years. He tried to push this horrible crime against his oldest son out of his mind. Maybe if he didn't think about it, this nightmare would go away. But of course it didn't. Whenever our poppa read or heard about hideous crimes, this ghastly crime against his son would come rushing back to his memory as though it had just happened.

To know that these evil men was free to go on with their lives as though nothing had happened, for them to attend their Sunday church services and enjoy their family, Poppa knew who they were. In these small towns, everyone knew who did what and what they did. The irony of it all, sometimes people with authority was involved in these hate crimes.

Sometimes while driving, our poppa would see these men in their pickup trucks driving in the opposite direction.

"Those are the men that raped my son. That's them all right!" Poppa said out loud. He prayed for the ability to function in his day-to-day routine because sometimes this cross was too heavy to carry. He felt so helpless. He couldn't undo what was wrong by retaliating because he knew he couldn't find justice in the court of law.

Poppa started giving serious thoughts about leaving Mississippi. Just packing up cattle, horses, chickens, hogs, the whole shebang! Leaving this hellhole. Living in a state where White people don't think you are fully human. With this mind-set, they can justify all kinds of horrifying and outrageous acts against their citizens without the fear of impunity.

*"Darkness is where all the wild beasts of the forest do creep forth."* Seeking their prey like a lion at night, the wild beast in men do much

of their work at night; bestiality in man can be evil. Men and wild beast motives are different. Wild beasts attack for food or to protect their young. Evil men attacks for "fun," their lust is to kill and destroy.

Reeling from the chaos spinning around in his head, he was torn between the decision to leave or fight to stay. His roots are here; in his heart of hearts, he really never wanted to live anyplace else. Our poppa's roots were planted deep in Mississippi's red, sometimes dusty soil. His mother was buried here. "Why, tell me, God, why Satan won't let man live in peace with his fellowman?" He was racked by emotional and mental pain and anguish, aware too that any moment and at any time this may be only the first chapter to a horror story. Family ties were his anchor; even during the turbulent winds of hatred, his anchor to land and family held.

These evil men had forced this unnecessary grief and fear upon Poppa's family. And they were still lurking out there like lions or bears waiting for their next victim. However, there had been many decent whites who had crossed his path. Mr. Coleman always came to him when he needed him. Like the time this cow of his kept getting choked, food lodging in her throat, almost dying because of it. He went and talked to Mr. Coleman, a nice white man, because he owned a large dairy farm about three miles away. "Sam, boy, all you have to do is get a rubber hose and shove it down her throat. This will force the food down out of her throat. Some cows don't take the time to chew, which causes large chunks of feed to get lodged there. A sure sign is when they are drooling lots."

He read the life of John Brown *To Purge This Land with Blood* by Stephen B. Oates, a book that everyone should read before hating all white people. John Brown was a white abolitionist who led the antislavery crusade, sacrificing his life and his family's life in the process.

Thousands of men had died in the civil war, the war in which the primary factor was slavery. Poppa's mind was made up; he was going to fight to stay in Mississippi where even during the turbulent winds of hatred his anchor to land and family held.

Poppa and Momma's teenage son, Junior, that's what they called him. The anger and rage Junior felt for these evil men emerged into hostility toward all white men. He saw them all as "blue-eyed devils."

Junior also struggled with, who am I really? What was a real black man supposed to be like?

When Junior was drafted in the military, his time spent servicing in South Korea in the midfifties at the age of eighteen added to his confusion and anger.

Our brother, like most young recruits, had never set foot on foreign soil. This huge cargo plane was his first flight. So when these young soldiers, after a twenty-hour flight, disembarked in Seoul, South Korea, the culture shock was hard to express in words. There was even an unfamiliar smell in the air.

This strange environment had millions and millions of people. Junior had never seen this many people before. They were yellow-skinned with jet-black hair. Even their eyes were different. The men wore dark suits, white shirts, and black neckties. Their black shoes were spotless. The women were dressed in dark two-pieced suits, their hemlines falling just below the knees.

Junior said he noticed right away that the men and women too were taking every step with pride and confidence. Is this what real men supposed to look like? he probably asked himself.

He watched them as they walked with their family, as their children went to government-run schools. He was amazed to see groups of people doing their exercise in the public square. Here in this strange environment, thousands of miles away from America, was the first time he didn't feel threatened, endangered, or harmed.

They showed respect for his humanness by greeting him with humility. Junior said the first time he came face-to-face with a Korean male, he was afraid, didn't know exactly how to handle it. "Can I make eye contact? Can I shake their hand?" The images of America were whirling around in his eighteen-year-old head. "Never look a white person in the eyes, they will think you are an upper nigger, you may get lynched because of it."

However, when he and two of his colored army buddies approached three Korean men, these humble men brought their hands together as in prayer while bowing their heads. *Annyeong haseyo*, which means "hello." Junior said he had to fight back tears; no one had prepared him for this godly moment. Never in his wildest dreams did he imagine that one man could possibly greet another man in this manner.

The only men he had ever seen who controlled their environment were the American white males. The Koreans did everything in order. Within a short time, these strangers became his heroes.

Poppa's oldest son started seeking out information about these unfamiliar people, reading everything he could about his new heroes. The more Junior read about the Republic of China and compared it to America's Jim Crow laws, he felt that China was more just with their citizens, wasn't blinded by the distraction of color. This knowledge opened the door for him to hate his homeland and the Christian religion of that land. "Christianity has turned colored people into 'Uncle Toms.'" Consequently, to add to his deep and strong feelings of injury and injustice, his own poppa was a Christian preacher.

The culture and the Korean people had a powerful influence on Junior. His experience there taught him to look differently at the world, that the world is much larger than black and white.

When Mao Tse Tung became the leader of China, he wrote *The Thoughts of Chairman Mao*. Everyone in China was required to read it or risk being arrested. From 1964 to 1976, when published, its publication rapidly spread around the world. Once Poppa's oldest son got his hands on *The Little Red Book*, the 267 quotations became his bible. Junior believed that all the quotations were true to life: *"U.S.A. Imperialism and European and domestic reactional forces represent real dangers-and this respect like real tigers."* Junior saw Mao as his leader and not the president of the United States in which he lived.

A few years later, as could be expected, this *Little Red Book* brought dishonor to our poppa's house, Junior quoting from this book, which conflicted with our poppa's quoting biblical scriptures. We all were amazed that our oldest brother actually thought that he could bring our poppa around to his way of thinking.

Ten years after being raped by the Klansmen and in 1958, after returning from South Korea, the awful and dark memories of Mississippi still haunted Junior and disturbed his past through his present, therefore these experiences continued to live in full motion in his mind and spirit. Everywhere he went, in glaring detail he had an awareness of surrounding danger; he smelled it, sensed it. Felt trapped and fenced in by a thick wall of racial hatred, the resentment intensified.

The resentment in Poppa's oldest son entangled him into a web of rage and hatred.

Many years later, when Junior got older, he married his young bride Eliose, and during this time, they had two children—a son named Dewey and a baby girl name Jackie. Hearing of the opportunities up north for Negroes, Junior went to Chicago, taking his three-year-old daughter Jackie with him, leaving his wife Eliose with her parents with the intention of sending for her and his one-year-old son Dewey at a later date when he found employment.

He, like thousands of other blacks, migrated up to northern cities during the 1910-1970s, which is called the "great migration" from the Jim Crow laws, which were the driving force behind these migrations.

After arriving in Chicago in the late 1950s, Junior found work in a shoe factory. Our sister Cozetta and her husband William Lee had settled in Chicago a few years earlier, and she baby-sat for her brother, keeping little Jackie while Junior was at work. Junior loved Chicago, especially being in the presence of so many well-dressed blacks, walking and talking with confidence because all the blacks he met seemed to have it together, so to speak.

Junior was at the bus stop the day his whole life changed. He had seen these black men in their black suits and black bow ties selling papers; however, on this day in 1958, while he was standing there with his hands in his pockets on this cool day with the chilly Chicago wind blowing off the great Lake Michigan, he was watching the tall black man selling papers after the signal lights turned red and the drivers had stopped in the intersection in the thick of Chicago's rush-hour traffic. The man started walking toward him with a stack of papers in his hands. Reaching out his hand for him to shake, the man said, "As-salaam alaikum." Junior said the man could see by the expression on his face that he didn't know what that meant.

*As-salaam alaikum* is the black language for "Hello, good to meet you, my brother." *Hello* is the language of the white slave master. Junior said that when those few words were spoken, he liked the man because he knew who the slave masters were. Junior said, "I have lived my whole life with him."

"Brother, what's your name?" the man asked.

"Sam Gathing Jr.," Junior replied.

"Oh, my name is Mohammed. I got rid of my slave name a long time ago. My father named me Charles. I was named after some white man. I had to get rid of that name."

Mohammed, looking at Junior, said, "My brother, I can tell you have been deeply wounded by these 'blue-eyed devils.'"

Junior looked at the man with a puzzled, bewildered look. Junior told me later, "Roberta, the truth of what he said made me feel weak in the knees. I felt dizzy, lightheaded. The words that the man spoke hung in the air around my head. Mohammed asked, 'My brother, are you all right?' Some of the images and experiences I had in Mississippi came flooding back into my mind. On that dreadful night on the dark dirt road in Mississippi where the only light was from the full moon. The awful act of rape and the horrible things those evil white men forced me to do. For some odd reason while Mohammed was talking to me, I smelled those evil men. It was like my mind was taking snapshots of those experiences. The fact of the matter is this nightmare that happened in 1947 at the age of fifteen hadn't gone away. It continued to live on inside of me. I heard myself say, 'I'm okay.'"

Mohammed said, "My brother, I am giving you this paper as a gift. Read it, it will free you from the bondage of these 'blue-eyed devils.' And here is my card. The address on the back is the address of Chicago Coliseum. I want you to come to the meeting Saturday night at 7:00 p.m. sharp. As-salaam alaikum."

The man left. Junior said, "I stood there and stared at the paper. *The Final Call* was written on the heading of the paper. Turning and leafing through the paper, the words on each page leaped out at me. 'Now is the time for the great black man to arise! Time to awaken out of their sleep and slumber!'"

Junior said that as he was standing there staring at the paper that Mohammed had just handed him, a black woman, a complete stranger, walked up to him and said, "Young man, I saw you talking to that black Muslim. My advice to you is leave those people alone, they are nothing but trouble. Do you think the white man is going to let the black man run anything? The white man sees how they run Africa." And just as quickly as she had appeared, she walked off.

"As she was walking away, for a split second I thought of Momma. However, my thoughts quickly returned to Mohammed and the paper I held in my hands," Junior said.

"I read *The Final Call* on the bus ride to my apartment on Jackson Street on the south side of Chicago. I finished reading it sometime through the night. I reread it on the bus to work the next morning."

That day at work, whites that worked there looked different to him now. He saw in them the "blue-eyed devil."

Junior arrived at the coliseum early and was glad he did because there were hundreds of black men dressed in black suits and bow ties. The women were dressed in long cotton dresses down to their ankle with beautiful scarves wrapped around their head, covering their hair.

He sat in the midst of the huge coliseum surrounded by thousands of black people. The year was 1960. Junior was twenty-eight years old the first time he heard Malcolm X speak.

When Malcolm X was introduced and was walking toward the mike, the whole coliseum stood up and erupted in applauses. Junior said he was surprised how light Malcolm's complexion was. This black man had a lot of white blood in him. Junior wondered what happened to him to make him call the white man "blue-eyed devil." From where Junior was sitting, he said Malcolm's eyes looked blue.

As though reading Junior's mind, Malcolm said, "Upon first meeting me, people are surprised how much of the slave master's blood is in me. Yes, it's true. I hate every drop of that blood. I envy my black brothers in Africa who haven't been polluted this way."

Malcolm X continued. "As long as the white man sent you to Korea, you bled. He sent you to Germany, you bled. He sent you to the South Pacific to fight the Japanese, you bled. You bleed for white people, but when it comes to seeing your own churches being bombed and little black girls murdered, you haven't got any blood. You bleed when the white man says bleed; you bite when the white man says bite; and you bark when the white man says bark. I hate to say this about us, but it's true. How are you going to be nonviolent in Mississippi and Alabama, when your churches are being bombed and your little children are being murdered, and at the same time you are going to get violent with Hitler and Tojo, and somebody else you don't even know?

"Dear brothers and sisters, it's time for the great black people to stop worshiping the white God of their slave masters. Allah is the true God of the black man" (the above quotation is from *Malcolm X Speaks*).

Poppa's young son Junior knew that this man Malcolm X without a doubt had the answer that he needed. With an urgency, Junior knew he had to share this truth with others, especially his brothers and Poppa too. Junior said that the next time he visited Poppa and Momma in Mississippi, he was going to share this great truth with them.

On this day in 1960 at the age of twenty-eight, Junior came to the realization that his own poppa was preaching and worshiping a white god. This was the first day that he felt Poppa didn't know what he was talking about or the lies he was preaching to his own people and his own family too.

From this day forward, Junior bought every *Final Call*— paper, book, cassette tapes he could afford to buy on the messages of the black Muslim and what they stood for. He went to the black Muslim meetings, and hearing them speak was the first thing on his list of things to do after work.

The man Junior had heard so much about, he read a lot about him in *The Final Call*, listened to some of his speeches from the cassettes tapes. The man was the head of the black Muslims, "the Honorable Elijah Muhammad." Junior was nervous with anticipation. He was standing in front of his dresser mirror in his apartment's small kitchenette, looking at his reflection. By now, Junior had seen enough of black Muslim men to know how a real black man was supposed to dress—dressed in a black suit, white shirt, and black bow tie. Junior looked down at his black shoes to make sure they were spotless too.

Junior said that looking at his reflection in the mirror, he realized how much he looked like Poppa. Poppa always wore a dark suit, white shirt; however, Poppa wore a necktie. Junior said thinking about Poppa that he realized he had never seen Poppa in a bowtie. He wondered why.

The line was four abreast and very long the night Junior went to hear the "Honorable Elijah Muhammad" speak at the national headquarters, Mosque No. 2 in Chicago, Illinois. On this warm spring night in 1961, Junior said he had never in his whole life felt this kind of joy. That he had a feeling of excitement, a warm, comfortable feeling in the midst of this crowd of so many black men. He felt an inner strength he had never felt before. He knew that this was where he belonged.

After what seemed like forever, he was finally seated by one of the many male ushers. Looking upon the platform, he recognized Malcolm X.

When Malcolm introduced the "Honorable Elijah Muhammad," Junior said he had to fight back tears. To be here in the presence of this great man was almost more than his twenty-nine years could handle.

As Malcolm introduced the Honorable Elijah Muhammad, Junior was expecting to see him up onstage. However, everyone started turning and looking back when Malcolm said, "Now I present to you the Honorable Elijah Muhammad." Mr. Muhammad would, to Junior's surprise, come walking down the aisle, rapidly moving from the rear.

Mosque No. 2 erupted into adoration and applauses, hundreds maybe even thousands standing, saying, "As-salaam alaikum! Praise be to Allah!"

Junior was amazed at how small and white this man was. His complexion was lighter than Malcolm X. Junior was probably thinking, "This is a white man." But it was said that if you have one-tenth of black blood in you, this makes you black. Although he looked white, he must have some black blood in him. There were handpicked Islam guards surrounding him. Junior noticed too that he was carrying his Holy Bible, his Holy Quran. Looking at this scenario, chills and bumps came upon Junior's body. These well-dressed men in their black suits were given the authority to protect this small man Elijah Muhammad, their spiritual leader, with their life if necessary. These men, through the Nation of Islam, was given the same authority as the secret service was given for the president of the United States. Shoot to kill if they saw a threat to their leader. They knew that their leader, the Honorable Elijah Muhammad, had as many enemies as the president of the United States, maybe even more.

The Honorable Elijah slowly climbed up on the stage with his security guards still following closely behind. Standing behind Malcolm X was a row of men dressed in black suits and black bow ties, standing like the British Royal Guards in London around the Queen's palace.

The Honorable Elijah Muhammad began to speak. "I don't have a degree like many of you out there before me have. But history doesn't care anything about your degrees. The white man, he has filled you with a fear of him from ever since you were little black babies. Held over you is the greater enemy a man can have—and that is fear. I know some of you are afraid to listen to the truth—you have been raised on fear and lies. But I am going to preach to you the truth until you are free of that fear.

"Your slave master, he brought you over here, and of your past everything was destroyed. Today, you do not know your true language. What tribe are you from? You would not recognize your tribe's name if you heard it. You don't even know your family's real name. You are wearing a white man's name! The white slave master, who hates you."

Everyone stood upon their feet with loud applauses. "All praise to Allah!" (excerpts from *Malcolm X Speaks*).

Mohammed saw Junior regularly at the bus stop. From their common interest in Islam, a friendship grew. Junior started selling papers, started shopping at the Muslim store and selling their products, especially their bean pies. He stopped eating pork because the Holy Quran says swine is unclean. This contact with Mohammed increased his interaction with other like-minded men. Their conversations with his new circle of friends were always about the evil white men and the great Honorable Elijah Muhammad. Junior loved this new and exciting reality. These new friend of Junior created for him a well-needed release valve to vent years of stored-up anger. I think Junior knew what it meant in "there is power in numbers."

During the 1960s, this time in American history, there were many militant voices on the public stage that were screaming that they were angry also. These voices of Malcolm X, Stokely Carmichael, the Black Panther, Elijah Muhammad were very angry black men, among others, that said with a loud convincing voice that they had the answer for the American blacks.

Stokely Carmichael: "Black Power!"

Black Panther: "Protect our neighborhood from police brutality!"

Malcolm X: "We are tired of catching hell from white folk!"

Elijah Muhammad: "Great Black men, don't let fear of the white man stop you any longer!"

Some of Poppa's two oldest boys Junior and Plaite were persuaded that these angry black men had the answer they needed. They turned their backs on the god of their father. They had forsaken the ancient faith and turned their attention to Elijah Muhammad and Islam.

# 18

## The Day Junior Went Home To Tell Poppa the Error of His Preaching

T he year was 1962. Junior and his young daughter Jackie hadn't been home to visit Poppa and Momma and his young family—his young wife Eliose and their two-year-old son Dewey—in almost a year. His daughter Jackie was always with her daddy. His son Dewey too was living with Eliose and her parents, about four miles from where Poppa and Momma lived. Junior had gone to Chicago to find work before bringing his wife and his son to live with him in Chicago.

Junior told me, "Roberta, one thing I am sure of, I will never, never let my children follow the white man's religion. Christianity is used to enslave the black man."

On the 650 miles' ride on the Greyhound bus from Chicago, every time he tried to read the *Final Call* or take a nap, his mind would see the white picture of the white Jesus hanging on Poppa and Momma's living room wall. The bitter taste of anger would rise up in his throat. My head swam with the words of his newfound knowledge—Malcolm X's "blue-eyed devils and the words of the Honorable Elijah Muhammad: "You are a people who think you know all about the Bible, and all about Christianity. You even are foolish enough to believe that nothing is right but Christianity. You are the planet earth's only group of people ignorant of yourself, ignorant of your own kind, of your true history, ignorant of yourself."

Poppa had seen some disturbing things about his oldest son. He was too angry to live down here in Mississippi. Poppa had seen and heard enough to know what happened when a black man became too aggressive. For that he would be killed; consequently, he and Momma both were glad when Junior went to Chicago to live and find work there.

Sometimes children are not aware of the depth of things going on in their parents' life. In the 1960s, our poppa was in his early fifties. We could hear him talking to Momma about the problems he was having in his churches, how he had orchestrated in building them, the four churches that over the years he had pastored, putting large amounts of his family income into. And now they were doubting his leadership. The deacon board were talking about replacing him in one of his four churches.

One of his members came to our poppa for help. Mrs. Powell told our poppa that she was afraid for her and for her three children. One of her brothers, Thomas, was threatening to kill her over a family house dispute. Thomas's family was uprooted when his sister got control of the family property after the death of their parent. His sister forced him and his family to move—a crushing blow to Thomas, and a rage developed. Poppa said, "When I talked to the dear lady, I saw how scared she was, but I knew her brother Thomas. Even knowing that he had a bad temper, it never crossed my mind that he would actually kill them over their daddy's land that he had willed to his youngest daughter. That's a law down here in Mississippi that when parents die, the family house goes to the youngest child.

"You know, this mad man, while Mrs. Powell and her three children slept, came in during the night and killed his sister and her three children with an axe. Lord have mercy, I had no idea Thomas was that crazy. When I talked to the man, I saw something in his eyes that wasn't right when I think about it now. Over and over again this scene is played in my mind. I keep thinking I should've known. I should have stopped that horrible massacre. Lord, I just didn't know."

When Junior came to tell our Poppa about the black god "Allah," that he could correct the false teachings of Poppa and that Poppa just didn't know any better, Poppa was dealing with his own problems.

Poppa believed in the God of the Bible, the one and only True God and His Son Jesus Christ.

Junior had been home for a few days. And every word he spoke was about his newfound religion, about the pitiful state of the black men. Poppa told Junior that he was talking foolishness. Poppa knew how false doctrine affected the mind. Seeing his son fall in love with these people, falling into a form of brainwashing, he was amazed that his boys were falling for this stuff. Now he could see his second son Plaite listening to Junior, bowing his head in agreement when Junior talked about the "blue-eyed devil."

Junior discovered on this visit that he hated what Momma and Poppa stood for. He loved them, but hated their lifestyle. The white Jesus picture hanging on the wall. Every time Junior looked at the white blue-eyed picture, he had to resist the strong urge to snatch it off the wall and stomp on it, releasing some of the years of pent-up anger he had held inside against the white man, the all-too-familiar smell of the filthy pig that Momma seemed to always be cooking. Ham hocks, bacon, even the hog's intestines, calling those stinky things "chitterling." Thinking this is soul food! "This has to be the food of Satan," Junior said.

Momma told me years later, "Roberta, your poppa didn't tell me at the time, but he was afraid of Junior. His eyes didn't look right. Your poppa also said that when he looked into his son's eyes, for some unknown reason he would think of Thomas."

Later that day, Poppa went to the barnyard to check on his livestock and to make sure one of his children hadn't left the gate open. Lloyd and Junior were in the barnyard feeding the cattle, giving them hay.

Junior was in an animated conversation with his fifteen-year-old brother, trying to convince Lloyd that all white people were evil. Lloyd didn't believe him. "What about the evil black folks?" They kill people too, don't they? Mr. Thomas just killed his own sister and her three kids."

"What about him?"

"He was black," Lloyd asked.

"That's different," Junior replied.

"Junior," Lloyd said, "man, you need help."

Poppa saw that his boys were in a heated debate as he approached the barnyard. He really wasn't in the mood to talk to Junior. Poppa said he had so much on his mind. On this day, he really didn't want to hear about "Allah."

As soon as Poppa opened the barnyard gate, Junior started walking toward him, talking about Elijah Muhammad. "Poppa, aren't you tired of jumping every time the white man say jump?" Junior asked.

Poppa raised his voice as though he was preaching. "Boy, I am pretty tired of this Muslim talk in my home and around my children! I am amazed you and Plaite believe this crazy stuff."

Lloyd said he knew this was a highly charged situation that was getting very scary and extremely dangerous. So he walked over to Junior to try and calm him down. Lloyd said, "As he was walking toward Junior, Junior reached down and picked up a big stick." And when Poppa saw this, he turned around and walked rapidly away." This was absolutely horrible, Lloyd knew. None of Poppa's children had ever confronted or challenged him before.

Lloyd, in total disbelief, put one hand on Junior's shoulder, looking him in the eyes and asked, "Junior, were you going to hit Poppa with that?" He was looking at the stick that Junior was still grappling tightly in one hand.

"What?" Junior looked dazed. "Hit Poppa? No. Er . . ." Junior looked like he was getting ready to cry.

Poppa rushed into the house to get his car keys. Momma was at the stove frying chicken. Her two youngest daughters, fourteen-year-old Betty and twelve-year-old Peggy, Betty said, were at the kitchen sink washing dishes. Looking at her husband, seeing the weighty, serious look on his face, Momma knew right away that something was terribly wrong. It seemed when Poppa was angry, everything in his presence paid attention. Rover, the family pet, on the back porch stopped wagging his tail. Peggy and Betty stood still, afraid to move. "Sam, what's wrong?"

"That boy of ours threatened me in the barnyard. Was getting ready to hit me with a stick."

"Oh my God! Oh no. Lord have mercy!" Momma knew it was Junior because she knew their oldest son was a very troubled man.

James, Poppa's fifteen-year-old son, the youngest of his five boys, was wishing Junior would hurry and go back to Chicago. Ever since he started following Elijah Muhammad, his oldest brother was obsessed with hating white people. Even at this young age, James showed great interest in ancient civilizations and looking for what he thought was the root cause of man problems. James was one of those people who if he didn't have something important to say would be silent. He was never good at light conversations or chitchat. When we saw the Jim Crow of our surroundings, this would trigger James into a discussion about the "first man, Adam" being black.

"No matter what the white man says, Adam was black. Common sense tells us that you cannot turn white to black, but you can, with the mixing of the races, turn white into black. That's why the white man has so much fear, the mixing of the races. He knows that his white skin would disappear. The white man knows mixing his blood with the blood of the black man his skin would turn brown. The picture of a blond Adam and Eve in the Garden of Eden is a joke!"

James continued, "Junior's behavior shows he has lost his mind. How in the world can he think he can come down here and run Poppa's house? Wanting Poppa to follow this crazy man Elijah Muhammad. This man is insane, he marries young girls. Saying he don't believe in the white man's law of one wife. So this crazy seventy-year-old man has several teenage girls as his wives. Elijah Muhammad thinks he is a Muslim; he has no idea who the real Muslims are. The real Muslim is the Muslims of the Middle East. The Arabs worship the true Allah."

When James was talking, all his listeners wondered where he got all his information from. I suppose the same were wondered by Socrates or Plato, their contribution to the field of ethics, trying to figure out the "good and the just."

"Sam, where are you going?" Momma said as she followed her husband as he rushed through the living room to get his car keys and grabbing his gray hat and his black suit coat that was hung in the living room closet door.

"Bracey, you will find out later."

Momma stood at the front door watching her husband as he got into his car. As he was speeding down the dirt road with the Mississippi dust trailing behind, she was thinking maybe that he was going to talk things over with his sister Mary who lived about ten miles away. Poppa and his sister Mary were close friends. They had a lot in common, both loving books, both loving the Word of God. Sam and his sister would talk for hours. Mary was a schoolteacher, a popular career for black women during the 1960s.

Momma said later that she had been worried about her husband. "Things weren't going well for him. There were some serious problems in some of his churches. They were losing confidence in his leadership. The killing of Mrs. Phillip and her three children, I don't think Sam will ever get over that. Preaching the funeral, looking down upon the four open caskets, everyone was so grieved over this unimaginable dreadful tragedy."

As Poppa stood at the podium to preach, looking out over the audience, there wasn't a dry eye in the church, including his own. "Lord, we don't know why evil strikes, evil driven by Satan." Momma said Poppa had preached many funerals in his forty years of preaching; however, this one was the worst to deal with. It was even hard for him to talk about it. And to compound it all, his two older boys thought he was preaching the white man's religion. Momma said, "Your poppa felt betrayed by his sons, to say the least, for not agreeing with his values and views about God, God of the Bible."

Poppa had talked to Momma about his reoccurring dreams. Dreams about snakes surrounding his house, trying to get in. And just the other night, he dreamed there were two crawling on his bedpost. Poppa was a big believer in the prophecy of dreams. He said the Bible spoke of them.

Peggy, Momma's younger child, came out of the kitchen and stood next to Momma. It seemed that wherever Momma was, Peggy was nearby. If Momma was sitting, Peggy would either be sitting on the floor near Momma's feet or sitting in a chair near her. Out of all Momma's fourteen children, it took Peggy much longer than the other children to have outgrown the soft comfortable cushion of Momma's lap. Peggy's siblings would tease her, "Peggy, get your big old self off Momma's lap. With your long legs, your feet are on the floor."

Peggy responded, "I ain't stunning y'all. This is my momma." Peggy had a strong emotional tie to her mother. Because Momma was still in deep thought thinking about her husband, Peggy patted Momma slightly on her wrist to get her attention, startling Momma out of her deep thoughts while she was still standing in the doorway looking out as her husband's car disappeared down the gravel road, leaving behind the trail of dust slowly settling from her husband's speeding blue 1960 Ford.

"What's the matter, Momma?" Peggy asked.

"Nothing, baby."

"But, Momma, why is Poppa so angry?"

"Baby, this is grown folks business. Now go back into the kitchen and help your sister."

Junior and Lloyd came in from the barnyard, both of them looking very solemn as they entered the back kitchen door with the smell of chicken frying and the delicious smell of Junior's favorite molasses cake that Momma had baked with him in mind.

Betty dried her hand with her drying cloth from washing the dishes. "Take those muddy boots off, leave them on the back porch," Betty said to her brothers, noticing too that something was troubling them. "What's the matter with y'all?"

"Nothing," Lloyd said.

Living on the farm, there was always dust or mud. The bare earth was never covered with concrete. Momma would say, "Whose turn is it to sweep this dirty floor?"

Junior and Lloyd were sitting near the heater, comfortable in the living room. Lloyd asked Momma, "Where is Poppa? I am getting hungry." They knew they couldn't eat until Poppa blessed the table. "I think he went to see Mary. He was upset about something," Momma said. "He probably will be right back."

*Knock! Bam, bam!* "Open up! This is the sheriff! Open up, we are coming in!" Junior and Lloyd jumped up so fast they both knocked their chairs over. Lloyd said, "What on earth—!" Junior was so shocked, face frozen in fear. Junior probably felt that the devil himself were at the door.

Momma's heart dropped; she thought her husband had been in trouble. "Oh my God, Lord have mercy!" Peggy and Betty came out of the kitchen. "What's the matter?" Lloyd rushed to the door to open it. When he put his hands on the doorknob, the sheriff, there were two of them, forced the door open.

Standing in the living room with their hands on their pistols poised to draw their guns if necessary and while watching Junior, their eyes were quickly scanning the living room. Sheriff Roy was short and fat, and his belt buckle wasn't visible because of it. Looking at Junior, Roy might have compared his out-of-shape body with the strong black muscled body of Junior. His strong arms, neck, and body were the results of his daily workout. Junior was the type of black man that white men knew that they would need backup with, never one-on-one to capture him. Roy and Billy both knew Junior could kill one of them with one of his hands tied behind his back. Knowing too that this was the type of angry nigger a white man didn't want to meet on an isolated road at night. Roy's eyes fell upon Poppa's bookcase. I am sure Roy was surprised to see Poppa's collection of books: *War And Peace, American Negro Slavery* by Ulrich B. Phillips, *Uncle Tom's Cabin* by Harriet Beecher Stowe, *A Collection of Biblical Commentaries* by MacDonald. The bookcase was filled with many books. There was also a stack of *Time* magazines on the coffee table and the daily paper *The Commercial Appeal* near Poppa's green high-back leather recliner. Roy had never associated books with niggers; this puzzled him, caused confusion in his mind. Roy was a reader also; however, he only read girly magazines. *Playboy* was his favorite. Sometimes he would read *Look* magazine. Like his buddy Billy, Roy's favorite pastime was telling nigger jokes. Pollack jokes were funny too, but the nigger jokes were the best.

"We got report from Sam that one of his boys threatened him," Roy said. They looked at Junior. Junior looked at them, knowing he had come face-to-face with the "blue-eyed devil." Junior's heart started beating so fast he thought he might pass out.

The words of Malcolm X and Elijah Muhammad came flooding through his mind. *You will bleed for the white man, but when it comes to your own you are scared. You bled in Germany, You bled in Korea.* Elijah Muhammad's also, *Great black man, don't let the fear of the white man stop you any longer.*

Junior knew these men wanted to kill him. Ever since he was a small child, these Mississippi "blue-eye devils" wanted him dead. The horrible night that he was raped by men like these, in fact, these might even be them. They all smell the same. Like wet dogs. Now the moment of truth has arrived. One thing Junior told me later, "Roberta, I knew I was not going to let these evil men kill me without a fight. Standing there, I knew that Poppa kept his shotgun in his and Momma's bedroom closet."

Junior made a rush to Momma and Poppa's bedroom, trying to get to the shotgun in Poppa's closet, hoping the gun was loaded. Roy and Billy were in quick pursuit. Momma, Peggy, and Betty started crying. Mommy was saying her favorite prayer with tears rolling down her face, "No! Stop! Lord have mercy! Stop, Junior. Please don't kill my son!" Lloyd pushed Momma, Betty, and Peggy out of his way, trying to get to his brother because he knew the sheriffs were going to kill him.

Roy had his gun ready to shoot. Billy held his gun for backup. Lloyd caught the barrel of Roy's gun. The bullet that was meant to kill Junior seared junior's head, going through Momma's and Poppa's bed room window.

For some reason, Billy looked at Momma and couldn't pull the trigger that would have killed her son. Billy and Roy knocked Junior to the floor, seeing that he was unarmed. Junior was lying facedown on the cold floor. Billy's foot was on Junior's back. He could feel the heel of Billy's cowboy boot, the spur on his boot very painfully pressing against his back. Junior felt the cold steel handcuffs as Roy twisted both of his arms to fasten them. Handcuffs secured, Billy and Roy pulled him up by his shirt collar, choking him. Saliva ran out of the side of his mouth. As Junior was dazed and staggering, trying to keep his balance, all eyes were on him—Peggy, Betty, Lloyd, and most of all, Momma, who couldn't believe what they were witnessing.

Poppa's family was leaning against the wall for support to clear the way for the sheriffs and Junior to pass by. The climate of fear was palpable. Soft sniffs could be heard from Peggy and Betty. Lloyd and Momma were afraid to move.

Momma was in total shock as the sheriff was taking her firstborn away. Peggy looked at her mother. Momma looked very tired. She was tired. Peggy put her arms around her to comfort her and to help her stand. Leading her mother to the sofa, Momma flopped down like a wet rag. This scared Peggy. "Momma, are you all right?" she asked.

In an almost inaudible whisper, Momma said, "Your poppa did this awful thing."

Peggy just sat there as she held her mother's hands, not knowing what to say, realizing that there was a lot about grown-ups that her twelve-year-old mind didn't understand. As Peggy held Momma's hand, her eyes fell on the floor to where Jesus's picture had been knocked off the wall. The glass in the fourteen inch frame was broken. No one was ever sure who knocked the picture down.

This late October day in 1962 had to be the worst day of Poppa's fifty-four years of his whole life—the day he went to get the sheriff to arrest his firstborn. The son he asked God for. Sitting in his parked car down the road from his house, afraid of his own son, Poppa would tell his children, "Yes, I remember the first time I held you." He remembered the first time he held Junior "looking like a carbon copy of himself. Everybody who saw Junior said, 'My God, Sam, he's a spitting image of you.' And he was, too." It seemed that his familiar world as a preacher, as the head of his family, was falling apart. A woman who trusted him, came to him for urgent help. He didn't know the seriousness of Mrs. Phillip's cry for help. Now she and three children had been murdered by a mad man, her own brother. Poppa had said that he was a part of this real-life horror story.

His firstborn son Junior bowing down to a foreign god, bowing down to Allah; the Bible speaks against this. His sons were rebelling against him and their Momma's belief. His boys were thinking the God of the Bible created these cruel Jim Crow laws. Before lynching a black man, the mob would sometimes read a scripture from the Bible: "Galatians 3:13, 'For it is written, cursed is everyone who hangs on a tree.'" Or Deuteronomy 21:22 "And if a man have committed a sin worthy of death, and he should be put to death, and you hang him on a tree."

The Jim Crow laws twisted the Word of God to commit crimes against the black man.

They shoved Junior in the back of their police car. The handcuffs were hurting his wrist as they pressed against his back. As the sheriffs drove off, Junior was wondering where they were taking him. Thinking maybe they were going to lynch him. Or maybe with handcuffs on, they were going to throw him in the Mississippi River.

He probably thought about his children—his little four-year-old daughter Jackie, his two-year-old son Dewey. Wondering what's going to happen to them when he was gone, he wished he could talk to his Muslim brothers. They would help him; he knew they would because they hated the "blue-eyed devil" as much as he did.

The smell in this car was making him sick. "Lord—I-I mean, Allah (he couldn't believe he said "Lord" instead of "Allah)." Junior told me later that he thought he was losing his mind, even in the backseat of their police car sitting behind the thick window barriers that separated him from the "blue-eyed devils sitting up front. Looking at their red necks."

Trying to hide his deep-seated fear of these men, he didn't want these men to see his fear. No matter what they did to him, he was not going to let them rob him of his pride.

Sitting in the police car, he saw Poppa passing by, going in the opposite direction. Probably going back home. Poppa saw him too. The emotions they both felt caught them both by surprise. Neither was angry anymore. They knew this was a bad situation that got out of hand.

Poppa said he started praying that the sheriffs wouldn't harm his boy. Junior wasn't like him, never did learn to play the game the whites down here wanted him to play. The horrible game that we are boys and they are men. When Junior was drafted at eighteen and going all the way to Korea, this changed him. His experience in the army made him see how men were supposed to be treated. The first time that he really felt like a complete human being was when he was in South Korea. These foreigners treated him like the man God made him to be. When he met them, they didn't spit on him; these humble people actually brought their hands together as in prayer and bowed their heads when they greeted him. Men, women, and children—they all showed him respect. On first experiencing this, he had to fight back tears.

With love replacing their temporary anger, Poppa knew that if his son were locked up in jail, he could be held captive too. "Lord, please don't let them kill my son. I don't see how I can go on if they did."

Poppa said that when he pulled up in front of their house, it was the first time he thought about his wife. "Oh my God! What have I done to Bracey? During the onslaught of events, Lord have mercy, I didn't think of what this is doing to her. Bracey must be terrified," Poppa said. "Sitting in my car, I was not sure how I was going to face my wife. I was aware too that this was the first time I ever felt anxious about facing her."

They heard the car pull up, heard the car door slam, the turning of the doorknob. Momma was still sitting near Peggy on the sofa. Lloyd and Betty were standing near the heater. The smell of fried chicken and molasses cake was still strong throughout the house. Although it was past dinnertime, no one felt like eating.

Poppa softly pushed the front door open. The delicious smell of the aroma from the dinner his wife and his daughters had prepared welcomed him. Eyes scanning the disarray room, chairs were still lying on the floor. His eyes fell upon the broken picture of Jesus lying on the floor. He looked at his wife. Bracey didn't look well.

"Bracey, I couldn't let that boy run my house. Everything is going to be okay," he said to his wife.

"Sam, don't tell me everything is going to be okay when you know good and well it isn't," Momma said. Lloyd, Betty, and Peggy looked at Momma in amazement. None of Momma's children had ever heard her speak in disagreement with their poppa. Momma started weeping. This was something new to her children also. And scary too. Peggy looked at Momma and then at Poppa. Peggy told me she started crying also.

Momma was sure they were going to kill her son. Momma, like all other Negroes who grew up in Mississippi, knew that the state did more lynching and killing of black men than any other state in the United States. Growing up in a culture were whites killed blacks with impunity, now these horrible people has her son.

Poppa wasn't sure what to do next. He didn't know how to comfort his wife. His children had never seen him show Momma affection in their presence. He would sometimes buy her things, like the time he bought her a box of Valentine candy.

His life was quickly falling apart. Looking at his children who wasn't looking at him but at their mother, he knew he was the bad guy in all this. His two sons Plaite and Junior bowing down to Allah, Poppa could see some of these tenacity in his youngest son James. His boys Fred and Lloyd didn't seem to be serious about anything. Fred and Lloyd both had talents that could be used for the service of God. Lloyd was an amazing singer. Poppa's churches loved to hear him sing. Fred was a good orator, skilled in the art of public speaking, could be used mightily by God. They both preferred hanging around with low-life people, going to these honky-tonky and drinking.

Poppa looked again at the broken picture of the blond stringy-haired and blue-eyed white Jesus lying on the floor, not sure whether he wanted to pick it up. The Bible didn't say what color Jesus was. He left the picture there. Lloyd picked it up with broken glass falling on the floor and laid the picture of Jesus on the bookshelves.

He was hungry. Smelling the fried chicken reminded him of this. Normally Momma would call her family to dinner. Everyone would follow Poppa to the table for prayer before eating. However, no one was now in the mood for prayer or eating. The food on the table had turned cold.

Momma jumped up the sofa, startling everyone, Poppa included. "They are going to kill my son. My son! They are going to lynch Junior! Lord have mercy! They are going to kill him like they killed Emmet Till." This panic attack, intense fear, began abruptly—trembling, problem breathing, shortness of breath. Lloyd and Betty joined Peggy at the sofa to comfort Momma. "Kill, kill, Junior." Poppa came over to try and comfort his wife. Momma pushed him away and ran into their bedroom and slammed the door. Momma had forgotten about the shattered window in their bedroom from the bullet that almost killed her son. A cool breeze was blowing through the broken window. Flashbacks of the horror of the previous incidents flew in her mind with the breeze. Momma thought Junior was still lying on the floor with Roy's gun held at her son's head. Momma screamed. "Stop! No! Don't kill him." Peggy and Lloyd came to Poppa and Momma's bedroom door, knocking softly. "Momma, please let us in." They could hear Momma crying.

Peggy starting crying again. She couldn't handle her momma being in this much anguish. "Momma, please open the door," Peggy said.

Momma couldn't resist her. Getting off the bed, she walked slowly to the door and opened it. Lloyd and Peggy were afraid. They didn't know what to say or do, so Lloyd said, "Momma, it's going to be all right."

Momma was always soft-spoken, never raising her voice—until now. "Don't tell me things are going to be all right when these men are going to kill my son! You children haven't seen what I have seen. The lynching, the killings. Junior hates white people. And when they find out he's one of those black Muslims, I know they are going to kill my boy."

Momma had real anger born out of real feelings. Momma followed Lloyd and Peggy out of her and Poppa's bedroom. Her face was wet with tears. Poppa was now sitting at the table eating. This angered Momma even more. "Sam, how can you eat when our son is being murdered?" The first time, Poppa was silent and Momma was doing all the talking. "You called the sheriff on our boy, now they are going to kill him."

Momma's life with Poppa was always "My husband knows best; wife, stand beside your husband." "It's up to your poppa," our momma would say.

This motto Momma couldn't live by. There was never a time she didn't want Sam; now she didn't want him anymore. Didn't remember a time he wasn't a part of her life. They had played together as small children.

Watching him eating the fried chicken thigh, which was his favorite piece of chicken, from the plate that she didn't service, this had never happened before. Her husband had never prepared his own food. Wondering if he blessed the food, Momma could momentarily see the pain in her husband; however, her anger overrode the compassion she would have had for him, the first time her feelings came before his feelings.

The sweaty smell of the sheriff would linger in her nostrils. Her firstborn with both hands cuffed behind his back. One sheriff pulling Junior by the waist of his trousers, the other sheriff having him by the back of his shirt collar, choking him, causing saliva to run out the side of his mouth. The flashbacks of this horror like a camera taking snapshots keep reoccurring in her mind.

"Lloyd!" Momma said at the top of her voice. "Come here!" Lloyd rushed to his momma.

"What, Momma?"

"I want you to take me to Momma and Poppa's house."

"I can't do that, Poppa won't let me drive his car," Lloyd said.

"I will not stay here, demons has come here and took my son to kill him!"

Poppa stopped eating and said in a soft voice, "Lloyd, do as your momma say. Here." He took the car keys out of his pocket and handed them to Lloyd. "Go now, take her to your grandmother's."

Peggy, upon hearing this, was no way going to let her momma leave while she stayed here. This was an awful moment for Peggy. "Lloyd, wait for me!" she said in a loud voice. "I am going with you."

Peggy grabbed a pillowcase out of the hall closet which was to be used as a suitcase because the only suitcase in the house belonged to Poppa. Momma didn't have the need for one until now. She had never spent a night away from her family.

With urgency, Peggy rushed into the girls' room, grabbing a few things she thought she needed and packed them into the pillowcase, repeating the same thing in her parents room, getting things that Momma might need.

With the pillowcase full, Peggy went to where Poppa was now sitting in his green recliner chair in the living room. His strong broad face was deeply etched from years of leadership. And his hair was white. Even under peaceful circumstances, Poppa's children felt intimidated knowing it was a strong possibility that he would say no to their request. Under the urgency of the events with her momma getting ready to walk out of the front door leaving her, Peggy momentarily forgot this possibility. This had never happened before. Peggy rushed over to where

Poppa was sitting. "Poppa, can I go with Momma?" she asked. He waved his arm toward the door, indicating silently that she could leave.

Momma wasn't the only one who was mentally exhausted. The reality for this situation had slowly sunken in. Poppa was probably searching his mind and replaying the series of events that had begun to deal with his heart. Junior in the hands and at the mercy of the sheriff. His wife has left. During his many years of preaching, he had counseled many people, telling them to never make major decision under distress. "Why didn't I take my own advice?" Like before, when he had problems, he didn't want to worry his wife; his sister Mary came to mind. When Lloyd returned with the car, I'll go and talk things over with her.

Sitting in their old wooden rockers on the front porch of their small framed three-bedroom house that had faded with age, Momma's parents recognized the red-and-white 1960 Ford right away even in the midst of the cloud of dust from the narrow dirt road that were mostly used for their mules and wagon.

To Momma and Poppa's children, this was Grandma and Poppa Johnny's house. Often, after church service on Sundays, we looked forward to going there to visit. Poppa Johnny was a small dark man who was also a preacher and a farmer. Grandma was of medium height with light brown complexion, pointing back to some white ancestry still lingering in her blood. Momma was the third of nine girls, including two brothers. Momma's sister, our aunt Earline and her family, lived down the hill from Grandma. As children, we loved playing with our first cousins. They were a large close-knit family like our own that maintained stable bonds in the union of their family where our family would unite for Sunday's dinners.

Our family gatherings promoted strong union between our families. These Sunday's dinners were served in a very formal setting—white linen tablecloth, best china, sterling silver flatware, and beautiful drinking glasses for brewed iced tea from whole tea leaves that were a summertime tradition. The centerpieces were usually a large platter of fried chicken, a large baked ham that came right out of the smokehouse of Aunt Earline and her husband (Uncle Willester). A bowl of fresh garden cooked greens, string beans seasoned with ham hocks and okra. Desserts of homemade chocolate cake and apple pies were waiting for us after dinner.

There were no vacant seats around this long mahogany table that seats ten. As the family was gathered, all standing behind their designated seating, our poppa and our uncle Willester, standing at the opposite ends of the table, with a quick glance and a tip of their head, gives a silent signal to who will lead the family in prayer. Once all heads were bowed, the chosen man gave thanksgiving to God for his mercy and grace for allowing this family gathering. After everyone standing had said their blessings and amen, they sit and eat.

Our uncle Willester took pride in his large carpenter's box with his hammers, saws, nails that reflected his love for creating beautiful structures from wood. This was a man with a hammer, highly skilled in craft. He and his three sons built the three-bedroom framed houses in which they lived. Later as their children got married, they as a family built their own houses too.

Our uncle worked at the whites-only Maywood resort near Oliver Branch in which he lived with several other Negroes that worked as maids and gardeners. Because of his love for turning a piece of wood into a beautiful structure, he paid close attention to the creation of badminton, tennis, the lake, pavilion, swings, seesaws, and all the activities on the resort; and these were used as an example on how he could create some of these things on his own property.

Consequently, when our poppa brought us to visit our uncle and aunt, we had so much fun at their resort. His oldest son of their five children Lavern said, "My mother (our aunt Earline) used to see toys in the store that she couldn't afford to buy for us. She would work with them and her children would make toy airplanes, toy cars, some of the same toys that was in the toy store."

As the car grew nearer, Grandpa Johnny stood up to greet them; Grandma continue to rock slowly in her old rocker. He knew something was terribly wrong as the car got closer and he could see that the driver wasn't his son-in-law Sam but Sam's son Lloyd. His daughter wasn't sitting up front without her husband; fear probably instantly flooded him. His son-in-law must have been seriously injured or even dead. *Oh my God*, he looked at his wife. *Something has happened to Sam!* Grandma stood up when she heard this. Grandma was alarmed and aware of immediate danger.

Lloyd said that as he was parking the car, Grandpa Johnny and Grandma rushed to greet them, looking at him. "What's the trouble, son, where is Sam?" Lloyd said he opened his mouth to speak, but Momma interrupted him through tears. "Sam had the sheriff to come and get Junior. Our son is in jail."

"Oh my God, no!" Grandma gasped.

"I knew that boy was headed for trouble ever since he got involved with those Negroes up north. Sam has talked to me about him. He was scared that the white folks were going to kill him down here," Grandpa Johnny continued. "For a black man to be at the mercy of the sheriff is not a good thing. Most of them don't know the meaning of mercy when it comes to blacks."

As Lloyd continued to tell the story, Momma started crying again. Peggy started crying, too. Four-year-old Jackie was crying, "I want my daddy." A heavy dark cloud of fear came upon them all. Lloyd opened the car door for Momma, assisting her out of the car. She obviously was very weak. Lloyd held her around her waist, thinking his momma may collapse. They all walked silently into the house.

Word travels like wildfire, and the news of Junior's arrest spread rapidly throughout the surrounding area, quickly reaching his brothers and sisters up north.

To my knowledge, Roberta said, no one we personally knew had ever been locked up, let alone a family member. Recalling it now, the year was 1962, and Roberta was living in St. Louis, Missouri, with my sister Ruth and her family when we got the shocking news of our oldest brother being in jail, causing intense surprise. As her sister Betty was breaking the news to her over the phone, she said she had to sit down to fully accept what she was hearing. "Ruth, come, hurry! Betty is on the phone. She says Poppa put Junior in jail!"

"What! Let me talk to her!" Ruth grabbed the phone out of her hands. "Betty, what in the world is going on?" Ruth asked.

Betty told us in detail why and how it all happened. Even about Momma leaving to stay with Grandma and Poppa Johnny.

We all knew our oldest brother had some serious coping problems dealing with the Jim Crow laws and with Christianity, our family religion that conflicted with the black Muslim religion. And we also knew that Poppa in his own way was fond of his oldest son, who bore his name and was a good deal like him in resoluteness and stubbornness.

Momma stayed with her parents, keeping little Jackie with her. Through tears, Peggy, because of school, had to return back home with Lloyd. With Momma gone, Betty said that an eerie quietness pervaded our home. Momma's leaving reflected gloom on her family.

It was evening, September 5, 1962, and the sun was beginning to set. Poppa was sitting with legs crossed in his green recliner with his face probably expressing the troublesome and distressing images of the terrible events of the day running through his mind—a day that far surpasses anything he had previously known.

His wife was heavy on his mind. Bracey had never turned her back on him before this. It never entered his mind that his wife would leave or he would have his life without her. *What do I do now?* he may have been thinking. They weathered so many things in their thirty-three years of marriage, she giving birth to fifteen (one stillborn) of their children, all at home with the help of God and a midwife, women who understood childbirth. She spent her young life pregnant, giving birth, nursing babies, caring for him and their children when they were sick. In the cold winter months, one or more of their children were always sick with the flu, measles, chicken pox, and others.

Poppa had never slept in their bed without Momma lying on the opposite pillow. Now he had to because Bracey wasn't there.

"It's time to go to bed," these were the words we grew up hearing our poppa say after the nine o'clock news had gone off, and he has given his commentary of Douglas Edwards, the anchorman on CBS in the 1950s and early '60s. Poppa always had an opinion about the current event, following them closely. "President Roosevelt is for the poor and working people. Social Security wouldn't exist if it wasn't for his compassion for the working man, now Harry Truman is for the rich."

Before the routine was broken by Junior's arrest, Momma would be sitting in her chair next to Poppa's chair in the warm comfortable living room, the cast-iron heater the source of this warmth. When Poppa looked at his wife and said, "Bracey, it's bedtime," he rose out of his chair with Momma doing the same. Their children would watch as Momma walked behind Poppa and he gently closed their bedroom door.

Recalling it now, it was hard to imagine Poppa in their bedroom without Momma.

"We were blessed," Poppa said. "That, with all the childhood illness the Lord spared us from any of our children dying from these diseases."

Poppa said the worst funeral is of children. Over the years he had preached some of them.

In facts, that was one of Momma's prayers: "Lord, please don't let me bury any of my children."

Poppa continued to reflect on the events of the day; how could these events not be running through his mind? *Our firstborn is in jail. I put him there. And Bracey thinks these men are going to kill him. The threat of impending danger for my son is hanging over my head also. Our children are living in different times than me and their foreparents lived. They can't accept the place assigned to them that the whites are 'men' and we are 'boys.' They expect more than their parents. Even in the midst of insults, injustice, and exploitation, most Negroes of my generation experienced a sort of racial peace living under these laws. We didn't like it; however, we were forced to accept the realities of the times.*

Momma found no release from the intense fear for her son's safety during the three weeks she had been in her parents' house. Her nightmares followed her there. On this early October morning in 1962, with the smell of coffee perking in the coffee pot on top of the stove, Momma was sitting in the wooden chair around her parents' old wooden table while Grandma was standing at the cast-iron pot below the wood-burning stove, frying sausages. Momma's crying started abruptly, trembling and shaking uncontrollably. Her mother walked over to her with great concern, putting her arms around her daughter's shoulder. Grandpa Johnny heard his daughter crying as he entered the rear kitchen door with a load of firewood in his arms. Gently putting the logs of wood in the wood rack near the kitchen door, he walked to where Momma was sitting, taking the chair near her at the table.

"Beatrice," he said, "look at me." Momma, with red and tear-stained eyes, looked at her poppa. "It's time for you to go home. Sam and those children need you there."

Taking the advice of her poppa, Momma agreed to go back to her husband and children. Our poppa had let Lloyd take his car to visit Momma; Peggy, Betty Joe, and James would go with him because they missed their momma so very much. Our momma and two-year-old Jackie was packed and ready to go when they arrived. The car was filled with unusual silence the fifteen miles' ride home.

The gravel road was silent and lonely for long periods of time that ran in front of Poppa and Momma's house until a vehicle would occasionally break the silence. Cars would pass by every now and then. Consequently, when one did pass, someone would look out the window to see who it was. "There is Mr. Phillip going home" or "That's old man Sanders's old pickup truck." So when Poppa heard a car coming up the road, he looked out to see who was going up the road. It was his red 1960 Ford, knowing his children were returning and they would tell him how Bracey was doing.

As his car was approaching, while he was now standing on the porch, he immediately noticed that the head count had changed. How could his heart not skip a beat, recognizing now that his wife was coming home?

With her family gathered around her, Peggy stood closer than them all. She hadn't slept well during Momma's absence, even having nightmares. Our twelve-year-old sister told her sibling about her reoccurring dreams during Momma's absence. "I dreamed that Momma was in quicksand. She was sinking deeper and deeper into the hole." Peggy continued. "I was so afraid. Trembling in fear because I knew if I didn't pull her out she would sink deeper and deeper. And every time I pulled her by her hands, because of the mud on her hands, my hands would slide off of her hands and Momma would continue to sink. After the dream, I would wake up and start praying, 'God, please bring my momma back home.'"

Although Momma was back home, she still wasn't herself. Her son was still in jail. Peggy said Momma would wake up through the night screaming, "Junior! Junior!" The image of the sheriffs pulling her son by his shirt collar and choking him, causing saliva to ooze out the side of his mouth never did leave her. Flashbacks from this scene kept running through her mind, like a movie playing in her head. Momma may have been thinking that was the way her son was going to look when they put a rope around his neck. She was still having these terrifying dreams about her son being killed. She was obviously still in a state of shock, experiencing feelings of helplessness, extreme anxiety, and sorrow—what psychology would probably call "posttraumatic stress disorder."

It was November by then, Robert said, three or four months after Junior's arrest before he was released. Meanwhile, Poppa was working behind the scene with the help of his schoolteacher sister Mary for his release. Having the reputation of being a good Negro and none of Poppa's five boys ever been in trouble with the law, the judge had mercy and released Junior under Poppa's care.

When Poppa picked his son up from jail, they both were silent. What was there to say? Everything had been said through their actions. Junior looked at his poppa. The look of authority was strong as ever. Junior said later, "When I looked at Poppa, this was the first time I wanted to tell him that I loved him. I just didn't know how to say it, but I felt it deep down."

On this cool November day, when Poppa and Junior walked into the house, Junior's brothers and sisters gathered to meet him. Lloyd and Peggy held Momma's hand. Like Jesus said on the cross as He looked down at John, "John, behold your mother" and Jesus looked at Mary and said, "Mary, behold your son" (John 19:26). Momma rushed to her son and started weeping.

"Lord have mercy, He has brought my son home."

Even though Junior had experienced this trauma, one thing for sure, he could never challenge the belief of Poppa again. Poppa does what he does because he believes what he believes. And nothing or no one can change the rock on which he stands. The Holy Bible was his "Rock of the Ancient Path." All else is sinking sand.

# Remembering Junior

## (June 8, 1932-April 9, 2010)

His experiences with the southern whites filled his consciousness with anger and resentment. Even in his anger, Junior never forgot to remember his younger sisters and brothers. When he would come home, we would rush to meet him so we could receive the candy and gum we knew he had in his pockets for us.

Junior was into bodybuilding. Being a real man was his thing. He had big strong muscles. He displayed his physique with pride. We enjoyed watching him flex and pose his masculine physique.

As young children, he would lift one of us up by his biceps to show us how strong he was. Sometimes we would watch him as he told us to count how many push-ups he could do or he would tell one of us, "Come, sit on my back. I'll show you how many I can do even while you are on my back."

Junior was very upset when society, the people, and government wasn't responding the way he thought they should have to current events. As could be expected, as he got older, he was angry and frustrated most of the time.

In 2008, Junior's daughter Jackie, the second daughter of his three children, took him in her home in Memphis, Tennessee, once he was stricken with cancer and he was in his last stage of this terminal disease. His son Dewey, his only son, and his younger daughter Shay both lived in Chicago. Junior's strongest passion in life was to train his children in the way they should go, "the black Muslim way, Elisha Muhammad's way." Consequently, his children were dragged from mosque to mosque, little Jackie and her little sister Shay dressed in head wrap and floor-length dresses. Jackie said she hated being different from other children her age.

Standing on the street corner in Chicago's busy traffic selling *The Final Call* and bean pies for the great black people that Elisha Muhammad said "the great black man forgot who he is, we must teach him." Jackie said, "I wasn't interested teaching anyone anything. I just wanted to be like other children and go to the same school as they did, but I couldn't because me and my brother and sister wasn't like them, people would stare at us."

Jackie said, "My mother wasn't always with us because sometimes my dad would leave her with her parents in Mississippi and Dad would sometimes bring her to Chicago up from Mississippi to live in his second-story apartment to live with us." Jackie continued. "I knew at a young age that my mother was different, she wasn't like the other women in my life. My aunt Cozetta who lived a few blocks from my dad, on south side Chicago, used to baby-sit me and would brush and comb my hair. She even tried to fix my clothes so that I wouldn't look so much as an orphan. As my aunt was brushing my hair, I would be wishing my own momma could brush my hair, but my mother didn't know how to do those simple things."

Cozetta said, "Jackie had a beautiful head of hair. I used to hate rewrapping her head with the scarf she had worn and covering her head of beautiful hair, but I had to because her dad demanded it."

Jackie said, "While my aunt was brushing and combing my hair, there would be the smell of a pork roast in her white General Electric gas oven. That's the only thing I didn't like about my aunt Cozetta's house—the sometimes smell of pork—because Allah Mohammed said pigs are full of demons, Jesus put them there (Matthew 8: 32). And when my dad took me to Mississippi to visit Poppa and Momma, I would go to their pigsty and look at the muddy pigs walking in their own filth.

That was probably the only thing me and my dad agreed on—pigs are not fit to eat.

"My aunt loved to cook and to talk. She was an animated talker like Poppa, sometimes sounding like a preacher like Poppa. 'Jackie, Jesus is the only way, He is the Truth, not Mohammed!'

"My mother seemed to be living in her private world, always waiting for my dad to return. He would leave her for long periods of time. He would be with other women because Mohammed said David, Solomon, the great men of the Bible, had many wives. The white man's law is trying to imprison the great black. My mother only knew how to sit and rock back and forth in her chair while tapping her feet on the floor *tap, tap, tap* with the squeaky sound of the chair."

Her face and eyes would light up when she saw Junior, her husband. She would even laugh when he entered the room and *tap, tap, tap* and rock faster in her chair. We are not sure when they met; maybe through our poppa knowing her poppa because her poppa sold our poppa his 150 acres of land.

Jackie said, "Other times after living with us for a time, my dad would take our mother back down to Mississippi to live with her parents because the Great Elijah Muhammad says, 'Great Black man stop living by the White man's law the Great men of the Qur'an had several wives.'"

Now, with Junior's eyes following other much younger women who probably didn't feel comfortable looking at his wife number one rocking and tapping, Junior would take wife number one back to Mississippi to live again with her parents where she would tap, tap, rock, rock; and when Junior entered the room, her face would light up as though he was returning from outside chopping wood although she hadn't seen him in over a year or so. Now some wives would nag at their husbands, "Where in the hell you been for a whole year! I dare you think you can just walk in and out of my life and spend this time away from me with other women!" My mother wasn't that type of woman, questioning him, accusing him. Whenever she saw her husband, her face would light up.

Although Eloise would answer any questions about her life past or present, expressing her good memory, when it came to her husband, however, she appeared not to remember that he would leave her at long periods of time that when he did return, she would say, "My husband is here."

While Junior was down in Mississippi, he tried to educate these Mississippi blacks about how great they were and teach them of the teachings of Elijah and sell them some bean pies and *The Final Call.* "These ignorant black people don't read and they said that they tried a bean pie once and they thought it would taste like their Momma's sweet potato pie, which it didn't. They would rather eat their slave master's food than the healthy food of the great Elijah Muhammad."

Jackie's relationship with her dad was an extremely difficult one— passing through many toils and snares. His belief in Mohammed, her belief in Jesus Christ—this drew a strong dividing line in their relationship. She said she didn't want to be a "black Muslim," she wanted to be like her grandpa and her grandma, a Christian. She said, "I would listen to Poppa talk and I love what he said about Jesus."

Poppa would say to Jackie, "Jesus is the only way. He died on the cross for our sin, Jackie. I pray that boy of mine comes to his senses. Mohammed aint't never save nobody. Why, that man is going straight to hell himself."

In spite of the fact that there was a line drawn in their relationship, she never stopped honoring him as her father even if he was confused about who he was for this was what she believed, "that her dad was a child of God."

Jackie, sometimes under and against great odds, always with patience in his final days, took care of her dad in her home with her and her family.

As she prayed for her dying father, she also asked her church, her aunts, and her cousins. Anyone who prayed, she would ask them to pray for her dad. With sobbing and weeping, she said, "I don't want Satan to take my dad."

Although Junior was a fighter, at the end he had to completely surrender to cancer.

Roberta said, "Upon one of my visits to see my dying brother in Memphis, Tennessee, and as Jackie and one of Junior's grandchildren would assist their mother in lifting their granddad's frail body, the love I witnessed moved me to tears."

*"The evil that men do lives after them"* (William Shakespeare).

## *Social Change*

C oming-of-age in the 1960s was a time that young people were releasing pent-up anger and freedom from restraints, fury over social injustice, victimization, and inequality, the humiliating racial signs over the doors of public restrooms that read, "White Only and Niggers get to the back of the bus." They were rebelling against the injustices of a system that treated their parents as children and second-class citizens. Their parents fought abroad in wars, and returning back to America, they didn't have the right to vote—this showed how ridiculously hypocritical this country were.

Poppa, while watching Douglas Edward, the news anchorman on television, found it difficult to comprehend the boldness of these young people demonstrating in the street. A new and different voice was heard; these voices belonged to the young and the bold, knowing that free speech is powerful, it can stir people to action. After a period of time, as his children continued to migrate up north after finishing high school, his daughter Roberta, now living with Ruth and her family, quickly joined hands with the militant voices that were expressing her own life experiences she had left behind in Mississippi. Roberta was seen with a protest sign in St. Louis, Missouri. "Down with the system!" We want justice now!" "We demand the right to vote." Quoting the Black

Panthers, "Down with the pig cops!" "Now is the time for change! We've waited long enough!"

Poppa said, "I had to admit that deep down inside with fear for the young people, I felt a sense of pride and hope—hoping for a change. Seeing my daughter speaking boldly before the whole world made me aware of my strong angry feelings that had been languishing just below consciousness. The words Roberta and the protesters were speaking could've been my own because I have lived in fear all of my life. Sometimes it's best not to know the odds you are fighting against—like those young protesters who are not aware of the odds they are fighting against the opposition they are going to face. Controlling power, not giving up control without a fight. This generation of young people is angry for what their parents had to endure because of the color of their skin. They encountered hundreds of years of tremendous amount of hatred and scorn."

It would appear, so at least for a time, these children of the Black Power revolution who had been galvanized by the young militant visions; their motivation and encouragement were coming from the young angry militant blacks like Stokely Carmichael, Malcolm X, and Rap Brown. That high, uplifted arm with a tightly clenched fist while screaming, "Black Power! Black Power! We want it now!" was also the answer—years past. Out with the old. In with the new.

The year 1960 introduced a young and new president. Hope and demands for change were thrown on the desk of President John F. Kennedy. When JFK was campaigning for president, his youthful looks and charming demeanor seized the imagination of young and old, black and white.

While Kennedy was campaigning, every word he spoke was words of hope. Poppa would lean forward in his green recliner, hanging on to every word the young John Kennedy spoke. Poppa said that living in the state of Mississippi had the similarity of an internment camp. Internment is the imprisonment or confinement of people, commonly in large groups, without trial.

In *Years of Infamy*, Michi Weglyn writes that in 1941, President Franklin Roosevelt issued an executive order "which permitted the military to circumvent safeguards of American citizens in the name of national defense."

The order set into motion after the surprise attack by Japan on the U.S. naval base and other military installations on December 7, 1941, near Honolulu, on USS *Oahu* when they bombed Pearl Harbor. The unexpected attack caused panic throughout America and the exclusion of Japanese Americans from certain areas.

During World War II, over 100,000 Japanese American individuals, the vast majority of which were actually American citizens, were rounded up and shipped eventually to internment camps.

They were put in these camps, not because they had been tried and found guilty of something, but because either they or their parents or ancestors were from Japan; and as such, they were deemed a "threat" to national security. Every Japanese was seen as an enemy and a spy. The theory that a "Jap is a Jap" was a deep-rooted racist view of Orientals.

Blacks who were born into that was similar in many ways to what was an internment camp. The Jim Crow laws were the fence that locked them in, with all the restrictions that were placed upon them like the Japanese American citizens. Negroes could not step beyond the fixed limit into forbidden territory. A willful transgression or overstepping of limitations that the Jim Crow laws had set, a violation of these limits would be asking for severe consequences, including lynching. The deep-rooted fear of Negroes was present. The separation of the races was present. The undesirability of mixing the blood of people was there also although there was some similarity that they were short-lived. The Japanese internment lasted for four years; in 1988, Congress passed the Civil Liberties Act of 1988. This act acknowledged that "a grave injustice was done" and mandated Congress to pay each victim of internment $20,000 in reparations. The Negroes' internment lasted for over three hundred years with the broken promise of "forty acres and a mule."

Through the Afro-American loud voices of protest and discontent, other groups joined hands with the blacks, including some young, some old, some white, some Quakers, some ministers plus rabbis. There was a powerful shifting of attitudes sweeping America. From indifference to involvement, organizing support groups to fight the local authorities. White women felt that they didn't have equal rights in the work force as their husbands. They saw their own needs and joined hands with the blacks.

President Kennedy in his inauguration acceptance speech in 1960 "The New Frontier" said, "The Frontier of the 1960's . . . unconquered problems of ignorance and prejudice, unanswered questions of poverty and surplus. In the words of Robert D. Marcus: Kennedy entered office with ambitions to eradicate poverty and to raise America's eyes to the stars through the space program."

During President Kennedy's administration, a significant amount of antipoverty legislation was passed by Congress, including education, welfare, civil rights. Scholarships, loans, and grants to advance one's education were available.

The meaning of these gifts wasn't lost on all. Some blacks took full advantage of these privileges while some refused to buckle down with books in hands. Some found it easier to hold protest signs rather than books, forgetting so soon the ladder their ancestors slowly climbed upward from slavery in 1850 to Reconstruction in 1877 through the Jim Crow laws 1876-1965, people like the Quakers risking their lives to teach blacks to read and write. John Brown saw men, black and white, the biblical meaning of their relationship with God; who sacrificed his wife, and children, a white preacher who believed what Jesus said about man "This is my command: Love each other." The Negro cause has had many martyrs, including Dr. Martin Luther King Jr., John F. Kennedy. Sojourner truth: Actually the list is too long to list all the names throughout history whose lives have been of special significance to the support of the Negroes. They saw the potential of blacks, and we must see it also. Consequently for blacks not to take advantage of these sacrificial giving of so many people, dropping the torch that was passed to us so soon, shame! Shame on us! We all found out that it would take more, much more than a protest sign to rise to the educational and economical level that other races appear to reach with ease.

Why are these accomplishments so easy for others and so difficult for blacks?

Colin Powell writes in his autobiography *My American Journey*:

> American Blacks sometimes regard Americans of West Indian origin as uppity and arrogant. The feeling, I imagine, grows out of an impressive record of accomplishment by West Indians. What explains that success? For one thing, the British ended slavery in the Caribbean in 1833, well over

a generation before American did. And after abolition, the lingering weight of servitude did not persist as long. The British were mostly absentee landlords. And West Indians were left more or less on their own. Their lives were hard, but they did not experience the crippling paternalism of the American plantation system, with white masters controlling every waking moment of a slave's life. After the British citizen ended slavery, they told my ancestors that they were now British citizens with all the rights of any subject of the crown. That was an exaggeration; still, the British did establish good schools and made attendance mandatory. They filled the lower ranks of the civil service with Black. Consequently, West Indians had an opportunity to develop attitudes of independence, self-responsibility, and self-worth. They did not have their individual dignity beaten down for three hundred years, the fate of so many Black American slaves and descendants.

In Poppa's home and around other blacks when no whites were present illustrated the thrusting growth of the man—his evolution, rapid growth toward the man he might have been if his intelligence hadn't run into resistance from the southern whites.

Some of us wonder what if, while Poppa was walking through life, he hadn't bumped into institutional signs of Caution, Doors Closed, Danger Do Not Enter, No Niggers Allowed, if these hindrance and roadblocks hadn't been placed in front of our poppa? How far would he have climbed as a full American citizen?

Poppa was dressed in his dark suit and tie on this Sunday morning in July of 1962. All eyes in the sanctuary was upon him. Comfortable and reassuring in his role as a pastor, in control, he stood at the podium to preach. Blacks did not see a boy as they looked at Poppa; they saw the fullness of the man. He had a particular pride in his leadership as a pastor. There, he didn't have any doubts about himself—unless some whites were present. When whites came to visit black churches, they were always treated as guests of honor, sitting in one of the high-back red velvet seats reserved for pastors.

With the "white special guests" sitting beside him, sometimes in his own high-back red velvet clergy chair, Poppa would trim his sermon so he wouldn't show his black pride, making sure not to offend the "special" guests' sensibilities on race. Never forgetting that in the presence of whites, even religious whites, he was a nice black boy. "Sam," they would address him. Never "Reverend." That would show him too much respect. Poppa didn't want any of his special guests to frown on him, Poppa not for a moment forgetting his position under the Jim Crow laws.

Poppa's family was sitting in the sanctuary watching the change in the way he presented his message when whites were present. Resentment for the whites built up within his children. Poppa's fifteen-year-old son James leaned over to his fourteen-year-old sister Betty Joe and whispered, "Every time whitey is here, Poppa is afraid to really get down and preach."

"Why do they have to sit in our poppa's chair?" Betty Joe asked. Watching our Poppa living a double life was hard; it affected his family, especially his boys.

There is, however, an inevitability built into the natural order of things—cause and effect are in fact joined. Poppa and Momma's children were deeply affected by the pains of their parents because the dehumanizing lifestyle they were forced to live was painful to ourselves too.

Poppa and Momma saw as their children reach their teens; they were getting more racial and militant, less and less tolerant of the system they lived in. They didn't like the directions their children were going. When Poppa wasn't around, we would come to Momma as she was sitting comfortably in her favorite chair, maybe hand sewing missing buttons on one of her children's shirts. Because of her easy, soft, and gentle ways, her children felt comfortable around her. We would come to her and vent our frustrations.

We would ask Momma, Why would Poppa change his ways around whites? Why at times we had a strong poppa and at other times he was weak and uninspired? Momma would say, "Your poppa is a good man who has to protect his family. Your poppa loves you more than his pride. It's more painful for him when his children has to watch him play this role than it is for your poppa to play this degrading, subservient, inferior role in the presence of his family."

When people's whole lives are lived in the midst of hatred and obstacles, it is natural for resentment to build. For rage to take hold, and take hold it did.

William H. Grier and Price M. Cobbs writes in *Black Rage*:

> Aggression leaps from wounds inflicted and ambitions spiked. It grows out of oppression and capricious cruelty. It is logical and predictable if we know the soil from which it comes.
>
> People bear all they can, if required, bear even more. But if they are Black in present-day America they have been asked to shoulder too much. They have had all they can stand. They will be harried no more. Turning from their tormentors, they are filled with rage.

Poppa had a yearning for more. Although Poppa had to play this role around whites, he took being a man very seriously. This Negro man knew what a man was supposed to be like God told him. For Poppa, read his Bible daily. He believed what God said about man, not what the southern whites said. Poppa's children heard him say many times, "When I was a child, I thought like a child, I reasoned like a child. When I became a man, I put childish ways behind me" (1 Corinthians 13:11).

The American Negro men, women, and their children in the 1940s were greatly affected by the 1857 U.S. Supreme Court decision in the case of Dred Scott that no black could be a U.S. citizen and that black people had no rights in America that white people were bound to respect.

These were very difficult times for blacks, to say the least. By reading their Bible, Negroes knew who God say they were; however, they had to obey the laws of Jim Crow that blacks were inferior to whites.

In today's times, it's hard to imagine the double life our poppa was forced to live. Although he died in 1986 over twenty-six years ago, as I write these words, my spirit still weeps for him. Openly, he lived by laws that blacks had no rights, but in his heart, he was a child of God and was equal to all men.

Living under the Jim Crow laws was like living under Adolf Hitler's Germany, where there was the similarity of the fear of the mixing of the blood. Hitler writes in *Mein Kampf*:

> What we must fight for is to safeguard the existence and reproduction of our race and our people, the sustenance

of our children and the purity of our blood, the freedom and independence of the fatherland, so that our people may mature for the fulfillment of the mission allotted it by the creator of the universe.

Consequently, centuries of violence against man is the fear, I think, of the mixing of the races or the control of territories.

Arnold Rampersad writes in *The Life of Langston Hughes* Vol. 2:

The Red Cross's insistence on separate blood bank for Blacks, while the blood of white felons, collected in jail, and even that of Americans of Japanese descent, in spite of the "relocation center," was pooled with the normal white supply. Hitler could hardly desire more.

The civil rights movement from 1954-1963 was borne from the First Baptist Church. This was the first Negro church built in 1867 in Montgomery, Alabama. The white religious leadership had painted them in a corner; proverbially speaking, there was no place for their "good Negroes" to worship. The whites didn't want the blacks in their churches.

Over time, blacks were allowed to stand behind the podium to speak to their own people publicly. There was one condition by the white authorities—that these black ministers could only teach from the Bible; problems of race or politics wasn't open for discussion.

Being able to speak publicly, although limited, this was a significant event in black American history. Like the first stone that was laid for the pyramids in Cairo, Egypt, the stone of growth, the meeting of the minds was a slow process for black men. However, these men were able to with their sovereignty organized deacon boards. And also, within their churches, other committees were formed. They were legally allowed to gather without the fear of being lynched. Subsequently, the NAACP, SCLC, and other black organizational stones were continued to be laid to be built upon. Martin Luther King Jr. and other like-minded men reached the top of the civil rights pyramids from the foundation of the first Negro independent Baptist church built in Montgomery, Alabama, in 1867.

White men like Socrates and his student Plato had been meeting around tables for thousands of years, debating and sharing information, writing this important material down in printed form and passing this information on to the next generation. Subsequently, black information was kept in their village, proverbially speaking, passed on by word of mouth. The information that wasn't built upon became fragmented, misquoted, or lost altogether.

Maybe the fear of black men organizing was the remembrance of Nat Turner who was fresh in the minds of whites. Nat Turner was a Negro slave turned preacher with whip marks covering his black body that his slave master had left there to remind him of his position in life. However, these scars also reminded Nat Turner how much he hated his slave master. Although Nat Turner didn't have a church to speak in, his loud, angry voice could be heard on the riverbanks or in the fields. He made sense to his listeners, and they followed him. With violent vengeance on his lips, he led an insurrection in Southampton, Virginia, in 1831 with a group of Negro men that shared his bitter desire to injure those who had wronged them.

With his group of men, they moved swiftly through the night, silently coming into white homes and massacring all the white inhabitants of that house. All in all, it took some three thousand armed white men to come to Southampton to put down the insurrection. Nat Turner was hung on November 11, 1831. The violent action of Nat Turner and his followers made the southern whites aware of the risk and danger of angry black men coming together as a group.

# 21

## *All the Gates Are Closed*

T hey would come over on this warm Friday evening in July just before the sunset, knowing that the gates were shut, that all the animals were accounted for and fed. Poppa and Momma were sitting on the front porch in their wicker rockers, sipping from a tall glass of Lipton iced tea. Poppa, as usual, was doing most of the talking about the problems of the world, churches, or his farm. If there were children around and, of course, if she and Poppa weren't in their bedroom there were always children nearby, Momma would be rocking and not really listening to her husband because she was paying close attention to her two girls Betty Joe and Peggy as they were sitting on the bare earth playing checkers with their checkerboard.

"Why, look," Poppa said as he saw the familiar figure of a tall, dark woman and the heavyset man walking on the dirt road leading to their house. "Well, Lord be if it's not the Rayfords." Mr. Sonny and Mrs. Lindie Rayford were longtime friends of our family. They lived across the pasture adjoining our farm. Poppa went into the house and got two more chairs for his welcomed guests.

Almost before the Rayfords were seated, the reflection of the times continued. Mr. Rayford loved to listen to our poppa talk, who had knowledge of many things. Mr. Rayford wasn't alone in his respect for

163

our poppa. It wasn't unusual for deacons from one of his churches or for one of his brothers to come over and visit with Poppa while Poppa was doing most of the talking. When Poppa's brothers were present, he would always try and convince them the importance of landownership, trying to encourage them to buy land and to give up drinking, telling them that alcohol is the devil's drink and that the Bible says, "Don't get drunk on wine." Our uncle Tussie and uncle BB just kept on doing what they loved—drinking. And they didn't share our poppa's passion for landownership. Many people knew Poppa and were influenced by his public speaking as a preacher; consequently, Poppa had little trouble getting an audience.

Poppa started the conversation about the foolishness of man, the risk some men would take in jeopardizing their lives in a no-win situation. "Now take Nat Turner, killing all those white people. John Brown thought he could kill all the whites who didn't think the way he did. Now, common sense would tell these men and men like them that if the civil war didn't destroy this country, a handful of crazy men can't do it. You would think they would know better."

The white authorities probably saw Poppa as an object of suspicion, that blacks would easily follow him if he let his anger show. Nat Turner's attempted slave revolt stayed in slaveholders' minds for decades, that it was a possibility that Poppa would lean in that direction. Consequently, Poppa had to reinforce his subservient role on a daily basis, making sure he didn't become an object of suspicion.

# 22

## *Negro Baptist Convention*

Amazing how this may sound during the ten years of Reconstruction (1867-1877). The American Negroes got a taste of freedom they never had before. The door that was open to be a full American citizen was never mentally shut. Our Poppa's great-grandpa Bill, born in 1828, had lived through those hopeful years of promises to actually live the American dream. Great-grandpa Bill passed this Negro experience through the voice of one man to the generations that followed. Our poppa talked about what his poppa told him about those years, what they could accomplish when obstacles and barriers are removed. By word of mouth, this experience was kept fresh in their minds.

A land fraught with difficulties and danger, this so-called Christian environment in which the Negroes lived that rebelled against the teachings of the Bible did not weaken their spirit. This horrific experience built up their courage and determination. Even though it was a law that a black man had no rights that a white man had to obey, with this law always hanging over the blacks' head and with the odds stacked against them, this drove the Negroes to pursue answers beyond their own realm.

With the foundation of the black churches and the building blocks of that groundwork, this created a powerful platform for creating unity for the American Negroes that never existed before. The rapid growth from this unity was amazing. In 1886 or about that time, the Negro Baptist Convention was organized.

Baptist churches would have a special fund set up to send their pastors to these conventions. And their pastors would travel to St. Louis, Missouri; Chicago, Illinois; California wherever these events were scheduled.

It was a warm clear day, the first of many in August 1958 and the first hint that the hot and dry days in Mississippi were coming to an end. Poppa was very excited about the Negro's Baptist Convention. Roberta remembered how he would talk about the convention as the time drew near. The joy Poppa was experiencing of the pleasurable upcoming event was noticeable to all. This was truly a red-letter day in his life.

Roberta said, "In my mind's eye, I can still see the black metal Samsonite suitcase that has some damage and signs from wear and tear lying open on Momma and Poppa's bed as Momma was packing her husband's suitcase for this four-day big event. His dark suit is on the bottom. Four white perfectly ironed shirts and matching ties and black socks are on top. And a bottle of Old Spice. Momma would check and recheck Poppa's suitcase, making sure she hasn't forgetting anything."

Our poppa said, "The convention promotes social interaction and a better knowledge of other ministers, encourages open discussion regarding religion, education, civil rights, and social interests of the Negroes."

Poppa talked a lot about his experience the first year he went to the convention in 1950. The knowledge and practical wisdom gained from that would always be with him. After returning back home, he would have a special meeting with his deacon board to give a report on the important issues that was discussed. The building of black schools were at the top of the list because before 1954, blacks in Mississippi didn't have public schools that went beyond the eighth grade.

To be in the presence of men like him, feeling instant camaraderie, in the words of Alice Miller, "by the presence of people who was completely aware of us, who took us seriously, who admired and followed us."

# 23

## $\mathcal{D}own$ $on$ $the$ $\mathcal{F}arm$

On this cool midsummer day in July, the morning sun hadn't yet risen. The sounds of the night owls and crickets could be heard. Poppa's older boys, Sam Junior, Obadiah, and young Alfred were milking cows. A pail, short stool, two hands, and a very gentle cow were all they needed to enjoy fresh milk every day.

Poppa sold the milk from his boys' labor to increase his much-needed income to $100 per month during the '40s depression.

It was also the boys' responsibility to make sure the milk did not spoil before the milkman came around before the boys went to school to pick up the milk cans. They did this by putting the full milk cans in cold water; this was before the refrigerator. Sam Junior, Obadiah, and young Alfred took turns getting up through the night to change the water around the milk cans to make sure the water stayed cold because if the milk was spoiled when the milkman got it to the cheese processing plant, the milkman would return the spoiled milk back to Poppa.

Milking cows were only one of the jobs of Poppa's boys. There were many others—cutting wood, feeding the farm animals, sometimes hunting for rabbits or squirrels for our next meal, etc. These were boys' jobs. Girls didn't do these things because there was a very clear line drawn that separated what girls did and what boys did.

167

The older girls assisted their mother and the boys assisted their father. The older children also assisted in the rearing of their younger sisters and brothers. The younger siblings knew that their older siblings were their second parents.

Most of the early years for Poppa and his family were lived in a traditional framed house with a tin roof and no indoor plumbing. Despite this fact, Poppa and Momma's children loved to hear the rhythm of the rain beating against the rooftop. It was soothing and comforting to hear the raindrops tapping on the tin roof as we slept through the night. Our poppa would recite stories and sometimes riddles to his children around the fireplace or during mealtime.

With the invention of the lightbulb in the late 1800s people's lives changed. Although the bulb was invented in the late 1800s, by 1940, it still hadn't reached Poppa's farm and other rural places. It took time to build power lines scores of miles into rural areas.

People who lived in rural areas kept their kerosene lamps burning long after most city folks had thrown their kerosene lamps in the trash. Most rural folks probably had lost hope during the forty or so years of waiting. Didn't believe it, couldn't figure it out in their minds. It was sort of like when the first airplane was built or when man went to the moon. Poor, uneducated people couldn't comprehend that with a snap of a switch, light would enter their homes; the only lighting they had ever known was oil, candles, or kerosene.

"Why, this 'lightbulb' thing sounds like magic." "Do you believe that?" "I'er believe it when I see it or naw, Lord I sure don't." These were some of the comment of the times.

However, it was true. And in the late '50s, the power lines reached the rural area of Mississippi where our poppa and other families lived. And once the power line was installed, indoor plumbing was close behind. The days of the night pail and oil lamp was finally coming to an end.

# 24

## *The Day of Rest*

Remember the Sabbath day by keeping it Holy.
Six days you shall labor and do all your work,
But the seventh day is a Sabbath to the Lord, Your God.
On it, you shall not do any work,
Neither you, nor your son or daughter, nor your manservant
or maidservant, nor your animals, nor the alien within your
gates.

—Exodus 20:8-10 (NIV)

O ur momma told her children, "Don't sew on this day of Holiness for sewing on this day is like putting needles through Jesus."
Our poppa and momma told us many things like parents do today to get their children's attention. However, everything stopped on Sunday except cooking, eating, and going to church.

Sunday was considered a day of worship and was set aside for a day of rest. Through the 1960s, "blue laws" were passed that made it against the law for stores to be open on Sunday. All attention was on singing, praying, and worshipping, a time for family to gather for Sunday's dinner after church. These meals were special meals, using the white linen tablecloth, the best china. Momma and her girl would start preparing for this meal on Saturday—the best roasted chicken and dressing, special desserts, homemade rolls, fresh home-grown vegetables. Our momma would have to put away the molasses cake or her chocolate cake out of view because someone in her family will cut it before Sunday's dinner. The three-tier system immediately goes into effect—men in the front room sitting comfortably, discussing church service; Momma and her girls preparing and putting on the final touches on our meal; the children playing out front. "Y'all come in and take your Sunday clothes off before y'all get them dirty!"

These were times of conservatism in America. Churches had a strong hold on which way the country should go. They had the power to demand and enforce strict moral standard. The public paid attention to what was being said from the pulpit.

After a long week of going to school, many chores, assisting our parents indoors and outdoors, it was easy for us to accept this reality that everything came to a squeaking halt on Sunday.

In Poppa and Momma's home like most homes during these times, children weren't confused on who played what role. Poppa was the head. Momma knew without a doubt that although her husband was gone quite a bit, she had his support; they were aware at all times that Poppa was coming home. "Y'all don't want your poppa to get his belt on you, do you?"

Poppa and our momma believed what the Bible said about heaven and hell. *Children, obey your parent that your life may be long.* These principles were adopted as a way of life.

It is to be observed, too, that the Negro man and his family were saddled with a lot of societal problems; however, in their own world, there were lots of good in those years of darkness.

Men showed women respect by never using offensive language around them. When a woman entered the room, men and children would stand and offer their seats. They also opened doors for women. When walking past a woman, men would tip their hats and say, "Howdy, ma'am." Men paid the bills. In return, women serviced men by cooking for them, cleaning, washing, ironing for their man, making sure their man was dressed for the occasion. These etiquettes of the times were rarely broken.

# 25

## The Cycle of Life

Over the years, Poppa and Momma owned eight mules and horses. Rock, Shorty, Ida, Ole Mike, Lucy, Scott, Beauty, and Twilight were their names. In these early years before machinery, animals and man depended upon each other. Animals were rarely thought of as pets by the grown-ups. Sometimes though the children on the farm would get attached to some of the domesticated animals and saw them as potential pets. Grown-ups knew these animals were not pets, but helpers, made to assist man, not toys to play with (that is, don't play with those keys, they are not toys) even though they were domesticated and trained to perform certain tasks and loved by their owner. In these times, farmers had an intimate relationship with their animals as work animals that assisted them on the farm. These animals were beneficial to the family—hauling, plowing, sources of milk, eggs, food, and much more. They would call them by name, and sometimes Poppa's children could hear him talking about his animals as though they were one of his children. "Beauty" did this or "Twilight" is acting like she is sick or some cows got out through a broken barbwire fence, a fox raided the chicken coop and got all the eggs.

Consequently, from these close daily contacts with some of their animals and the ones they had close contact with were names: Twilight,

Beauty (our two horses) Doc the bull, Bessie the cow. Domesticated farm animals were equally dependent on man. The kind, gentle daily pats on their head or their body that farmers gave their animals daily reinforced the animals' love for their master. Even though there were daily dependencies, unlike pets, these domesticated animals were not kept as companions. They were restricted to their own neighborhoods— the barnyard, pigsty, the chicken coop.

During mating season on our poppa's farm, his young children were immersed into the realities of mating, birthing, and death. Dogs, cats, hogs, cows, etc., we saw day by day the consequences of this. When these animals conceived and their bellies grew and the mother's tits hung heavy with milk, we knew even as small children that their babies will be born soon. And often we would witness the live birth.

Our poppa's young children saw the care and attention that was given to his creatures that made his children aware how special they all were. He gave them a gentle pat, and we did too. We saw the fruit of these animals' labor and reaped the rewards of it. Our brothers milking old Bessie, we drank her milk. The eggs that the chicken laid were often witnessed when her egg passed out through her reproductive opening. The egg would drop from the hen onto her nest. If we were told "leave the eggs alone," the hen would come and sit on them; and in about two to three weeks, little baby chicks would pluck their little, tiny heads through the eggshell.

The live birth from farm animals is amazing to see even for grown-ups. The smaller animals, like cats and dogs, would try to find a quiet, private place to give birth; oftentimes when children wandered or roamed, they would stumble upon these births. The birth of larger animals, like mares and cows, who probably needed the space, would give birth in the wide open spaces. Children while walking across the pasture, which they did often, would witness these births. Consequently, as small children, seeing a live birth from one of our poppa's large animals was totally amazing, to say the least. Subsequently, when one of them died or was sacrificed for our meals, we felt the loss.

Momma's youngest child, eight-year-old Peggy, paid close attention to one of our roosters. She even named him and started calling him by name. "Come here, Jean," she would say while feeding him. Jean started recognizing his name. He started following Peggy. Peggy said Jean would follow her into the house. At night he would roost by the head of her bed.

Momma would say to Peggy, "Baby, you're turning many animals into pets."

"But I like them, Momma, and they like me too. I like them because they are my friends and when I am not with them, I missed them."

Momma, looking at Peggy, showed concern. "Now, Peggy, you have Tommylinnie the cat, Jean the rooster, now Doc the bull. It's a risk getting too attached to animals because it's so painful when they die. Besides, some animals are not meant to be pets." And with a slight giggle, she added, "It's hard to eat something you have named."

Early TV had only three channels, and during this time, TV was not aired all night like today. Man and woman were not allowed to share the same bed. Kissing was allowed, though. If Poppa walked in the room and saw his children watching a white man and woman (blacks weren't allowed to kiss in public) kissing, we knew as children we were caught red-handed. Opps! Poppa caught us watching this trash, and he would say, "Cut that junk off now! How dare you watch these white folks lapping themselves in the mouth!" So one of his children would rush to the television and cut it off—this was before the remote control.

Peggy had made friends with Doc, Poppa's big red bull that let Peggy ride him. She first saw this on television an old black-and-white Western. A cowboy was riding a big old bull at a rodeo. Little Peggy said, "My goodness, I would love to try that with old Doc."

When Doc was just a yearling, about two years old, the young girl would go to the barnyard and rub Doc's back and gently rub him on his side. Doc would turn his head ever so slightly and, with his big eyes looking at the little girl, felt the love from her gentle touch.

Once, we were exposed to the possibilities of what we could experience with animals through watching the Lone Ranger, Roy Rogers, and Dale Evans. They all played in a highly successful Western television series during the 1950s. The farm animals that we saw on their programs were the same types of animals on our poppa's farm. With the rodeo movie fresh in her mind, Peggy was talking with her fourteen-year-old nephew Henry, our oldest sister Cynthia's son.

"Henry, I've been thinking about the movie we saw last night."

"What about it?" Henry asked.

"I bet we could ride old Doc that same way." Peggy told him, being the type of person he was, always ready for a good adventure, easily persuaded to meet a challenge. Like the time he tried to ride Twilight,

Poppa's red horse, who wasn't happy with anything on her back. Henry got on her back pretending that he was the Lone Ranger. "If the Lone Ranger can do it, I know this will be no problem for me."

With a gang of family members coming out to enjoy the show, Momma even stopped working in her garden to watch. "Oh Lord, that horse is going to hurt that boy. No one has ever rode her," Momma said.

Twilight is saddleless. Poppa had not bought his first saddle. We would throw an old blanket on Beauty's back, a beautiful white horse that enjoyed us children riding her. No one had succeeded riding Twilight. Anyway, Twilight was minding her own business, eating her midday lunch in open pasture—grass.

All eyes were on Henry as he started running toward the horse. We were all laughing and rooting him on. As Henry got near Twilight, he slowed down to a slow walk. Then just as quickly, he ran and leaped upon the horse's back. She instantly started bucking, making jolting motions. The ride lasted approximately four seconds, jolting him about two feet into midair before Henry landed like a bag of beans on the ground. Everyone erupted in loud laughter.

Young Doc was a friendlier foe. Peggy loved Doc. And the yearling loved her. Riding her was easy. Henry joined her in the fun of it all. They both were caught up into their imagination that they were actually in a live rodeo, just like on television.

Western movies on television greatly expressed the possibilities that could be done with our farm animals. We learned by watching *The Lone Ranger*, Roy Rogers, and Dale Evans and other Western programs of that era how they would throw their lasso and easily get their projected target. How could our brothers resist trying to do the same things? They had the same animals in our poppa's barnyard that was on these TV shows.

Fred, our eighteen-year-old brother, invited two of his friends, Tee Toe and Edward Lee who lived down the road from our house to watch him while riding Beauty using a lasso that he had made just like the one he saw Roy Roger use. He had no doubt that he could do the same thing to catch our poppa's big old bull that we called "Blackey." He was the ruler of the pasture. All the cows belonged to him. He didn't have to compete to mate because he was the only bull in the pasture. Blackey's long horns kept everyone at bay.

Everything about Blackey appeared peaceful. Watching him as he was grazing in the pasture, it seemed as though he was at ease and in control of his environment that he loved. By instinct, he knew when it was time for him to mate. He had the cream of the crop to choose from, proverbially speaking. He knew by instinct that man was his owner (our poppa) and loved him. He could tell by the way this human would pat him on top of his head and even sometimes let him eat hay right out of the palm of his hands.

Tee Toe and Edward Lee was anxious to see the show. Lloyd, our ten-year-old brother, tried to talk Fred out of trying this, especially on old Blackey. "Man, you should be scared of that old bull, he can be awful mean sometimes."

"Watch me, that's not as hard as you think, I saw Roy Roger do it, and besides I've been practicing. You just stay way on the other side of the fence with Tee Toe and Edward Lee while I rope old Blackey, okay?"

With the three boys standing on the opposite side of the fence that separated the pasture from the dirt road, they were watching while Alfred was slowly riding Beauty toward old Blackey who was peacefully grazing near his beloved cows. Blackey didn't feel threatened as he smelled them even before he saw them come nearer. Fred slowly approached the bull close enough to comfortably use his homemade lasso. A few feet away with grace and speed, he threw the lasso, and it actually landed on the bull's neck.

The watching boys gasped, "Oh my God, he did it. He roped old Bla—" Well, this old bull had never had anything around his neck before. This scared old Blackey. He started swinging his head with great force, bucking and jolting. The great thrust pulled Fred off Beauty's back, landing him with great force. The boy landed on the ground and still held the rope tightly in his grip. The big bull started pulling him, dragging him on the ground. The watching boys panicked, leaping over the fence to help Fred. "Oh God, he's going to kill Fred." The bull stopped pulling him and turned around and started rushing back toward Fred.

Oh, Blackey was full of rage, without pausing, bending his head and with one big scoop, like a man with a shovel full of dirt, scooped Alfred up, throwing him in midair before dropping him and throwing him back on the ground and piercing him in the leg with one of his large horns. Blood started oozing out of the boy's leg. With overwhelming fear, Tee Toe rushed and picked up a stick and hit old Blackey in the head to try and distract him from Fred. Hysterical was at an extreme. A wave of panic flooded the boys. Watching in horror, Lloyd started to cry. Finally, old Blue lifted his head and walked slowly away back to his cows.

They all huddled over Fred. Lloyd lifted his brother's head. "Man, are you all right?"

"My leg and back hurt some terrible."

"Hurry, we've got to stop the bleeding." Edward Lee took his shirt off and tied it around Fred's bleeding leg.

The boys managed to lift Fred up. Using their shoulders as human crutches, he placed his arms around each of their shoulders for support. Alfred was dragging his wounded bleeding leg while standing on one foot between each boy who gave him support.

Lloyd had run the quarter of mile to tell Poppa and Momma what had happened. They were both sitting on the front porch when Momma saw Lloyd coming toward them running down the path that led from the pasture. "Sam, something is wrong." Poppa looked up from the *Commercial Appeal* newspaper he was reading and knew something had happened. Our poppa stood up like he always does when someone was approaching with news. Maybe he does this while he still have the strength to stand, maybe it's easier to flop back down than to stand after receiving the bad news. Anyway, as Poppa was standing there, Lloyd reached the porch completely out of breath. "It's Fred, Poppa, old Blacky hooked him in the leg while he was trying to rope him and he is bleeding some awful!"

The first reaction from our poppa was anger. "I've told that boy a thousand times to leave those animals alone. All, naw, he refused to listen. I already know what he did watching those television shows, he think he can do everything he see those white folks doing. That boy is going to get himself killed."

They all saw the three boys coming down the path, Momma rose to meet them. Poppa stayed standing on the porch, wanting to get his belt out and beat "the living daylights out of Fred."

"This wasn't the first time he had done something stupid. Like the time he thought he could pick up a garden snake without getting bit. The snake bit him. Even stole my family Bible with the record of births and deaths of my family history. Sold my Bible! Mind you. That's the last time I hit that boy. I got my big belt, tried to 'beat the living daylights out of him.' He was thirteen and I knew then I would never hit my son again. Besides, Fred is taller than me now. The Bible says don't provoke your children to anger. What about when a son provokes his poppa to rage? There comes a time in a father's life that he stops hitting his kids. Instead of hitting them, he just throws up his hands, asking God for help. My son's own stupidity created this mess. And it's always a risk that once a bull attacks something or someone, it's easier for him to repeat this violence. Creatures and men alike, quite often violence is a learnt behavior.

"But you know that boy of mine has pulled off some amazing things being the type of boastful, show-off person he is. Like the time that red-and-white heifer of mine slid into this big mud hole and Fred pulled her out singlehanded. Mud was all the way almost to his knees as the boy pulled, pushed, until he got her out. Once, Fred and Lloyd was herding several cattle out of the pasture onto the barnyard. A large oak tree that buzzards would perch up high on the dead branches overlooking the horizon for dying or dead creatures waiting, anticipating their next meal, had been rotting for some time from age and couldn't stand under the wind and the rain the night before and which had fallen, obstructing their path. Without giving it any thought on can we do this? Just using their big arms and shoulders and their large scarred dirty fingernails working-man hands with a few grunts, you know those boys of mine actually moved that tree."

Momma and Poppa walked down the path to meet the boys. Fear set in when our momma saw the bloody shirt wrapped around her son's leg. "Oh, Lord have mercy, Fred are you all right?"

"Yes-sum, it hurt real bad though."

Looking at the boys, she asked, "What happened?" They explained in great detail.

Once Fred was in the front room, Lloyd and Momma elevated his leg upon a chair. Several of Fred's sisters and brothers that were present gathered around him to get a closer look at his wound.

Alberta began to weep out of compassion for her brother. Momma, looking briefly from her son's injured leg, cast a quick glance at Alberta. "Go, and get those scissors near the sewing machine so I can cut these pants off his wounded leg, and stop running, you may fall and hurt yourself." His wound was exposed once Momma had removed the bloody shirt. "Oh my God! Look at that!" Fear and murmuring spread throughout the room. The horn of old Blackey had left a silver-dollar-sized hole in Fred's right thigh. His thigh started bleeding again once

Edward Lee's bloody shirt that he had wrapped around Fred's leg was removed.

"Sam!" Momma exclaimed. "Come and look at the boy's leg." Fred was looking as though he was going to pass out.

"Momma! Look at him, he's closing his eyes, I think he's dying!" Ruth said in fear. Ruth had said she wanted to become a nurse someday. She would read medical articles from *Reader's Digest*, sometimes reading *Family Health Guide & Medical Encyclopedia*, a big hard-back book with over five hundred pages that Poppa had bought for Momma to aid her when one of her children got sick.

"Hold his head up! Don't let him go to sleep!" Ruth said. We all thought she knew what she was talking about because she read medical books.

Poppa came in when Momma called. Once he looked at his son, he said, "Come with us, Lloyd, we are going to the doctor."

Lloyd climbed into the backseat of Poppa's 1954 Chevrolet. Looking at his brother with great concern, he asked, "Man, you okay?"

"Am feeling real cold." Listening to the boys at the back, our poppa had seen enough sick people, including his own family, to know that chills are a bad sign. Poppa probably was hoping that the only doctor in Holly Springs was a white doctor, a Dr. Walker, and if the white-only waiting room was full, Dr. Walker would have to wait on all the white patents before seeing his son. "Lord have mercy."

When they entered the back room that was reserved for "colored only," which was the custom of the times, there were only five other colored people there—Mr. and Mrs. Hawkins with their ten-year-old daughter Rosie and Mr. Hattaway and his wife Mrs. Mary Lou. Our poppa knew them well. When Poppa entered the waiting room with his boys, they all stood up to greet him. He had preached as a guest speaker at their churches.

"Reverend Gathing, my God," one asked, looking at Fred, "what happened to your boy?" As Poppa told them about what had happened to his son, they all had a horror story to tell about their own children, especially about their boys. Mr. Hawkins recalled how his ten-year-old son CJ had fallen from an elm tree and landed with a broken right arm and two broken ribs. Mr. Hattaway told how his eight-year-old son was standing on a barrel that was lying on its side. He was standing on top of the barrel, rolling it with his feet while he was standing on its side.

His son fell, hitting his head on a stick when he landed on the ground. Bled some horrible his ma had to keep putting a cool damp cloth on it to stop the bleeding.

I was sure hope filled our poppa's heart seeing that the colored section wasn't crowded. Maybe the wait won't be very long. The people in the colored-only waiting room couldn't see how many whites were in the white-only waiting room. Our poppa could only hope and pray that the room wasn't crowded. Fred was shaking from chills and a fever. There was a blanket lying across a chair near Lloyd. He took the blanket and laid it across his brother's shoulders. Lloyd couldn't see how his brother could be cold. The waiting room felt very warm to him.

The friendly, soft conversation continued with silence occasionally falling in the room before someone would break the silence. "Did you hear about the deacon board of Mt. Oliver forcing Reverend Levey out after twenty-seven years as their pastor?"

Poppa said, "Lord, I heard about that. Poor man, I knew him well, a good man. His mistake is he tried to please everybody. That's something a leader can't do. No matter what, most church members has no idea and could care less about the responsibilities of their pastors." Poppa fell silent because he had learned over the years that what you say in public can be twisted, misquoted, and used against you. "Reverend Gathing said . . ."

Mr. Hawkins tried to continue the conversation along those lines, but Poppa had nothing more to say about it. He must have felt deep emotions on the things that were being discussed, stirring up some emotions within himself that he didn't want to share with these people. To discuss these things, memories of some of his own painful experiences would start to surge up within him, memories he preferred to forget.

During this silence, he told our momma later who was sitting there in the waiting room, "Bracey, with them casually discussing Reverend Levey with indifference to the awful pain that poor man experienced. The lack of concern is shocking. Most of these ministers give their whole life to their church. And what they get in return is a bunch of tight-fisted murmuring people who do not love their pastor. Of course, there are exceptions. Without deacons like Brother Franklin and Brother Pattison, Sister Frances who have stood by me since the very beginning of my ministry at age twenty-three, I would not have survived. Their encouragement was a gift from God. Without their prayers and emotional support, the murmuring that was thrown against me I couldn't have endured. Their amens are so important when I stand at the podium to preach. Looking out over the congregation, I could feel the negative murmuring flowing from some of the people in the congregation who thought I shouldn't be there. It's a painful thing when a pastor stands at the podium to preach and some in the congregation murmurs against him."

As he was preaching in the pulpit, he tried to ignore the two ladies sitting in the fourth pew. Instead of them saying amen to the truth of the Gospel, the lady in her large white hat that was partially blocking the view of the three small children sitting in the pew behind her was leaning over, whispering something in the ear of the lady sitting on her left and was occasionally glancing at him in the pulpit as he was preaching. Most preachers had this kind of detractions, and it was always a struggle to resist this powerful negative energy that was controlled by Satan trying to stop the Word of God.

Standing at the podium, our poppa probably remembered when most of the congregation loved him. Now as he was reaching old age, his popularity was waning in the generations of his younger members. This must have stirred up some painful realities, but yet he had some support that still remained.

Finally, after what seemed like forever, a young white nurse dressed in a white nurse's uniform came out. "Who is next please?" They all looked at our poppa. "He can be next," Mr. Hattaway spoke up. The nurse looked at him with a surprised look on her face. "You are telling me who is going to be next?"

"Oh no, ma'am, ma'am . . . er, it's just that his boy is in great pain." The nurse's first impulse was to turn and walk out of the room. "I dare this colored man think he can tell me what to do." However, when she looked at the young boy, she asked, surprising herself, "What happened to him?"

Poppa said, "He got hooked by my bull."

"Come," she said, looking at Fred, "follow me."

Dr. Walker was a pleasant white man with blond hair and very blue eyes. His eyes always made Poppa think of the eyes of a snake because snakes had very bright sparkling colorful eyes. White people's eyes, like snake eyes, were of different colors. Poppa noticed that the only time colored people had eyes other than light or dark brown, they inherited their eye color from some white that disowned them, but with a slight smile, he said that "eyes don't lie."

While examining Fred's wound, Dr. Walker said, "Boy, you are lucky your pa brought you here right away. I've known patients who have lost their limb once infection set in. At this early stage, a penicillin shot and here's a small jar of antibacterial cream and you should be fine." Looking at Poppa, he said, "Sam, bring the boy back in a couple of weeks. I'd like to take another look at that leg."

"Yes-sum, Dr. Walker, sure will, and thank you, sir."

"You know, Sam, we all have the same problem with our boys, white and colored alike. They just have the tendency to demonstrate their courage and physical power."

"Yes-sum, sir, that sure is the truth."

"Thank you, Doctor." Closing the door behind them, Poppa overheard Dr. Adams speak softly to his nurse, "You know, that Sam sure seem like a nice boy."

Peggy, her best friend Calla Mae, who lived right up the road from our house, and Henry were all in their midteens taking advantage of this warm Saturday day in May of 1962 from school and work. They were taking a leisure walk through the pasture to escape boredom. They heard an animal at a short distance that was in extreme distress. Following the sound of the call for help, they saw the beautiful white horse that was a big part of our farm life.

"Oh my God, it's Beauty! Henry!" cried Peggy in great compassion and fear as the three of them rushed to the aid of the animal they loved. A horse that was always a presence in their young life. They rode her. They brushed her beautiful mane. She also played an essential role in their well-being.

"Come here, Beauty," Peggy said with an apple in her hands just like she saw on the television show *Mr. Ed*. Mr. Ed's TV show was about a talking horse. Peggy used to try to get Beauty to talk just like Mr. Ed. "Peggy, horses can't talk." Peggy, by the look in Beauty's eyes, felt deep down within that just maybe she could talk, that Beauty had something to say.

Beauty lay on the ground panting, exhausted. Thick white-and-green discharge was oozing out of her large nostrils. "Oh my, Beauty is in labor!" Henry exclaimed. Our beloved horse was having a birth that was life-threatening to herself and her foal.

Peggy and Henry fell down on their knees to assist Beauty. One of her foal's legs had broken through the birth canal. Young Henry pushed his hands into her birth canal, trying to free the foal's other leg. His hand was slick and slimy because of the placenta and the amniotic fluid that prevented him from getting a strong grip. Henry quickly removed his shirt. Calla Mae rushed to assist him to take his shirt off. With shirt off, Henry used his shirt to try and clean his hands, also wrapping his shirt around the foal's leg, trying to get a better grip.

"Hurry, Henry, hurry!" Peggy said, making eye contact with the dying horse. "Beauty is dying! Oh God! She isn't going to make it." Peggy looked the dying horse in her eyes; she could almost hear Beauty say "thank you" before her last breath.

When Peggy was a little tot, Momma had picked her up so she could rub Beauty's face and move her little fingers through the horse's silky mane. Beauty fell in love with her then as the horse's wide nostril sniffed the small child. Poppa said, "Animals don't forget." And as the horse was dying, she remembered that moment when she first sniffed little Peggy. When Henry finally pulled the foal out, it was dead too.

Peggy was panting from exertion, out of breath from the fourth-of-a-mile run from the pasture when she burst through the back kitchen door, tears rolling from her grief-stricken eyes. Her friend Calla Mae was close behind. Henry stayed for a short time with the dead horse and her dead foal; the smell of their death consumed him, her life with him rolling through his mind, resonating there. Looking down upon their lifeless bodies as they lay there in Beauty's afterbirth still hanging from her dead body, grief swelled within him and he began to weep.

Looking up in the sky, he saw the buzzards soaring at a great height. Even before the horse's death, they were there, but at a distance because they were made to smell death. They were hungry, ready to eat, and our beloved horse and her foal would feed them for days. Henry had said how he hated buzzards "waiting on lifeless trees, hoping for death, scavengers feeding on the remains of the dead, plucking pieces of their carcass before flying away with large chunks of animal flesh hanging from their very large beak to feed their young that were waiting in their nest with their beaks wide open."

Although the buzzards were first, there were other hungry scavengers lurking behind tall weeds and branches where the floor of the pasture and the floor of the forest join—raccoons, foxes, possums, and many others waiting for their meal. As Henry stood looking down upon the horse that he loved, he looked over at the edge of the forest where he could sense their presence. The movement of the weeds and the branches testified that they were there, peeking through the weeds and branches like small children peeking through the curtains, expecting their parents to bring them sweet treats from the store. The buzzards hovering overhead had announced that a great feast was waiting for them.

The kitchen was filled with the smell of fried chicken when Peggy and her girlfriend burst through the back kitchen door. Momma quickly turned from the pan of dishwater that she was washing dishes in and with haste dried her hands on her apron. With great alarm, she opened her arms and Peggy fell into them weeping.

"Baby, baby, what's the matter?" Her sobbing was so intense she couldn't speak. Calla Mae spoke for her. "Mrs. Gathing, Beauty is dead!"

"What do you mean, how can this be? What happened?"

"Momma, her baby is dead too," Peggy said through acute sorrow.

"Lord have mercy, wait until your poppa hears about this. He loved that horse as much as we did." The word spread like wildfire throughout the family about the death of our beloved horse at age twenty-five. She had been in our family longer than most of Poppa's children.

# 26

## A Time to Celebrate

In mid-October, the leaves were putting on their fall colors of red, gold, and orange; the harvesting season has finally ended. The long, hot, dusty summer days has ended. It was time to put away our cotton sacks, set aside our water jugs that we had to drench our thirst with as we worked in the dry heat. It was time to hang up our beloved straw hats, the hats that Poppa's children had grown to love because our straw hats were the only thing we had to separate us from the awful heat of the Mississippi sun while working in the fields. Planting and harvesting season always end the same way year after year.

At the end of the planting season in June and the end of harvesting season in late October, Poppa and Momma always took their children shopping for spring and fall clothes. We were all excited at the end of harvesting season. Poppa always celebrated with his family by taking them about forty miles to Memphis's state fair.

Like sardines packed in a can, our poppa packed his kids in his car or truck with brand-new clothes and brand-new shoes, feeling good and looking new. This song comes to mind: "Don't you step on my blue suede shoes."

With his children's hearts filled with great expectations of amusement, cotton candy, soda pop, popcorn, etc., Poppa sped toward Byhalia,

Mississippi, about ten miles from where we lived. He drove through this small town on the way to Memphis, and as Poppa approached this small town, there was a steep hill. Before our poppa got to this hill, he would press down on the gas pedal and climb this steep hill as fast as he possibly could. When his car reached the top, it felt like, for a moment, the car was actually flying for a second or two.

I think the tires didn't touch the ground before descending.

All of his children screamed. We loved it! It reminded us of the rollercoaster we were getting ready to ride.

Poppa's children wasn't allowed to listen to worldly music in his home. The blues, swing, or R&B was not acceptable. Because his children weren't allowed to sing worldly music, they turned their attention to spiritual songs. With a gang of fourteen children and two nephews, you could always hear church music and songs' high rhythm, sweet melodies, clapping hands, and stomping feet. And sometimes shouting as they sang to their poppa, momma, and one another. With windows wide open, music and songs would vibrate and could be heard at a distance. Some of the children in the area said they used to sit on the roadside nearby so they could hear Poppa's children singing.

# 27

## *Feeling Like a Winner*

J oe Louis was the world heavyweight boxing champion from 1937-
1949. Nicknamed the Brown Bomber, Louis helped elevate boxing
by being an honest, hardworking fighter. Louis was named the
greatest heavyweight of all time by the International Boxing Research
Organization. Few men had a great impact on society or on our poppa.

Louis's cultural impact was felt well outside the ring. He is widely
regarded as the first Black American to achieve the status of a nationwide
hero within the United States. On June 22, 1938, between Joe Louis and
Max Schmeling, the fight was held in Yankee Stadium before a crowd
of 70,043. It was broadcast by radio to millions of listeners throughout
the world.

Each time Joe Louis won a fight in those depression years, even
before he became champion, thousands of colored American would
throng out in to the streets all across the land to march and cheer and
yell and cry because of Joe Louis's one-man triumphs. No one else in
the United States has ever had such an effect on Negro emotions.

Why Poppa would invite friends and family over? For this was a
day suitable for a gathering. The festive energy was upbeat in the house
and filled with excitement. Everyone was bustling about, watching the
wind-up clock that was sitting on top of the large battery-operated

Philco radio as the minutes tick away before the boxing match starts because when the ringside bell rings, everyone would be rushing to the radio because they didn't want to miss a punch.

Momma and her teenage girls Cynthia, Cozetta, Ruth, and Christine were busy in the kitchen, noisily chatting and giggling, getting everything ready for the party. Ruth was making homemade vanilla ice cream made in an old hand-cranked churn, and Momma had baked one of her family favorite molasses cakes for the huge Joe Louis's fight. Cynthia and Cozetta were cleaning while Christine prepared the large bucket of iced tea. I guess you could say Poppa had one of the first "superbowl" parties while they huddled around his huge battery-operated radio, hollering, stomping their feet just like the superbowl parties of today.

Joe Louis's boxing with a white man in these segregated years added to the excitement.

Joe Louis hit Max Schmeling with a right and then a left. And as these men continued to huddle around the radio, each man in his own way acted out what they heard the announcer was saying.

Joe Louis jabbed him in the chest! Oh my! A blow to the head. Uppercut to the chin—he's out! Max Schmeling is out!

The fight lasted two minutes and four seconds.

Everyone burst into indescribable excitement and emotions. For Joe Louis, a black man, to knock out a big white man against the backdrop of all the racial stereotypes of the black man—men and women, even children, who had been slain for no other earthly reason than their blackness—it was like every black man in the world had finally kicked the white man's ass!

# 28

## *Escalating Violence*

O ur poppa, born in 1908, living his whole life under Jim Crow laws, was a man who believed in law and order, a man who paid his bills on time—"nothing in the world like good credit"— paid close attention to current events, especially those that affected his family and his people's lives. Living during the 1950s, the time of escalating civil disorder, a time that the winds of change were blowing with a great force. Fear was closing in, getting more intense with each report of the daily news.

"The men who controlled power were very powerful men," Poppa said. To challenge their authority and go against their man-made laws is risking yours and your loved ones' lives with the possibility of causing anarchy. Our poppa was very aware of the possibility of American citizens being killed because of rebellion. Poppa discussed men like Marcus Garvey and Elijah Muhammad. "I don't see anything these angry men has done but talked." Our poppa couldn't imagine these men running the United States government.

Preaching and being the pastor of several churches kept our poppa at the center of the events surrounding his environment. His awareness was always at its highest peak living under the Jim Crow laws. The fear for his family, especially for his boys, and his people were always present. These were times of lynching and living in Mississippi, a tough state that was run by the Ku Klux Klan. Black people had no rights—the law wasn't on the side of the black citizens. The fear of lynching in the South, the threat, was always there.

Our poppa personally knew of someone who had been lynched or of the body of someone's son found floating down a river. One of our poppa's members came to him with red swollen eyes, weeping and sobbing out her story. "Our boy has been killed. The Klan did it, Rev."

Poppa didn't have an answer for this dear lady; he feared for his five boys himself. It always seemed that it was the boys the racist white men wanted to destroy. After counseling this weeping mother, he very well may have told her to pray. To ask God for mercy, that's what he did himself.

The civil rights struggle escalated in the early sixties. These events had a lot of impact on the blacks at the times, and we were no different. In 1960, these issues continued to escalate, and the civil rights struggle increased.

The big news of the week was Dr. King leading a protest against the dreadful Bull Connor, the most determined mayor in the Deep South that said no Negro would ever sit next to white children in their schools or anywhere else. Mayor Connor ruled the city of Birmingham as though he was a cruel dictator; even the whites were afraid of him. Our poppa's family was huddled around our television as the black-and-white images rolled in the widespread violence against the Negro children in Birmingham, "probably the most segregated city in the United States." We watched in horror as the dogs attacked the children. "My God! They're actually letting loose their German shepherd dogs on those children!" As the dogs lurched forward on the children, everyone in the room gasped in disbelief. Meanwhile, other policemen were using high-pressured fire hoses, overwhelming the children, knocking them to the ground. Roberta and Alberta started crying. Momma turned her head. "Lord have mercy, I can't watch this!" Our poppa was sitting on the edge of his chair. "Lord help us!"

The words of fifteen-year-old Betty Joe and fourteen-year-old Peggy came out in gasps. "Poppa, oh my God, those are the same dogs those white men sent to attack us from the back of their pickup truck!"

Everyone present knew what and who the girls were referring to. The terrorizing experience that Betty Joe, Peggy, and their friend Calla

May have happened while they were walking the mile walk on the dusty gravel road that led to the corner store. Our momma had sent the girls to get some Clabber Girl baking powder and sugar so she could bake some tea cakes for her family. The girls were enjoying their walk on this warm pleasant April day in 1963, giggling and talking like teenage girls do.

They stopped giggling and stood on the side of the road to let a truck pass when they heard the sound of it approaching. These evil men saw the girls before the girls saw them. The old muddy Chevrolet farm truck's cab was full, with four men crammed in there.

"Let's have some fun. We can watch our dogs scare the hell out of these nigger kids," one of them may have said. Without warning, the pickup truck pulled up and stopped in front of them, and before the dust settled, the girls knew this was serious trouble when they saw the four white men up front and the three German shepherds in the truck's bed barking.

This created horror in the minds of the girls. When these men released vicious, growling dogs showing their canines from the back of the truck, the German shepherds walked slowly toward the girls. These evil men were laughing while telling the dogs, "Get 'em! Go! Damn you, I said get those niggers now!"

Betty Joe said the dogs walking toward them were barking furiously. The girls were terrified, trembling, nearly fainting. The dream Peggy had the night before came with great force back into her mind. She told Momma about it. Our parents were strong believers in dreams. They would ask us, "What did you dream about last night?" Poppa said dreams are important. The Bible speaks of them. After Poppa had blessed our breakfast, he thought it was a sin to eat without first blessing the food. We sat down to homemade biscuits, rice, and scrambled eggs.

"Momma," Peggy said. "Guess what I dreamt about last night? It was real scary."

"What, baby?"

"I dreamt that there were three mean dogs walking toward me. Momma, they had long white teeth."

Poppa said, "That's not a good dream, I don't like it, child."

As my sister Betty told me this horror story in the summer of 2012, she was sixty-two years old, and the pain of this experience hadn't fully left her.

She said that as the dogs walked toward them she could hear Poppa's voice as plain as day. *Never, never run from dogs because you can't outrun them. Stand still and look them dead in their eyes.* Betty said that as these three snarling dogs were walking toward them, she obeyed the voice of our poppa. "Whatever you do, don't move," she whispered to the girls. "Look them dead in their eyes." As they stood there trembling in fear, they obeyed, the dogs turned slowly around, walked back, and jumped back into the truck's bed.

Growing up in Mississippi, we encountered so many evil whites we thought they all had invisible horns and hooves like the devils in the book of Ezekiel. And we believed they had evil power—and with absolute power.

Before Dr. King and his followers came to Birmingham, they were warned about the giants there. Bull Connor was the biggest giant they would face during their civil rights struggle. The powerful local and state national guards took their orders from him once Governor Faubus ordered them into the city. Hundreds of power rifles were held by men behind body armors to protect themselves against the peaceful demonstrators of men, women, and children. And all demonstrators were so afraid to face the evil giants. I'm sure Dr. King was afraid; however, he knew he had to face the giants to overcome the biggest hurdle of all, Bull Connor himself.

It appeared that Mayor Connor, like other men in power, was full of pride. Who do these niggers think they are coming in my city intruding in our peace?

As King and his followers faced the giants of hatred and enraged mobs, photographs of the images that flooded American airwaves shocked the unaware American citizens, causing them to be outraged by the millions. Consequently, the images that the rest of the world was witnessing were tantamount to the world population, looking behind the Iron Curtain that divided Europe in the 1940s into two separate areas. Most people who never lived nor visited the southern part of the United States really were unaware of the conditions that the Negroes lived under and had never heard of "Jim Crow laws."

When the media beamed their camera on Bull Connor and his cohorts, they were focused as obviously the evil giants. With the images that were spread all across the nation, the outraged public demanded to know, "Who are these people that can send vicious dogs on defenseless men, women, and children?" The public wouldn't have known the depths of hate in Bull Connor if the demonstrators or the media hadn't appeared. The protestor and the media manifested Bull Connor's true character. "There is Blessing in the Storms."

> From its dedication in 1927, Little Rock Senior High School (its name was changed to Little Rock Central High School in 1953) was recognized as more than a typical American school. The massive structure, a handsome blend of Art Deco and Gothic Revival styles, was named by the American Institute of Architects "America's Most Beautiful High School." Central High was celebrated for its size (100 classrooms; capacity for more than 2,000 students; a huge auditorium and stage) and for its academic excellence. The school also served as a civic center in Little Rock, hosting concerts, plays, and other events. It was a focus of community pride and a cultural symbol—perhaps one of the reasons so many fought so fiercely against change at the school.

In the book *A Hero for Our Time* by Ralph G. Martin, he writes about how John Kennedy had to come to terms with the civil rights struggle.

To quote from his book, "The pragmatic President was now also more passionate about civil rights. Earlier, he had told liberal Joseph Rauh not to push him on civil rights because his criticism was 'quite wrong.' Rauh remembered how 'Kennedy turned on me with great force.' After Birmingham, John Kennedy told Rauh that the civil right struggle was going to be a long, tough fight but we have to do it."

What helped change him, what horrified him, what made him sick, was a photograph of a police dog lunging at a black woman. "A snarling police dog set upon a human being," said TV commentator Eric Sevareid, "is recorded in permanent photoelectric file of every human being's brain." Television amplified the horror, showing Birmingham's police slashing with their nightsticks, using pressure fire hoses, methodically beating people, one policeman even sitting on a fallen Negro woman.

By all accounts, our poppa was witnessing the wide gulf between the races getting narrower, closing in like a deep hollow abyss. The great wall of separation was slowly crumbling. The symbol of division, White Only, No Blacks Allowed signs, were pushing against a thick wall of resistance from five major Negro organizations—SCLC, NAACP, SNCC, Urban Core, church and major groups: "A city that is broken and without walls" (Proverbs 25:28).

The death of so many Negroes over the span of our poppa's life and the generations before him who lived during the times that "Negroes has no rights" made fear loom ever in his mind, the terror that the white ruling class can force upon their Negro citizens. The tide of change was pushing strongly against the walls of separation that Jim Crow had built.

Years in the future, in 1989, President Ronald Reagan would challenge Mr. Gorbachev, the general secretary of the Communist Party of the Soviet Union, "If you seek peace, Mr. Gorbachev, tear down that wall!"

On August 13, 1961, the Berlin Wall was built. The purpose of the wall being built was to keep the Soviet Union citizens locked into their Communist system so they wouldn't be tempted by another freer life and flee to seek that freedom.

With encouragement from President Reagan and other parts of the free world, the Soviet citizens took advantage of the words of President Reagan and by the hundreds stampeded toward the ugly wall that held them captive for twenty-eight years, separating them from their family and loved ones who lived on the other side. From the sound of the hammers banging, chiseling, clanking, the sound of let freedom rang under their hammers and chisels beating down the twenty-eight-year-old wall that has been said to run twenty-eight miles long through the heart of Berlin's capital, imprisoning their citizens. And in 1989, the wall came tumbling down. How could their families and loved ones hearing the crumbling of the wall that separated them for so long could not pick up their own hammers and chisels and whack away at it from the other side?

Throughout the span of time, man has held other men captive; and throughout the ages, man has fought to be free.

Our poppa often talked about what it would mean to live life as a "man" should because he knew what a free society meant. Even in America, there were large pockets of freedom in the northern states. Poppa said he wasn't aware of the huge difference in lifestyles until he started traveling to different northern cities like Chicago, Philadelphia, Detroit to the National Baptist Convention, the largest

Negro organization that at its peak had up to ten thousand preachers and some five million members.

The walls of separation were continually before him. The dichotomy of separation that had been in existence for hundreds of years now had obviously run its course and was running out of steam, so to speak.

The Bill of Rights cannot be locked up to keep some of its citizens from receiving those rights of personal security and personal liberty. Blacks knew about their constitutional rights, and the whites, of course, knew them too. Abraham Lincoln had the vision to see that this nation could not exist half slave and half free. In their separate black and white churches, they both read the same Bible about "brotherly love." This brotherly love the Bible talks about wasn't viewed man to man but color to color. Blacks and whites could not see that in the eyes of God, they were all brothers. If someone had told a white that in the eyes of God blacks were his brothers, they probably would have been lynched.

The Bible is the truth. Poppa knew that reading his Bible, the Book of Truth, would lead him onto all truth. It must have been difficult for our poppa to feel this brotherhood that Jesus preached about. The thick walls of separation blocked his view. No way did he feel the words that he read in his Bible about brotherly love when around whites. How could he? The whites are men and black men are old boys.

Dr. Martin L. King Jr. was led into these truths through reading these truths. No man should be a slave to another man or a second-class citizen. "We hold these Truths to be self-evident, that all men are created equal," Thomas Jefferson said.

The powerful words spoken by Martin L. King are as follows:

> So we've come here today to dramatize a shameful condition. In a sense we've come to our nation's capital to cash a check. When the architects of our republic wrote the magnificent words of the Constitution and Declaration of Independence, they were signing a promissory note to which every American was to fall heir. This note was the promise that all men, yes, Black men as well as white men, would be guaranteed the unalienable rights of life, liberty, and the pursuit of happiness. ("I Have a Dream")

The segregationists knew instinctively that the words that Dr. King spoke were true, and this was the beginning of the end of old man Jim Crow. And because of his spoken words, they put Dr. King to death. "Woe unto you, Scribes and Pharisees, hypocrites" (Matthew 23:23). Because of the truth that Jesus told, the Pharisees killed him.

Our Poppa, like many people, believed the truth. However, their surrounding culture couldn't accept this truth. "That all men were created in the image of God. Jesus said to love one another."

It's impossible to understand that the whites that passed the Jim Crow law in 1857 that stated that "Negroes had no rights that a white had to respect" read the same Bible that the Negroes read. They read the truths in their schools, churches, and home. But they didn't believe these truths. Many people died because of their unbelief.

Even under these circumstances, there were many whites who, throughout our history, took a stand with the Negroes. The Quakers and John Brown comes to mind. Surrounded by throngs of hatred, like flowers on a cactus, they took a stand. And some died because of it. And Negroes shouldn't ignore these powerful acts of love.

## John Brown, a Hero for Blacks (May 9, 1800-Dec 2, 1859)

John Brown was an American abolitionist who advocated and practiced armed insurrection as a means to end slavery. He attempted in 1859 to start a liberation movement among enslaved African Americans. Brown demanded violent action in response to southern aggression.

During the Kansas campaign, he and his supporters killed five proslavery southerners in what became known as the Pottawatomie Massacre in May 1856.

During the raid he led on the federal armory at Harpers Ferry, Virginia, he seized the armory. Seven people, including a free black, were killed. Brown intended to arm slaves with weapons from the arsenal, but the attack failed. Brown was hanged after his attempt to start a slave rebellion failed.

In behalf of the poor and the oppressed, John Brown believed in the divine authenticity of the Bible.

The Quakers gave the runaway slaves support by putting candles in their windows to let the slaves know they could come to their house for food and shelter as the slaves were fleeing the south on their way up north or to Canada where they were seeking freedom.

The civil rights struggle had escalated in the early sixties. These events had a lot of impact on the blacks at the time, and we were no different. In 1960, these issues escalated, and the civil rights struggle increased.

Our poppa knew firsthand the danger that Dr. King and his followers were facing. The nightly news brought the horrific struggle into everybody's living room. Our poppa was deeply affected by what he saw on television. When peaceful people came face-to-face with the evil dark forces of racism, these two energies clashed in a horrible force of violence.

There were bombings, attack dogs, fire hoses on small children. Killings of innocent people.

Poppa knew the violence the racist white could create. The terrorist Klan was a perfect example of the evil one man could create on another man. Our poppa personally knew of someone who had been lynched or of the body of someone's son found floating down a river. One of our poppa's members came to him with red swollen eyes, weeping and sobbing out her story. "Our boy has been killed. The Klan did it, Rev."

Poppa didn't have an answer for this dear lady; he feared for his five boys himself. It always seemed that it was the boys the racist white men wanted to destroy. After counseling this weeping mother, he very well may have told her to pray. To ask God for mercy, that's what he did himself.

# 29

## They Will Kill You

O ur poppa was a man who believed in law and order, a man who paid his bills on time—"Nothing in this world like good credit." The men that controlled power were very powerful men. Our poppa was very aware of the possibility of American citizens being killed, the ones that rebel against the authority. Poppa had serious problems with men like Marcus Garvey and Elijah Muhammad. "I don't see anything these men has done, but talk." Our poppa couldn't imagine the man running anything, let alone overthrowing the United States government.

He was also concerned about the escalating violence around MLK's messages. So our poppa watched the earthshaking events on this hot summer day in August in 1962 of the images of the civil rights movement, the Freedom Riders, Dr. King speaking out in a strong voice, "We hold these truths to be self evident that a people has the right to the pursuit of happiness. Some truth is God given."

Dr. King and his followers stood so close to this evil they even rubbed the racist white spit off their faces. King and his followers stood their ground. Unyielding, they stood. Attack dogs, high-pressure water hoses. They stood. Police bully clubs. They stood unyielding. Singing their freedom song "We Shall Overcome."

What our poppa and the others were watching on television and throughout the world was hard to believe. Words that were whispered from their mouth, talked about in their homes.

Secret words about those "white folks." Because to speak them openly would cause death to you or one of your boys.

Lynching, burning, being dragged with a rope tied behind a truck while a white driver and his buddies inside laughing and telling nigger jokes. Our Poppa knew the evil of these southern whites. He lived his life while in the midst of their horror. So when Poppa said to his family and to God as he watched Dr. King on TV, "Lord have mercy, they're going to kill that man," Poppa knew what he was talking about.

Dr. King and his followers knew that Americans had not lived up to its promises. America had to face the lies they were telling the world. Foreign countries thought all of American citizens were free. As late as the sixties they were not.

MARTIN LUTHER KING IS SLAIN IN MEMPHIS; A WHITE IS SUSPECTED: PRESIDENT JOHNSON URGES CALM (*New York Times*, Friday, April 5, 1968)

## Reflection

Looking back to the mourner's bench era that was written about in great detail in the chapter about "Mourner's Bench" on page 22 in the year of 2010, it may seem foolish now. Was all that necessary? you may ask.

You decide. Today's youth, thank God not all of them, the satanic rap music, low-slung-style pants that hangs below the butt and underwear visible for all to see and passersby would glance at and wag their heads in shame, too horrified to look ("Even with their buttocks uncovered, to the shame of their people" [Isaiah 20:4]), these kids are blocking the light from their grandparents' generations.

They, especially the teenage black boys, are bringing in so much darkness that the hope and prayers through their grandparents' struggle has been weakened. They've given the civil rights movement a black eye.

What happened to them? many are asking. Some of their parents and especially their grandparents who migrated up north from the rural and agriculture lifestyle often talked about their social history. The daily contact with the cycle of life—the birth of a calf, the struggle the cow goes through to bring that calf into the world. The old agrarian community was replenished with birth and death. "I can hear that cow mooing out, weeping for her dead calf," our momma would say.

The rhythms of life is felt at every turn; even plant life is a big part of this life. "Lord, I pray that it rains, the fields are awful dry." The labor of your hands that was supportive of life felt mercy for the newborn calf, held a baby chick in the palm of your hands. Experiencing the cycle of life causes people who live on the farm to value life more.

The following story of Bo-Bo is based on facts; however the names have been changed to protect the identities of the ones involved.

The horror and fear that parents go through each time their son walks out the front door into the night to join his friends waiting in the car out front, looking out the window as their son gets into the red 2006 Chevy Impala—the four boys that are waiting, they wonder who they are—the danger that's clocked over the car is palpable. Will this be the last time they see him alive? They've tried over and over again to warn him the danger surrounding urban life. Telling them to walk the path of caution, don't step on anyone's $200 Jordan shoes because saying you are sorry may not be enough. You may get killed because of it.

The young men are very much aware of their culture. They know they cannot escape, where will they go? This is their home, all of their friends are here. The fellowship of brotherhood is also in the narrow area in which they were born and will probably die.

The horror became a reality when she answered the phone at 2:00 a.m. on a Saturday night. She probably knew at the first ring it was her son. "Ms. Lennon, we found your number on the back of a picture in his wallet. We need you to come down to the city morgue to identify the body."

How could she not gasp for breath? Fear and grief, the emotional and physical loss, the crushing blow of her sixteen-year-old son who by her gut feeling knew that it was him lying under a white sheet on a gurney covered from head to toe. The great love and now the great loss. She heard herself say, "Yes, office we will be right now." Edward, awakened by the ringing of the phone, heard his wife talking over the phone. As she hung up the phone, weeping, Edward, like his wife Frances, knew it was their son.

When her son Bo-Bo—he earned that nickname when he began to walk at age fifteen months because of his bowed legs—was a happy toddler, he laughed a lot, would even go to a complete stranger. His interest in numbers and airplanes was apparent at a very young age. As he got older, we started giving him toy airplanes for his birthday and for Christmas. When he started going to school, even in kindergarten at five years old, he would play the game "2x2=4 and 2x4=8 and 2x5=10. During holiday celebrations, we would call for Bo-Bo, "Come and count for your cousins! Our little son loved the attention."

When he first entered junior high at age thirteen, this was when she and her husband started worrying about their son. Bo-Bo's friendly, easygoing personality was attracting boys that concerned his mother and his dad. His clothes were the first sign of rebellion. "Bo-Bo, pull your pants up, what's the matter with you!" His dad didn't like it either; however, his dad was more tolerant until one even he saw Bo-Bo standing on the street corner with a group of boys with their underwear showing. Edward, rolling down his car window, hollered at his son, "Boy, pull those damn pants up! Have you lost your mind?" Bo-Bo pulled his pants up while his buddies just laughed.

Bo-Bo's grades started dropping. He and his dad were arguing now, and that was something that had never happened before. Edward asked his wife, "Do you think our son is on drugs?"

"Honey, I think the music they are listening to is driving them crazy, have you ever listened to any of that stuff?" She handed her husband a rapper's CD that she had gotten out of their son's room. Edward placed it into the CD player. The awful foul language blasted through the speaker, words that were designed to kill and destroy, entice and glamorize rape, criminality, destructive force against other people, death and other extremes and excesses of brutality, seeing their peers as not human but a "thing."

Bo-Bo's indifference to his parents' feelings was something that left them groping for answers that didn't come. His self-assuredness, full of pride in his good looks, and his friends was all he needed. Their son acted as though he didn't need them anymore; his friends were enough. His attitude left them in a permanent state of anxiety, stress, and fear.

Bo-Bo's potential was revealed to his parent at a very young age. They envisioned him becoming an airplane pilot; now they painfully watched as he was taking the low road. Reinhold Niebuhr writes, "Groups are more immoral than individual." The awful reality, they now realized, was that their son was a member of a gang and was getting immoral support from them.

Although Bo-Bo was the product of a two-parent home, the breakdown of the Afro-American family in the culture in which he lived had a huge effect upon him. The influence of peer pressure and the undercurrents of group activities of boys in his neighborhood weakened his resolve to resist.

Unlike Bo-Bo's, most of his friends' dads were in prison or had served time there and were very angry men because of it. Playing the "blame game"—"It's not what we did but what was done to us"—they were deeply affected by the growth of the black male in the prison population.

It is true that there's extremely high violence in the black male population. However, there is an always unseen story behind what we witness. It's always more to it than we think.

His heart (an angry black man) was filled with anger against his black brother to the point of threats of death by shooting. Some middle-age men would rush and get their pistol, speed off in their automobile to wave their pistol in another black man's face. "If you don't pay me the money you own me, I'll shoot you, m—!"

Most of the time, this angry outburst was just a threat, just to get their attention. However, their teenage sons heard their dads or another angry black man say these awful angry words filled with extreme hostility. These boys took it to the next lowest level and actually pulled the trigger, killing their perceived enemy that looks like themselves.

It may not be acceptable to talk about it. Sometimes they don't believe the facts. The facts, however unpleasant they are and they include the high murder rate in our young black male population, are that it's obvious the threats these young men hear dismantles their love they should have for their brothers.

The melodrama of it all: "It all happened so suddenly," they say, speaking of the teenage son. The mother amidst sobs and tears says, "What happened? My baby was here yesterday, today I'm at the morgue."

There are enough black males and females in college, though, which gives us a ray of light, a gleam of hope. It also shows us too that our grandparents' prayer hasn't totally been lost, that some seeds that were planted generations ago fell on fertile ground. By all of this, we are encouraged.

# 30

## Reminiscence beyond the Crossroad

The writing on BI (Baptist Industrial College and Seminary) is based on the writings of Ruth Gathing, our poppa's fifth twenty-one-year-old child who attended the school during 1953-1957.

Our poppa, as I've stated in a previous chapter, shared the philosophy of Booker T. Washington that education was the answer to the American Negro's problems. Consequently, he talked a lot about education and the foundation of the building of those school and the Negro and white men and women who played a major role in the building of schools for Negroes. The generous philanthropy of missionaries and northern churches became a compelling force, with their power to influence donating their time and money to assist Negroes.

In the middle of the 1800s, blacks were forced into independence because there were no public schools for Negroes that went beyond the eighth grade in the southern part of the United States.

During this time in our history, the impoverished black communities made large contributions to the first black schools: 1865, Fisk, Lincoln; 1866 Talladega, Howard, Morehouse; and many others. The remembrance of slavery was fresh in their minds. The Negro men and women didn't take their freedom for granted. The promise of "forty acres and a mule" didn't happen. Blacks learned a hard lesson. The whites' controlling power was not going to do it for them. The more Negroes were denied the privilege of education, the more value they placed on education; so with self-determination, they buckled down and were determined to do it for themselves. Philanthropists and missionaries saw that the time had arrived that the Negroes were serious. "God help those who help themselves."

During this segregation era, there were eighty-three private schools that were started by and run by Negroes where Negroes could pay for a high school education in Mississippi because there was no public school for blacks that went beyond the eighth grade.

The Baptist Industrial Academy, also known as BI, in Hernando, Mississippi, was one of those schools (1887-1957). BI, in fact, was the only place in Desoto County, Mississippi, that Negroes could pay for a high school education.

These children came from all over the county in search for a high school education. Most parents were following the teachings of Booker T. Washington (up from slavery): "If the Negroes were to succeed in America, they must be educated."

Our poppa was in the midst of this zeal for education. A love for BI was embedded deeply within Poppa's heart.

Our poppa was the moderator of Sardis East Baptist Congress that was held up by a conglomerate of churches that spread throughout several adjacent counties in northern Mississippi, with unified control that pooled their resources, time, and money to build schools for their children.

As moderator, Poppa held the gavel, seeking ways to solve internal disputes these churches encountered. Poppa's children would hear him discussing plans, hopes and disappointments, progress, and setbacks that deeply troubled him after some of those meetings.

He sent his oldest son Junior and his two daughters Ruth and Cozetta to BI, and his younger children were looking forward to going also.

"My memories of BI," Poppa's daughter Cozetta reflected upon those long past years, "were some of the most memorable days of my life. The school was rich in our black history and culture, having great worth in building our character. Giving us a rich supply of issues to discuss and debate. The writings of W. E. B. DuBois, Booker T. Washington, and Marcus Garvey were a few of them.

The large trees—and five-stories buildings and the separate gender dormitories on the ten acres of land were nestled cozily in the shades of red maple, dogwood, and magnolia that were indigenous to Mississippi landscapes. The three hundred or so students that came from throughout Mississippi expanded our awareness of other people, increasing our once narrow world.

It appeared that the planners of BI was competing with the white schools in the state. "We will have what they have, only better because the whites were the standard in which we judged ourselves. We took pride in our parades on homecoming day, parading down the main streets of Hernando. Even the whites would stop and watch, some even standing in the doorways of their business to watch. Our floats were the prettiest of all. Ruth would be right up front with the other majorettes, twirling her baton, throwing it high up above her head and catching it in midair and continuing to twirl it without missing a beat as she and the other four majorettes continued to march behind the band as though they were trying to touch one of their knee to their chins."

"Cozetta," Roberta interrupted, "how did Poppa feel about Ruth wearing shorts even in a parade, knowing how he never did approve of his girls wearing shorts?"

"That's a good question. I don't really think he ever approved of it. I think under the circumstances he just compromised his standards, came to terms with it. Ruth was so active in school. She wrote speeches, was the one most chosen to give the 'welcome' to events at school. Always ready to volunteer for whatever."

Cozetta continued. "After classes and on weekends, we would go to our favorite shade tree with a blanket with some of our girlfriends and would be quickly joined by some of our boyfriends." The memories still brought sparkles in her eyes. "Girl, now those were the good old days."

To be away from home, out of the watchful eyes of our parents was more than our poppa and our momma's younger children could hope for, and to live in a dormitory, to share a room like Ruth and Cozetta, wow! When we visited our sisters in Hernando, Mississippi, with excitement, we saw a glimpse into what we anticipated our future would look like.

Poppa said he read somewhere that "if you think education is expensive, you should consider the cost of being ignorant."

Those were the years before the Supreme Court declared that segregated schools were unconstitutional. The white authorities were pressured by white liberals and the Negro leaders into building their Negro citizens' public schools that were being built in the midst of Negro schools already standing so they could escape the churches, lodges, and poorly constructed buildings that between the cracks of these framed structures you could feel the wind and rain and the leaky tin roof on a windy day.

Although this was a momentous event in black history to have brand-new bricks and mortar, sparkling large windows to let the sunshine in, this excitement slowly started to wane as the days and months passed and reality set in. Black schools therefore received far less financial support than white schools. Used books and used school supplies that were rejected were passed down by the white schools because the white students were getting the brand-new books and new supplies.

Roberta remembered being issued her ninth-grade books, and after leafing through her history book, several pages had nasty, spiteful notes from the previous white student who used the book to humiliate the black student he or she knew was going to receive the books. In big bold letters using black crayon, they would write, "Kiss My Ass Nigger!!" Roberta said that she was so disturbed by this she wanted to throw the book in the trash right then and there, realizing just as quickly that if she did that, she would not be getting another book. So she did the next best thing—she took a stick of black crayon and covered the cruel message, but now every time she saw the blackened message, she was reminded of what was underneath and was still disturbed by it.

Consequently, building Negro schools did not solve the school controversy; "separated and equal" wasn't a reality. These separate schools were far, far from being equal, and the reality weighed heavy on the Negro leaders like Martin Luther King Jr. and many others. It became very obvious that for Negroes to have the same level of education as whites, they would have to sit together in the same classroom.

The southern whites found this so extremely outrageous. No way was any nigger kid going to sit in the same classroom with their children. There was great resistance to this possibility, it even came to the point of extreme violence, including black churches and homes being burned, bomb killings of many black men, women, and their children.

The terror from the whites wasn't of the Negroes' imagination. The headlines in the weekly paper was proof of the reality of the times in which they lived. The headlines and stories changed daily on violence against Negroes.

With the fall of 1957 approaching, segregationists in Little Rock predicted that violence would erupt (*New York Times*)

10,000 view body of lynched colored man on Sunday

President sent troops to Little Rock, federalizes Arkansas National Guard; tells nation he acted to avoid anarchy (1957) (*New York Times*)

White supremacist groups that made a solemn oath to resist racial change were extremely powerful and had great influence and controlled the state's politics. There was a long history of controlling their interest by force like a pack of wolves no one dared challenge because these brutal, barbarous men were the controlling power, sitting in high positions of authority.

In 1954, the U.S. Supreme Court declared segregated schools unconstitutional in the *Brown v. Board of Education*. When public high schools opened for Negro kids, it threw these black private schools into confusion and chaos. For the first time in Negro history, Negroes didn't have to pay for a high school education.

Once the law was passed, BI, like other private Negro schools, stood at the threshold of change and a tough choice had to be made—should they fight to stay, or flee from the circle of which they were the center, through the doors of sparkling new government schools that were being built for Negroes that went through the twelfth grade? Anyway, Negroes were contributing through their tax dollars the same as whites supporting education in public schools, and ultimately it was against Jim Crow laws for them to attend. They stood at the crossroads knowing a vital decision had to be made, debating the issues, the pros and cons. Should they hold on to the building blocks of their independence? The control to teach their own children. According to the Talmud, parents are required to teach their children The Five Books of Moses, a Trade and to swim. "Jews taught their own children even though they were slaves in Egypt." The paths of Negro private schools and government public high schools led to opposite directions.

The following was written by Sir Edward Elgar of BI, 1887-1957:

1887-1957 represents a period of seventy years. It was at the former date that a group of men themselves loss that a quarter of a century removed from slavery realized what an education could mean to every individual started Baptist Industrial College. Their very heads were filled with dreams of having a college second to none on this campus. Toils, sacrifices meant nothing to this humble group of men and women. Their soul [sic] ambition was to make it possible for the next generation to live a little better than themselves.

For seventy years now men have been toiling on these grounds. These men must not lose sight of the noble heritage handed them by their forefathers. The job started by these noble men is far from finished, the dreams held by those men and women are far from being realized. Today as in 1887 we need men or vision, dedication, and resources to make our college what it should be. The job is not impossible. We of this generation can conquer the giants that are in our paths. Not only can we conquer the giants but we must! There are still thousands and thousands of young people who needs the outlook on life being offered here on this campus. Once again people in all walks of life are looking forward to a moral and spiritual maturity that will enable them to conquer the giants of our day and time. Baptist Industrial College and Seminary is trying to send her sons and daughters out into the world that they might be able to take whole where ever they find themselves.

YOU CAN MAKE A GREAT CONTRIBUTION TO THE BATTLE WAGED ON OUR CAMPUS IF YOU PUT YOUR SHOULDER TO THE WHEEL AND LEND US YOUR WEIGHT AND YOUR HAND. Can we count on you!

In 1957, the debate began on the pros and cons of "Should Mississippi have integration in public school?"

Against integration was Herman Hudson Logan, a senior at BI in 1957. He was probably in his late teens or early twenties when this was written:

To the question should Mississippi have integration in the public school? I answer firmly and with no reservations, No! One listening to the question may raise another question as to the time element for this integration to begin; and for clarification this debate today, is interested in the time of the present day. Should integration begin today? Since we are interested in the present time, than I say we should not have integration in the public schools of Mississippi.

It might well be remembered that integration is the last thing that many of the members of the Caucasians and Negroid races want. Majority of people do now and will continue for a time to believe that "men and "boys" should remain in their places. Where this "place" is, I do not know; but I can assure you that the Negro will die to reach it's (the place). With such a defeated attitude, integration will not be popular; for in order to combat such an attitude, the Negroes must be organized. Just how far will one get in Mississippi trying to organize people who constantly live in the realm of fear? A sincere believer in organization would only have to speak once in behalf of such before he would be shot down in cold blood. A trial to avenge the murderer, then, would only end with a verdict of not guilty since the deed was done in self-defense. This action would serve only to thwart the remainder of the gallant heroes who might fight for the same cause. Negroes, more than anything else, are afraid to die.

In light of this point, the action should now be not to integrate, rather to educate the Negro; so that the fears and superstitions that have so long been embedded in him will be shortly erased and then the Negro would be better able to move toward the goal of integration. Something needs to be done now toward pushing first, our leaders to better prepare themselves to take their places in society. And then, secondly, the prepared leaders should impart that acquired knowledge to the remainder of the Negro people of Mississippi; ever urging them to climb to heights undreamed of and acclaims once thought unapproachable. No, there should be no integration until the Negro uplifts himself educationally.

Alongside education, the Negro should be lifted from the gutter of vulgarity to relinquishing heights of moral and spiritual character. It is a known fact that the Negro is not the only Mississippian in the gutter, but criticism of the gutter, Caucasians cannot be constructive until the "backyard" of the Negro is thoroughly cleaned. Spiritually, the Negro ministers are not doing their part to help the people. The Bible, our greatest guide in this world, tells us that the "blind shall lead the blind" and it seems that this bit of the Bible is certainly being fulfilled among the Negro people. The Negro minister is stumbling blindly along, groping for a banister to rest upon and his flocks are toddling behind, racing toward damnation. How then, can there be integration in the public schools of Mississippi when the spiritual and moral aspects of the Negro are reaching a new low in the upper depths of chaos?

Due to the seemingly irresistible circumstance no organization, poor education, and low moral and spiritual guidance among the Negroes. Mississippi cannot and must not integrate its public schools.

The following was written by Ruth Gathing, our Poppa's third daughter, a student at B.B., age twenty-three years old, "pro" for school integration:

## SHOULD MISSISSIPPI HAVE INTEGRATION IN ITS PUBLIC SCHOOLS?

To the proposed question—Should Mississippi have integration in the public schools?—I say with pride and emphasis yes. There should be integration in the public schools, not only in Mississippi, but all over the world. However, since we are concerned only with Mississippi, I shall present points that will prove that Mississippi more than any other state, needs integration in the public schools.

First, there should be integration because the Supreme Court issued the proclamation that segregation in the public schools is unlawful. This judiciary body, the Supreme

Court, has as one of its primary functions that of correctly interpreting the Constitution of the United States. One can readily see that after studying the constitution carefully no other law could have been passed concerning segregation and integration. The whole government, as set up by our forefathers, is founded on the principles of democracy; a democracy where freedom itself reigns supreme. There was no battle among our forefathers as to who shall be free and where, when, or how the freedom is to be administered. These able-minded men were concerned greatly in a government where man could exist as a man, void the trepidations which might be thrust upon him; and as a result of their thinking, the constitution of the United States was formulated so that those who were to follow would have those before said principles on which to continue to build. In light of this, then, there should be integration in the public schools of Mississippi.

Second, several other states in the United States have fallen in line and integrated their public schools and have done so with much success. Why, then, cannot Mississippi do the same? Is the race hatred among the leaders so deeply rooted that they have been and will continue to be the blind that will lead the blind? Does Mississippi stand at such a pinnacle that she cannot be reached? Is Mississippi so independent that she can produce without any outside aid? Without giving too much thought one can arrive at no answer other than no to these questions. Perhaps, one might say that integrating the public schools would serve to justify more bloodshed; but one should think of the fact that more blood is already being lost for a cause that Mississippi itself cannot define. There was one poet who said that "anything worth having is worth fighting for" and for integration in the public schools of Mississippi, there must be a fight because such actions as integration is good and worth having.

Thirdly, integration in the public schools of Mississippi would bring better equipment and materials to the Negro child who has so long not had the access to. The Negro would now have the advantage of a nice complete, comfortable

211

building with several rooms which are so lighted to the advantage of the eye. The child will no longer have the strain his eyes to visualize the objects before him, thus causing him to fear no more the thought of blindness because of poor lights. On days when the weather warrants such, the rooms will have adequate warmth so that the child would not freeze. And now there looms the Negro child a world of books for him to enter and devour as he wills. No longer will he have to worry as to whether or not the information contained in the books is outdated for with much changing scene comes a new book to make it a living reality.

And lastly, the Negro child will be faced with teachers who have prepared themselves for their life's profession. As my opponent has pointed out, "progress itself cannot be imparted to youth when they, the Negro teachers, have not kept and are not keeping abreast with the changing times." There must be progress, especially in the Negro race, and only better teachers can make the idea of progress a living reality. We cannot stop to think that the Negro teacher will be given the opportunity to exemplify his ability. Integration would then either open the eyes of those incapable teachers and cause them to go back and prepare themselves for the great task lying before them, or cause them to seek the profession for which they are prepared and make room for a replacement.

Due to certain unquestionable data: The Supreme Courts' demand that segregation in public schools is unconstitutional and must be abolished; that other states in the United States, previously having segregation, having abolished the same with little or no opposition; that integration would bring better schools and equipment and materials to the Negro child; and that the Negro child will have advantage of progressing through a better prepared and more enlightened teacher;—I feel strongly that there is nothing to do but embed in the minds of all Mississippians the idea that Mississippi should have integration in the public schools and make this idea living reality.

Ruth Gathing

There came a time when the majority of the faculties and the student body rejected BI for the attraction of the public school. This must have been hard for the ones who wanted to stay.

Later, when our poppa saw BI crumbling, the years of pride and hope for his people faded. I am sure that after years of hope and energy it took to come to this point of seeing his own children reap the rewards of his and many other like-minded men and women's labor that went into the building of BI and now to see their beloved children choose to abandon their school for the new state school that they viewed as bigger and better he felt despair. How could despair not seize these men and women once BI became vacant buildings that were closed because of declining enrollment where hope and growth were for seventy long years, now in 1957 these building stood there in eerie silence from once full of life, active and vigorous that came from the young student body. With boarded-up doors and windows.

# 31

## Poppa Talked to Roberta under the Pear Tree

R oberta and Alberta, like their siblings before them, had migrated up north to live with their sister Ruth, her husband Airest, and their three small children in a second-story three-room apartment in north St. Louis, Missouri. They did so after graduating from high school in 1962 to find work and to flee from the restraining laws of Jim Crow.

After being away for a year, Roberta returned back home on the same Greyhound bus that she took to St. Louis. When she stepped off the bus there, she and Alberta, like so many before them, breathed the fresh air of freedom from Jim Crow. She stood there as her sister Ruth and her husband came to welcome them and took a deep breath of fresh air because they had uprooted themselves from the rankled soil of Jim Crow.

Looking forward to seeing her family while gazing through the large bus side window to visit her family, especially her poppa and momma, sitting in the back half of the bus because of the Jim Crow laws that was against the law for Negroes to sit in the front half of the bus that was reserved for "white only." The five hours' bus ride from

St. Louis, Roberta said that she was so homesick because she had never been separated from her parents and younger sisters and brothers so long. And this was the first time she had been separated from her twin sister who had gone to Chicago to spend some time with Cozetta and her family. Finally, the bus pulled up to the bus stop in Byhalia, a small town that her parents lived about ten miles away. The bus stop was right in front of the general store. The store had a snack bar where whites could sit and eat and where Negroes could buy snacks, but they couldn't stay inside to eat; they would have to carry it outside ("take home a sack"). The first person she saw was her poppa, standing right beside seventeen-year-old Lloyd and fifteen-year-old Betty Joe. She felt joy in seeing her family; she missed them so. Looking up at the large back window, their faces lit up when they saw Roberta smiling and rapidly waving at them. She could read their lips as they were saying with great excitement, "There she is! I see her!"

The union Roberta felt for them was so strong during the year's separation. The small things about them that I missed the most were the smell of Poppa's pipe tobacco and the early morning aroma of Momma's homemade biscuits baking. I also missed my brother Lloyd's making beautiful music with the spiritual songs he sings. Even the sounds of the farm animals, the night sounds of crickets, owls, and the distant wolf howling were some renewing and refreshing sounds from the heavy traffic, car horns, and the occasional sounds of sirens rushing to an emergency in St. Louis.

All the blacks stayed seated while the whites exited out the front passenger door. Once they were all safely off the bus, now the blacks can make their exit through the back side exit door.

Once Roberta was off the bus, her two siblings rushed to her with Lloyd picking her up, giving her a very tight hug. Poppa raised his voice. "Boy, don't drop your sister." Lloyd said while grinning from ear to ear, "I picked up more than this skinny girl and didn't drop it!" The joy Roberta felt was apparent to all. When Lloyd finally put her gently down, Poppa came over to join them with a warm smile. "Girl, I see you made it."

"Yes-sum, Poppa." Our poppa was a man who never showed physical emotions. Consequently, there was a moment of awkwardness. Roberta, standing very close, leaned to him and gave him a hug; and to her own amazement, while her arms were around his shoulders, her cheeks rubbed against his cheeks without thinking about it. For the first time in her twenty years of life, she kissed her poppa on his cheek. Later as time passed and this memorable moment was known throughout the family as "that was the day Roberta kissed Poppa," the love and welcome she received was new to her. To her surprise, her parents treated her not just their daughter but as a special guest. "Poppa and Momma treated me like 'company.' Being separated from my parents for a year, I discovered how dear I was to them." As someone has said, "Absence makes the heart grow fonder."

Roberta had been home for a few days and was sitting comfortably on the sofa in the front room chatting with Momma. At the sound of a knock at the front door, Momma rose up out of her chair to answer the knock. Roberta recognized the pleasant medium-height white man right away, a tax collector known as Mr. White. "Beatrice, I know I'm a little early. I told Sam I was coming tomorrow."

Roberta noticed that her momma was acting a little strange as though she didn't have the slightest clue who this man was. Momma reached down and started balling the corner of her apron in her hands, the first sign that Roberta knew something was wrong with their momma. Momma said Sam as though she didn't know how he fit into this conversation. Roberta stood up and went to where Mr. White and Momma were standing, putting her arm gently around her waist to comfort her.

"My poppa isn't here at the moment, sir."

"That's fine, girlie, I'm scheduled to be here day after tomorrow. I just stopped because I was in the area."

"Yes-sum, I will tell him you came by."

Momma knew something wasn't right with her. Momma asked Poppa, "Sam, what's wrong with me? Things just keep going out of my head before I can say them." Of course, our poppa probably knew something was seriously wrong with his wife. "Something is wrong with Bracey. She just keep forgetting stuff."

Momma was scared. Our poppa started seeing a gradual change in his wife. Our poppa told his children, "There's something wrong with your momma."

On the last two days of Roberta's two-week trip to visit her family, she went to Poppa's orchard of pears, peaches, and apples to pick some fresh fruits.

Poppa was in the barnyard checking on his livestock, making sure no one had left the gate open, when he saw me picking pears from the tree he had planted a few years earlier. He walked toward me with a serious, familiar look on his face. It seemed as though he always had important weighty issues on his mind. Sometimes Poppa would laugh a hearty laugh. It seemed that he was set free just for a moment. I mean, really free. Free from the cares of raising a large family, farming, and all the worries that comes with it—church folks, white folks. Just plain old free. And it would all come back; the laughter stops as quickly as it had started. The serious weighty look is back. An intense struggle of the inner man, dealing with these two opposite forces—being the man God made him to be and playing the role of a boy that Jim Crow demanded him to be, this conflict of reality, knowing what God said about man "made in His image." These are the evil forces our poppa, like Dr. King and other like-minded men, wrestled with.

Roberta's basket was almost full when she looked up and saw Poppa approaching. She was probably wondering if there was a problem because it was unusual for Poppa to have small talk with one of his children. He always had a word of advice. Preaching was what he did. His Sunday sermons never ended. The Bible said in Hebrew or in Ezekiel, "You will reap what you sow. Never use the name of God in vain. Save for a rainy day that's sure to come. Do not get drunk on wine. Leave that stuff along. Alcohol leads to great bondage; it's a playground for Satan."

"Howdy, Poppa," Roberta said as he neared.

"Roberta, come and sit for a moment. I want to talk to you."

"Yes-sum."

Once we were comfortable sitting on the ground, Poppa began to talk. Pointing while moving his arm around after we were seated comfortably on the ground under the pear tree, he said, "See this land? There's nothing like it. Roberta, I rented from racist whites for years. Me and your momma had to put up with more than you can bear to hear and, girl, even living in the most violent, feared states in these United States where the KKK runs things. More lynching, rape, and terrorist acts against our people than any other state. Not all whites are evil. It's the 80 percent that lives down here in Mississippi that gives the other 20 percent a bad name." Roberta giggled at that. Poppa laughed before turning serious again.

Poppa continued talking to me on this warm autumn day in 1963 under the pear tree. The soft autumn breeze carried with it the scent of the barnyard and the smell of the fruit trees, and as Poppa continued talking, we smelled both. A cow mooed at a distance, and her calf responded with a "bah-bah." Old Fido came and joined us, coming to me for a pat and a warm gentle, reassuring hug. Fido was one of Lloyd's favorite hunting dogs. Poppa said, "Girl, be careful rubbing dogs. Most have fleas." Roberta stopped. Fido was disappointed.

The first wild geese of autumn convened noisily in perfect V formation, flying south, providing a perfect visible display of God's creation and beauty. Poppa paused to comment. Looking up, he said, "See those geese God told us to pay attention to nature? Roberta, you will never see different types of bird flying together or different breeds of animals mixing. Animals stay with their own kind. This makes you wonder about men, doesn't it?"

"You don't think people should marry outside of their race?" Roberta asked. "It seems that in some cases, it works out okay, but in most cases it's more trouble than it's worth. You see, marriages can have more than its share of problems within its own race. I have married many, many couples over the years and I have also seen more trouble in those marriages than you can imagine.

"Roberta, it's one thing I love about you, you have joy. Laughing a lot, that alone will take you a long way in life. People enjoy being around that type of energy. This makes them laugh too. You have the personality that attracts men. Beware of that because there's a big difference between love and lust. I see these boys from church looking at you, some even following you. Be careful, girl, that's not always a good sign. Old men can be a problem too. One thing I can tell you about men, they pay attention the way a woman walks. They can see a lot in a woman's walk."

Roberta said she was beginning to feel a little embarrassed. That she wasn't aware of the way she walks. "The way I walk, how can you change the way you walk?"

"You and Alberta, although twins, are different as oil and water. Fraternal twins they call you all because y'all don't look alike. But you and Alberta can learn from one another. You spend money like it grows on trees and your happy-go-lucky adventure spirit will probably be used to your advantage in life.

"Alberta will never be broke. She doesn't waste money like you. Like those rings on your fingers, you can't eat those things. I don't even want to know what they cost." Roberta may have been thinking, "Thanks for not asking."

Poppa continued. "You and Alberta both has some of my ways. I have always wanted to travel, wanted to see more of the world. Wanted to go to Israel where Jesus walked. I have been to California, lived for a while in Madison, Illinois, before marrying your momma, living with my uncle Luscher, working in a steel mill there. I was only eighteen years at the time. My mind was made up even then to marry your momma. Your momma by her own nature was so trusting. Even at sixteen years old, there was innocence, a purity about her. This made me want to not disappoint her. I started saving money. A man don't want to marry until he can take care of his family.

"Alberta, like me, is very interested in things of the Bible. When I talk about Scriptures, she pays close attention, also asking lots of questions. I see in her maybe becoming a Bible scholar someday. I see that gift in her if she doesn't waste it."

With a slight smile, he continued. "She doesn't waste her money and she probably won't waste this gift either. The only way the nature of a person can permanently be denied is if their life is shortened. Alberta has seen enough poverty living here in Mississippi to make sure she doesn't fall into that trap. I'm tight with my money too, had to be that way. If I wasn't, I couldn't have bought this land. I couldn't afford to waste money. A man looks at the money in his wallet and if he's not sure of how he's going to replace it, he hangs on to the sure thing, the money that's in his wallet.

Poppa said, "Living through the 1930s depression, me and your momma only saw thirty cents in one year. The whole year, it's hard to believe, isn't it?"

"Yes-sum," Roberta replied.

"White folks didn't have any money either. All poor people black and white was pretty nearly in the same boat. Men talking about the life they used to have, where they used to work. You could see grown men, me included, walking with their head hung down looking at the ground hoping to find a coin, but finding none. From the loss of hope, despair seized us all.

"I read that President Franklin Roosevelt became a polio victim at thirty-nine. Was never able to walk again, that this is probably some of the reason he had so much compassion on the poor working class. Creating social programs like Social Security, during the Great Depression, seeing that the dream of the American lifestyle falling apart at the seam, so to speak. Roberta, so many people are not aware of how blessed we are to have had a president like Roosevelt, and there were others who care about the old, poor, unemployed, widows, and fatherless children within their citizenry.

"Millions of American were desperate. Most were caught up in these 'hard times.' The government opened up soup kitchens and bread lines. One line for the blacks and another line for the whites, both lines were long, it was staggering odds against even surviving. Know too that I had a calling on my life. I knew I was called to preach at age nine. Consequently, my heart and mind was always on that calling. Being aware of this, small things always seem small. My heart and mind were on bigger things. I didn't have money to waste.

"Now, Alberta can learn from you. She takes everything too seriously, don't laugh enough. She's too serious to be so young. Life can be difficult for both of you because people, by you all being twins, will expect you both to be alike, always comparing you as if you should be one. Nothing you can do about that, it's just the price you have to pay for being twins. No matter how old twins get, it's a lifetime of comparing, stereotyping. Even surprised when they see differences. Some would say, 'Roberta enjoys travel, Alberta doesn't. That's odd, don't you think, by them being twin and all?'

"Roberta," Poppa continued. "I have wandered away from what I really want to talk to you about, and that's about your momma." He looked sober at the thought of talking about our momma; a faraway troubled look in his eyes showed how troubled he was.

"Your momma forgets stuff, I'm sure she has senility. And I'm not sure what to do about it."

"Poppa," Roberta said, looking at her poppa in his eyes. She felt great pity for him, her own eyes filled with tears. The memories of her momma standing at the front door talking to Mr. White came vividly back into her mind with Momma twirling the corners of her apron in her hands. Her momma was obviously afraid because she didn't have a clue to who this man was.

"Poppa," Roberta said, looking at him. "They call this Alzheimer now when a person has symptoms of forgetfulness and loss of the ability to reason and think clearly." Silence fell upon them. Roberta probably didn't know how to comfort her poppa.

Of course, with the slow, inevitable downhill progression of Alzheimer, our poppa saw day by day that his and his wife's life were getting more and more burdensome. Betty Joe and Peggy, his last two children, had finished high school, Betty Joe in 1969 and Peggy in 1970. They followed the path of their older sisters and brothers and migrated up north to live with them for the same reasons their sisters and brothers migrated—to flee Jim Crow and seek out a better life. Their sisters and brothers who had migrated up north and returned home the younger children who still remained were attracted to their now northern sisters and brothers' city lifestyle and were pulled in that direction.

The once bustling house was silent now. Poppa said, "Your momma would ask all day, 'Where are the children?' She never did get used to the silence."

I'm sure, Poppa didn't either. Now with all his children gone, his independence for the first time has been taken away. He couldn't jump into his car and go wherever he wanted to go; those days are gone now.

Roberta remembered on one of her visits home after Momma had been diagnosed with Alzheimer; the year was 1980. Poppa told her, "Roberta, there's one thing I regret."

"What's that, Poppa?"

"That I never learned to cook. I don't know how to cook for me and your momma."

After giving it a little thought, Roberta said, "Poppa, in St. Louis, they have something called 'meals on wheels' that's a government-assisted program that bring hot meals to seniors who can't do for themselves."

"Lord have mercy, girl, that would be such a blessing. Where is the phone book?" Poppa, with haste, got and handed Roberta the yellow pages.

Roberta found family services in Holly Springs, and after talking briefly to the girl on the other end of the phone, she said, "Poppa, I'm sorry, she said they have a waiting list, but we could pay for the services until some of the senior dies and then they will have a spot open for you and Momma."

"How much would that cost?"

"Seventy-four dollars per month, and they will deliver two hot meals per day, one for you and one for Momma."

"Lord have mercy, that would be such a blessing. I will pay that, I can afford it."

"No, Poppa, don't worry about it, your children will pay for it."

And within a short time, our poppa sat on the front porch waiting for their hot meal because he knew what time the driver would arrive and hand him their hot daily meal, a simple meal that usually consisted of baked chicken, fish, or a small piece of beef, mashed potato, something sweet, and some fruit juice. These meals were so important to Poppa.

Roberta said later that on this October day, this time under the pear tree was one of the if not the most wonderful one-on-one time she ever spent with her poppa.

# 32

## *Poppa's Death*

At seventy-eight, our poppa was a man who had never been sick. His children had never even seen him lying down. Once he and our momma were in their bedroom lying down in their bed, of course, their bedroom door was closed.

He kept his pain and problem with his bowels to himself, tried to ignore the difficult, painful urination and frequent bouts of diarrhea until he confided in his beloved daughter Ruth whom he was so proud when she got her nurse's license: "My daughter is a nurse." This must have been very hard for him to do, to even discuss such a private matter.

"Poppa," Ruth said after coming from St. Louis to visit her parent. "You need to see a doctor." He put it off until the stomach pain got so severe he couldn't stand it any longer.

On this cold day of December 22, 1986, our poppa was home with his wife who had Alzheimer's, a brain disorder that she had suffered for nearly twenty-five years. Twenty-six-year-old Jackie, his oldest son Junior's daughter, was there visiting her grandparents.

Our poppa was a hardworking, extremely independent man. He had many heads of farm animals, was a community leader, and at one point in his life was the moderator of Sardis East Baptist Congress, playing a

223

major role in the building of Negro schools and churches by organizing committees and support groups through his pastoral platform, appealing to large groups of people for financial support. His reputation as a public speaker was well-known. Our poppa's dedication to public service drove him on in his sixties as relentlessly as when he was in his twenties.

Pastoring several churches was a product of our poppa's leadership. Consequently, his family was blessed to have him standing, uncompromising at the head of them. He was a strong believer in what the Bible says about children: "Children obey your parents in all things, for this is pleasing to the Lord" (Colossians 3:20); "If any work not neither should he not eat" (2 Thessalonians 3:10); "The soul of the sluggard desires, and have nothing" (Proverbs 13:4); "Lord knows there's nothing worse than a lazy man"; "What you sow you shall reap"; "Save for a rainy day that's sure to come"; "Leave alcohol alone, that's a devil's drink"; "Gambling run neck and neck with alcohol"; and "A gambler will always be broke." Poppa's children grew up with these words ringing in their ears. It wasn't until our hair turned gray and our poppa was no longer around that his children realized how important and blessed we were to have a poppa as the head of our family.

This day in December, a couple of days before Christmas, whatever was wrong with him he probably knew that day by day it was getting worse. He knew men and women with this same problem who died because of cancer. He may have been thinking, "I have cancer. Lord have mercy, what's going to happen to Bracey?"

Jackie said later that she was sitting up front on the sofa with her grandmother and was thinking of her grandpa because he had been in his and grandma's bedroom with the door closed, and she was worried about him like everyone else in his family. She heard a car pull up, and she went to see who it was. The old Ford that pulled up was her aunt Shug and her daughter Teresa. Her aunt Shug had lived in Chicago for a few years, leaving the gloomy presence of Mississippi, expecting a glorious bright future up north to Chicago because Poppa's children viewed their life under the agriculture farm life and Jim Crow as gloomy and the northern lifestyle as a glorious future. And after spending a few years up north, some of Poppa's children returned back to Mississippi, finding that the big city life wasn't all it was cracked up to be, proverbially speaking; Plaite and Shug were two of them. Shug now lived about three miles from her parents.

Their faces were full of concern for Poppa when they entered the room. "Where is Poppa?" Shug asked. Jackie said, "He's in their bedroom, have been there all morning."

At the sound of their voices, Poppa came out of the bedroom and into the front room with his worn KJV Bible in his hand; and upon seeing his frail, feeble body and his worsened condition from the few days past that they had seen him, Shug and Jackie both started to weep. "Oh my God, Poppa."

"Yes, girls, this old thing have gotten the best of y'all Poppa. I need to go to the hospital right away."

The emergency of our poppa spread rapidly, quickly becoming newsworthy throughout the area. The alert of "code blue" got urgent immediate response. "Have you heard Rev. Gathing is in the hospital?" "Have you heard Uncle Sam is in the hospital?" "Oh my God, our poppa is in the hospital!"

Cozetta received a call from St. Francis Memorial Hospital in Memphis, Tennessee, in her Chicago north side surburban home. "The hospital official on the other end of the phone said, "Mrs. Jones, I hate to alarm you, but we have your father here in the hospital and we see here that we need your permission to do emergency surgery."

Cozetta said she almost dropped the telephone. "What, er . . . what are you saying? My Poppa, you have my poppa?"

"Yes, ma'am, he has you down as the emergency contact and we have to have your approval before we do surgery."

"Oh my God, our poppa! Tell the hospital to do what they have to do to save my poppa's life."

The nurse said, "We have to have your signature."

"I'll be at your hospital tomorrow," Cozetta said, responding to the urgent message.

The red Suburban was headed south on Highway 55. The big green sign above the highway read 55 South to Memphis, Tennessee 540 miles. Cozetta, Plaite, and her husband Clem were in the 1985 red Suburban; Clem was the driver. Cozetta said she kept reminding her husband of the seventy-miles-an-hour speed limits.

"Clem, you are going too fast."

"Babe," Clem said, glancing quickly at the radar detector sitting on his dashboard, "that will beep when a highway patrol is near."

They arrived in Memphis early the next day. Cozetta said that once in Memphis, they did not know the direction to the hospital. Clem was driving real slow, not sure which way to turn, and then a couple pulled up right beside them in a white car. The driver asked, "Do you people need direction? You look like you need some help."

Clem said, "Yes, sir, we do. We are trying to find St. Francis Memorial Hospital."

The man said, "Follow us."

Cozetta said they thanked the nice couple once they followed them right to the front entrance of the hospital, and as they turned and walked away and she turned to wave them goodbye, they weren't there. Just like that, they were gone. Within five to ten seconds, they weren't there anymore."

"Clem, what happened to those nice people?"

"Don't know, babe, I guess they just left."

"No way could they be out of sight that quick."

Plaite said, "That is pretty odd, but strange things happen sometimes."

"For some reason, the memories of those two kind people stayed with me," Cozetta said. "Don't forget to entertain strangers for thereby some have entertained Angels unaware" (Hebrew 13:2).

When Cozetta, Clem, and Plaite entered the emergency room, both men removed their hats because during these times men removed their hats when entering a room. A pleasant short rosy-cheeked nurse dressed in traditional white nurse's uniform greeted them.

"We are here to see Rev. Gathing, our poppa," said Plaite with great concern in his face and voice over his Poppa's emergency condition, nervously turning his hat in his hand. This was obviously a nervous moment for them all.

"Follow me." The nurse led them to a room a few doors from the nurses' station. When they entered the room, Shug and Teresa were sitting quietly with Roberta and her twenty-two-year-old daughter Pamela who had already arrived the day before from St. Louis. They all were sitting near the hospital bed where their poppa lay between pearly white hospital sheets with the head of the bed tilted up. They rose and walked over to meet the new arrivals with hugs and kisses, expressing their shared grief and sorrow over their fallen leader. As Cozetta and Roberta neared the bed looking down on their poppa, tears rolled down their cheeks as Cozetta gently held her poppa's, hands sobbing for the sadness of the moment.

"Girl, it sure is good to see you all. Yes, this old thing has knocked me clean on my back," Poppa said in a feeble and weak voice.

Plaite, our poppa's second oldest son, came to the bed filled with emotion and gently held his poppa's hands. The large working man's hands, the old-man body was lacking in strength. His hands were weak and frail, but his mind still reflected the strength that his frail weakened body had given up on. Plaite told us later that he was surprised how weak our poppa's hands were.

Plaite continued. "That's when I knew the angel of death had entered the room, even hovering over our poppa. This was a man who used an ax with skill, slaughter a steer, a fattened hog with the help of his boys, not sparing the rod when one of his sons disobeyed him." The slaughterhouse was sometimes full of their labor where Momma would send her girls for the main course of the day.

"Clem," Poppa said, "thanks for bringing them so soon."

"Oh, Mr. Gathing, God blessed me to be able to do it."

Pam said, looking at her grandpa, "I told Grandpa he didn't have to get sick to bring us all home for Christmas." Everyone laughed, including Poppa.

Within a short time, the waiting room was crowded with people responding to the news of our poppa's emergency trip to the hospital.

Once Cozetta gave the authorization, Poppa was rushed for emergency surgery. After a couple of hours, Dr. Briski, the surgeon, came into the crowded waiting room and announced that the cancer had spread and there was nothing that can be done. "He's in recovery and when he's brought to his room, you all can see him there."

"Thank you, Doctor." The gloomy news created a heavy cloud of despair and sorrow within the crowd. Sniffing and weeping could be heard because of the loss of hope.

After what seemed like forever, a nurse entered the room. "You can go in and see him now, only four at a time." Many went in to see our poppa. Family members, neighbors, some elders of his churches came and prayed for him. He thanked them all. "Thank you, Brother." "Thank you, Sister, for praying for me."

He closed his eyes, his mouth slightly open. Just like that, our poppa, their minister, their uncle, brother in-law, and grandpa was gone. He died with his Bible near his bedside.

He died believing that some white men were God-fearing men, that some rebelled against the terrorist KKK; believing there is a God and He sent His only begotten Son Jesus Christ to die on the cross to redeem them who believed in that Sacrifice; believing that a man was the head of his household; believing that children should obey their parents; and believing that if a man don't work, he shouldn't eat.

His favorite song was "Lord I Stretch My Hands to Thee."

# 33

## After Poppa's Death

Note: Some of the materials regarding our momma's Alzheimer's behavior that Roberta has written about deals with events she wasn't aware of during the time of her momma's dreadful disease, but all the actions and confusion of her momma's mind actually happened. However, years later, Rosalyn, a nurse who was a dear friend of Roberta, gave her a book to learn more about Alzheimer's that was an amazing insightful look into the minds of these dear people: *The 36—Hour Day* by Nancy L. Mace, MA, and Peter V. Rabins, MD, MPH.

After Poppa's death, Shug, whom I've stated before lived in Mississippi and near Momma and Poppa, cared for Momma. Cozetta knew that Shug didn't have the necessary skills to manage or meet the special needs of our momma. It appeared for a few months that Shug could handle Momma's Alzheimer's; however, after a few months, it became apparent to all that the twenty-four hours wearying burden of constant care was too much for Shug.

Cozetta, Momma's fourth child, couldn't bear the thought of putting our beloved mother in a nursing home that was used as a dumping ground for the old unwanted people. The thought was too depressing for her. The image of nursing homes kept running through her mind. Old people lined along the corridor. Some in wheelchairs, some with hands gripping walkers to support themselves as they shuffled along. Lonely old people sharing a room with strangers. Eating food they didn't like.

It was a decision that she had to make. Night after night, Momma was on Cozetta's mind while she lay in her bed beside her husband in a Chicago suburban middle-class neighborhood, a mother of four. Her oldest was Larry, then her oldest daughter, Gwendolyn, both of them living independently in Chicago. Cozetta's second son Michael volunteered to make the United States Army his career. With her older children living away, it was now just her, her husband Clem, and her youngest daughter, Phoebe, a lively, animated, spirited person and who, through her conversations, brought laughter. Cozetta was content with her life, content with being a wife and mother, running her and her husband's small business, the store of antiques and used furniture.

She loved doing what she was doing. She loved talking with her customers. Looked forward to going to her church on Sunday.

But Momma, the woman that nursed her babies, gave them the home remedies that was passed down from generation to generation when her children were sick, made and mended their clothes when they needed mending. This was often, for you see back then, poor people didn't buy their children clothes until the old clothes were worn out and one pair of shoes. So the need for our mother to sew on buttons, sew on patches, to mend ripped clothes was always there.

"Child, come and thread this needle, for your young eyes are better than mine," Momma would say.

Cozetta remember so clearly Momma giving birth to her younger siblings at home. Natural childbirth we call it today.

But back then in the '30s to '50s, Momma was just having another baby. Cozetta said, "For some reason, the children were home during this delivery which was unusual because back then when women gave birth, the fathers would take the children to a neighbor's house so they couldn't hear the travails of labor, maybe our poppa had to leave for some reason, all I know we were home." Cynthia, Cozetta, and even little Ruth could hear the agonizing pangs and intense struggle of their mother in labor.

It was easy for Momma's children to hear what was going on in this old framed shack. The walls were thin for if they could search they may find a crack and peek and see what that midwife woman was doing to their momma.

It seemed to Cozetta's six-year-old mind that it took hours and hours even maybe a whole day before they finally heard the cry of their new baby girl they named Christine. Cozetta remembered Momma being so tired.

Cozetta remembered too how Momma and her sisters would sometimes get together all eight of our Momma's sisters talking quietly when there were no men or children around. They would tell her little secrets about how not to get pregnant so often. When Momma's girls were old enough to understand, Momma would share these same secrets with her girls. During these times there was no legal birth control for women. Momma, it seemed to her sisters, that she was always pregnant. Our mother and poppa thought that children came from God. So with this in mind, Momma gave birth to fifteen babies.

All eight of our aunts were very pretty, fiery women full of life and fancy as they puffed on their cigarettes. Momma didn't smoke. Momma's girls loved it when they came to visit us.

Momma's girls wanted to be like their aunts. Wow! We thought they were so cool.

They all had shoulder-length hair with their light brown skin. Their dresses were just below their knees with shapely legs accenting their pretty high heel shoes.

Cozetta knew Momma couldn't take the kind of change that a nursing home would require. And Cozetta couldn't stand the thought of her "sweet pea" (a nickname that Cozetta gave Momma and was only called by her) living with the indignities of a nursing home. She knew she had to leave the comfort of her lifestyle; and after talking with her family, especially her husband Clem who gave her his blessing, in 1987, one year after our poppa's death, Cozetta went down to Mississippi after closing their small business and brought our mother to live with her and her family.

Our momma was a country girl used to life in the great outdoors. Now living in Chicago was like living on another planet. The noise was strange to her. The sounds of sirens, car horns were scary too. This house had nothing familiar to her. Cozetta was the only person she recognized. Momma would call her by one of her sisters' name. "Pauline, where is Sam?" Or "Earline, where is Momma?" (speaking of her own momma). These strange people would come and gently hug her. They were her grandchildren, Larry, Gwendolyn, Michael (when they came to visit), but she didn't know that. The big very dark man would be walking around this strange house. He was her son-in-law, but she didn't know that neither. She wanted Sam, the only man she knew. He was dead, but she didn't remember that.

"Where is Sam?" Cozetta said.

Momma would ask that question over and over again. "Where is Sam?"

Cozetta had to make sure that all exterior doors were locked because Momma would wander outside. With her impaired mind, she probably wanted to go to her vegetable garden or to the chicken coop to get fresh eggs, try to go to the front porch and sit with her husband. They both had their own chairs, one for him and one for her where she would listen with him doing most of the talking. Sometimes her mind would probably be elsewhere, mostly on her children, but it was obvious to all she enjoyed just being near her husband. Those were the things she had done all her life; now she's so confused. "Where is Sam?"

After several months of trying to get outside, she gave up and she would sit in a big comfortable pink floral chair all day in this strange house with these strange people. Sometimes this nice woman that in her spirit she knew this house belonged to would take her outside, but by this being a strange place, she started wanting to go back into this strange house with these strange people.

Then one day, Cozetta said, "I couldn't get Momma out of bed, she just didn't want to get up. I called family services and a visiting nurse started coming in to help. Then one day Momma stopped eating and the nurse said sometimes Alzheimer's patients forget how to eat." Cozetta and Clem took Momma to the doctor. In very soft, gentle words, the doctor explained to them their options. "Mrs. Jones, you have two options—we can insert a feeding tube or you can let her starve to death." Cozetta said she was totally unprepared for what the doctor said.

"Let my momma starve to death? Are you crazy!" Cozetta said the thought of it made her heart start to palpitate.

"Babe, are you all right?" Clem asked with great concern for his wife.

"Clem, did you hear what the doctor said?"

"Mrs. Jones, this is a difficult decision to make, one that we all struggle with. Of course, the final decision is yours and your family," the doctor said.

As Momma lay in her hospital bed with a feeding tube used to feed her in Cozetta and Clem's sunny bright family room, the wall had a series of rows of family pictures reaching back and forward over several generations. Near the large windows were several large beautiful house plants that absorbed the sun rays filtering through the windows.

Roberta and Ruth would drive up from St. Louis to see their momma, and other family members who lived in Chicago would join them at Cozetta's house. We would gather in Cozetta and Clem's very comfortable living room before going to the lower-level family room where our momma lay. Her extremely frail body, weighing less than a hundred pounds where the only signs of her once strong self was in her eyes. As Ruth, Roberta, and Alberta stood looking down upon their dying momma. She cast her eyes upon them; even though she couldn't speak, her warm gentle eyes spoke to them. Alberta started to weep. Roberta put her arms around her twin sister and started weeping also. Alberta lifted our momma's very thin bony hand in her hands. "Oh, Momma, we love you so."

Ruth and Roberta would return back home with a very heavy, grief-stricken spirit, knowing that their momma was dying and that Cozetta would be calling them, "Our momma is gone," but they had jobs and families back in St. Louis. However, every time their phone rang, they feared it would be Cozetta on the other end, saying, "Momma is gone."

A visiting nurse came through the week to assist Cozetta and show her how to care for a hospice patient. Our sister did what she'd been doing daily for the past three years. After adjusting the feeding tube and with a soft, damp, warm face cloth, she would wash her mother's hands and face gently. As usual, Momma would go to sleep.

On this cool November 11, 1989, day in Chicago, Cozetta stood looking down at her "sweet pea" for a few moments, thinking to herself how peaceful and beautiful she looked, making sure Momma was comfortable. Before she started to go back upstairs, Cozetta picked up her basket of freshly washed folded clothes and headed upstairs. As Cozetta was climbing the stairs, she heard the Holy Spirit say so clearly, "Your mother is dead."

She turned so quickly, dropping the basket of freshly folded clothes and running back down the stairs to her dead mother she almost tripped. With uncontrollable weeping and trembling hands, she dialed 911. "She's dead, my mother is dead."

Momma was eighty years old when she died.

Momma died believing that her husband was the head of his household, that God was merciful (Lord have mercy), and children must obey their parents; always loving her babies, never abandoning her children; not sparing the strap because they understood the strap more than words ("This hurts me more than it hurts you"); and never forgot her nightly prayers.

Her favorite song was "Lord Don't Move the Mountain, Just Give Me the Strength to Climb."

Momma's age approx. 46

Roberta at the Great Wall of China—Beijing 1999

Church of the Holy Sepulcher—Jerusalem, Israel 1988

Egypt—Ramses II—Roberta in Egypt 1988

Roberta with a Masai Tribe, Kenya, Africa—1992

Roberta with African village in Senegal, Africa—2000

# 34

## *Roberta, Overcoming Jim Crow/ The Land No One Wanted*

Scripture from the Bible has been mentioned many times throughout this book. This chapter will show the anger and rebellion of young people who felt they were wiser than their parents.

Roberta, like her siblings, especially her brothers, were caught up in the "power to the people," "we want it now" era. Angela Davis, Malcolm X were some of her heroes too.

A few weeks after high school graduation, in 1962, my twin sister Alberta and Roberta packed all of our belongings in one suitcase. We caught the Greyhound Bus to live with our sister Ruth and her family in North St. Louis, Missouri.

As the bus took us through Arkansas and Missouri, with nervousness and excitement, our eyes were glued to the scenery passing outside the bus window because at the age of eighteen, we hadn't seen the world outside of Mississippi and Tennessee.

With anger and resentment still burning within us, the way our family, especially our Poppa was treated, the more distance we put between us and Mississippi, the better. We hated Mississippi, the Jim

Crow laws, the work in the fields, the awful Mississippi heat, all the worms and insects that went with it!

## The Land That No One Wanted

The land that Poppa paid such a high emotional price for, his children didn't want. We rejected the land and its people. This illustrates what damage resentment can do.

Jim Crow laws had gained a stronghold on Poppa's children. His children rejected the white ruling class and the land that was stained by generations of our people's blood. His children couldn't separate the hard labor their family put into the land from their resentment of the oppressive laws of Jim Crow. And his children also wanted freedom from the restraints of no social night life our poppa held over them, especially his girls. Consequently, his children joined the great migration like the thousands of Negroes before them. They were tired of living as though they were living in quicksand; if they moved even a little to freedom, they would sink even deeper into a garment of bondage tied in knots by Old Jim Crow himself. The way out was the Greyhound bus going north. In 1962, one suitcase was enough. "We felt like a calf when someone had left the gate open, leaping and jumping for joy. Does not a dog runs when his leash is broken? We are getting the hell out of here!" Consequently, we deserted our poppa's land. As the years passed, Poppa's children were caught up in a quagmire. They didn't move back, but most paid their taxes on the land. Others, by not paying their taxes, said, "Mississippi, you can have your land, I don't want it." Others asked, "What are we going to do with the land?" This became a lingering unanswered question to this very hour.

We were young, and a great change was sweeping America. Young people all over the land was speaking out, black and white. "These old outdated leaders don't know what they are doing!" The generation of the sixties, the rebellion generation, we thought had the power to change America. We were encouraged by the black power movement to put pressure on the slow snail's pace of our outdated leaders.

Consequently, we took to the streets, young black and white people throughout America with mass protests against the Vietnam War, civil rights, women liberation, anything our young inexperienced mind told us that weren't just and right.

Roberta said that as a young woman and doing her militant years in her twenties and even through her forties, she was very attracted to tall, very dark-complexioned black men. She read books about their personal struggle, the writing of James Baldwin; W. E. B. DuBois; Richard Wright; Ralph Ellison, just to name a few. Her disillusion came slow and gradual; she wanted to discuss these books with the man she was dating at the time, but he didn't read those type of books. However, the men she knew when she came to their apartment had lying on their coffee table a stack of *Playboy, Hustler* magazine, or the like. Some of them were open to the centerfold. Now, by her being a black woman, her hairstyle of a bushy afro and sometimes wearing a dashiki, she found this to be offensive, sitting beside him on his sofa and his eyes cast upon the very colorful uncovered and bare blond young woman in the centerfold. Being the preacher's daughter and a country one at that, she found this difficult to handle. "Dan, will you please close that magazine?"

"What's wrong with it?"

"You got something against white women?"

Perhaps even worse, no matter how hard the young black women tried, living in the midst of the white ruling class, most felt inferior, it seems, to that. The lighter the complexion of the woman, the closer the black woman's skin color was to the white woman, the more our black men were attracted to them. This rejection was deeply felt, especially when she looked at her black man we felt in our heart. "The blacker the berry, the sweeter the juice" or "We don't want no cream in our coffee," proverbially speaking.

We tried hard not to see our blackness as not being ugly and undesirable. Straightening our kinky hair and using bleaching cream on our face didn't improve our self-perception. The psychological consequence from this rejection has been huge. A feeling of being rejected by the one you love, but they don't love you back. The black men, with some exceptions, eyes were drawn to women who were not their own. Too many of our black men compare their women to the white women, her hair, her figure; she's more sensitive, more gentle they say. Their black women are meaner, our black men also says. These are the ones their black mothers prayed for, nursed, licked their wounds, so to speak, went to little league and Sunday school for, clothed, and fed. And to see most of them not remembering those things, they see their own black women as second-class citizens and the light-complexioned or white women as first class; their own black women as a Ford and the white woman as a Mercedes Benz, proverbially speaking. Now, what if we compared our black men to white men, would they pass the test?

Leaving Mississippi didn't stop Roberta's desire to leave America where she believed this country was the cause of the Negro's problems. Like so many others, herself included, she was blinded by her resentment for America, which caused her to ignore all the blessings and the people who had sacrificed so much for her to receive those blessings.

During her "militant" years, she was ready to go to war against America through the 1960s and 1980s wearing her large afro. If there was a protest, she was in the midst of the crowd holding her protest sign high so that others could see—"Down with America!"

This anger with America intensified when within a short time, an assassin bullet killed the men where she had placed so much hope on were all killed with one bullet to the head:

November 22, 1963, JFK assassinated while sitting near his beautiful wife Jackie waving at a crowd of supporters while in Dallas, Texas.

Martin Luther King Jr. while standing on the balcony of Lorraine Motel in Memphis, Tennessee, April 4, 1968, after a major protest in support for the Negro sanitation workers. One bullet in his head, and he existed no more.

Bobby Kennedy, after winning the California primary, one bullet in his head from an assassin bullet on June 6, 1968.

It seems that a light had been turned off, that someone had hit a light switch and turn the lights out on America.

Roberta said so much hope was placed on the words of President Kennedy from the Negro community. Senator Kennedy won the heart of Negroes when Martin Luther King was locked up in a Georgia jail and the senator actually called and talked with Coretta, King's wife, showing her and her husband great concern and he said he would "do all he can to help." The senator called for King's release. Negroes were so amazed that a call from a senator and a white man would do this for their Negro leader. Instant praises went up to this white man, and he became a friend to the Negro. When John Kennedy ran for president, he got a large majority of Negro vote because of that one call that he made to our leader's wife.

A brighter day quickly turned into darkness and despair each time the men of great hope were murdered. When President Kennedy was assassinated, our hope was still on Martin Luther King. Then five years after President Kennedy's assassination, it happened again. One pulled off a trigger from James Earl Ray's high-powered rifle, and another light was turned out. Roberta said, "I remembered so plainly I was in my 1965 white Buick driving to work to a catering service for the airlines in St. Louis, Missouri, where I worked at the time. The news came across the radio. 'Dr. King has been shot.' Lord, oh God no! Not him too. I started weeping so hard I had to pull over on the side of the highway because I couldn't continue to drive for the tears. I remember that on this warm sunny April fourth day, how could God continue to let the sun shine so brightly? All I could feel was darkness, gloom, and despair and the sun was shining. How could this be? Now what?"

Then there was Robert Kennedy, the last one left standing. Maybe Bobby Kennedy can finish what his brother President Kennedy and Martin Luther King started. Maybe Bobby can carry the torch of liberty and justice for all to the finish line.

Twenty-five-year-old Roberta was in her apartment in St. Louis until late into the night watching the California primary, praying that Bobby would win, knowing that he would continue what his brother and Dr. King had started once he became president. And as she was sitting on her sofa in her second-story apartment's small living room smoking a Kool cigarette, Bobby was standing on the platform in the Ambassador Hotel Embassy ballroom in Los Angeles; they had just announced he had won. "Thank you Jesus Bobby has won!"

And just as quickly, he was lying on the floor from the sound of *pop, pop,* with the room filled with chaos. His only security was provided by former FBI agent William Barry and two bodyguards. A single gunman, twenty-four-year-old Sirhan Sirhan, pulled the trigger from his .22 caliber revolver that sent bullets flying into young forty-two-year-old Kennedy's head, and he died twenty-six hours later.

It seemed that the spirit of assassination filled the country, left us all wondering who will be next, that assassins were lurking behind every bush, every dark alley, every crowded room. "That's why we came to kill and destroy."

Roberta said she felt so hopeless it seemed time stood still, everything was moving in slow motion. With the strong emotions she had for these men in power, now with them all being killed, she didn't know how to channel her emotions. The thought of fleeing kept running through her mind—another country where they didn't kill good people.

She even toyed with the idea of changing her name. "Who wants to hang on to the names of their slave masters?" she asked. Influences of Malcolm X.

Sometimes she would visit Moslem Mosque, which threw her into a spiritual identity crisis: should she continue to stay in the Christian religion, or change to the Muslim religion?

Reading other people's history, traveling to developing countries, especially Africa, standing in the "Doors of No Return" where the slaves passed through the doors to be forced to America. She said she wept for her ancestors. She also witnessed abject poverty. In Egypt, she was in a group of about ten tourists led by their tour guide—Happy, she wanted them to call her—on a walking tour down a busy Cairo city street. Cairo has a population of over 7 million people, where the ethnicity was very diverse—Africans, some with tribal scars across their dark faces, Senegalese women dressed in their beautiful floral head wrap and full-length dresses, Arab men dressed in white with heads also covered in white, making their copper-tone skin more pronounced. They were told they were very rich Saudis from Saudi Arabia.

Roberta said on this particular tour that she noticed a couple of men, probably in their late forties, that had one of their hands missing. "Happy, what happened to their hands?" she asked.

"They were caught stealing, and the judge sentenced them to jail and also the removal of their right hand." Roberta, upon hearing this awful, horror thing, said she felt sick to her stomach. *Lord, don't let me throw up.*

Seeing the ruins of antiquity and standing on the Great Wall of China that was built 220 years before Christ makes one appreciate times past and present, that a lot happened before the slave ships to America. And after a one-on-one conversation with some of their citizens, I found out that everything in their country wasn't peaches and cream either. Learning more about the discontent of some of their citizens changed my ungrateful attitude about America. Getting out of the forest, I definitely could see the trees.

After reading "We wish to inform you that tomorrow we will be killed with our families" (*Stories from Rwanda* by Philip Gourevitch).

These African men who killed—an Aid worker guessed that 100,000 to 500,000 men, women, and children were axed to death—and committed these horrific crimes against their own people came straight from the pits of hell. "So much for I'm black and I'm proud."

After reading Benazir Bhutto's autobiography *Daughter of Destiny*, I loved her kind and gentle ways and the love she had for the Pakistan people. Her father Zulfikar Ali Bhutto was prime minister before he was assassinated in 1979. In January 2008, she won the parliament election with most of her people shouting for joy; and after entering her bullet-proof vehicle, standing up through the sunroof waving at the crowds, thanking them for their support, someone shot and killed her. "So much for the goodness of humanity."

I strongly suggest that anyone who is still crying in their soup, saying, "poor me," I strongly recommend them to read *Bury My Heart at Wounded Knee* by Dee Brown, an extraordinary book that changed the way Americans think about the native inhabitants of America. Of course, there are thousands of books to choose from, to learn about the horror of people's life experiences.

The experience of reading and traveling grew me closer and closer to America. Roberta said she had heard it said that America was one of the best places to live in, and she slowly started seeing the truth of what was being said.

In later years in 1992, Roberta was vacationing in Kenya, Africa, with Tanzania and Zimbabwe included. A safari was included in this seventeen days' trip. Our tour group of twelve had a three days' visit to the Masai Mara National Park while in Kenya. Also we visited a Masai's village. Upon entering, the smell of cow dung greeted us. This made me think of our Poppa's barnyard. We were welcome by the sound of beautiful African drums. Standing in their center court surrounded by huts that were made of straws and cow dung and built by their women because that was women's work, there was a group of about fifteen to twenty natives dressed in their traditional colors of red, and they were obviously expecting us. I was even invited into one of the huts by a beautiful young girl of about fifteen with pretty white teeth with two bottom teeth missing, and then I noticed that all the men and women too had two bottom teeth missing. Later we were told that was a sign of beauty.

Once inside the hut, the smell of cow dung was almost overpowering. The pretty young girl pointed toward what looked like a bed made out of straws and mud. After I was seated, she gave me her baby that was wrapped in a rag blanket. As I held the baby, it began to cry. With a smile, I gave the baby back to her mother. Everyone laughed. Poppa said, "A smile is a universal language." They didn't speak my language of English and I didn't speak their language of Swahili, but we all understood the laughter.

The Masai men's job was to get dressed in their pretty red and black cloth wrapped around their tall, thin, very dark bodies. Even wearing their best very colorful red, blue, orange multicolored beaded handmade jewelry now, they were dressed for work. Their work was to let their cattle graze all day. The only thing they were carrying was a tall walking stick. And when there wasn't enough grass to feed their cattle, they and their families take all of their belongings and move to greener pasture where their women will build more huts, another village.

Upon hearing this, being an American woman, I wanted to scream, "You men are nuttier than a fruitcake! How on earth can you expect this of your women? Why, some of them are pregnant, others have your babies on their backs, and the only thing you are carrying is your walking cane!"

A strong feeling of rebellion surged up in my spirit. I wanted to get a picket sign. Down with these crazy men! I need to call Gloria Steinem who strongly believed in women liberation, even wrote a book about it, *Outrageous Acts and Everyday Rebellions*. Of course, I knew there was nothing I could do.

I remembered good advice from the travel agency: "Thou shall not expect to find things as thou hast them at home, for thou hast left home to find things different." Good advice.

As James Baldwin once wrote, "You think your pain and your heartbreak are unprecedented in the history of the world, but then you read. It was books that taught me that the things that tormented me the most was the very things that connected me with all the people who were alive, or who had ever been alive."

As I write this book, I am a senior citizen. The God I service is the God of my father.

The scriptures I quote daily are the same scriptures Poppa quoted. The flag I once want to burn I now proudly display on the Fourth of July, Veterans' Day, and Labor Day. God bless America!

# Momma's Home Remedies

- A teaspoon of flour for diarrhea.
- Gargle with warm salty water for sore throat.
- Check temperature, a slight touch on the forehead or the side of the neck.
- Epsom salt for upset stomach.
- Baking soda for brushing teeth and for deodorant.
- 1 teaspoon of sugar with 1 or 2 drops of turpentine for digestive tract worms.
- Vick's Vapor Rub for stuffy nose.
- Cold sores—a little earwax.
- Corn husks tea—for bedwetting.

This bedtime prayer was required of the Gathing children:

Now I lay me down to sleep
I pray to the Lord my soul to keep
If I should die before I awake
I pray to God my soul He shall take
Bless Momma, Poppa and everybody
Amen.

# Momma's Recipes

*Molasses Cake*

1/2 cup of Crisco shortening
1/3 cup of sugar
1 egg
1 cup of molasses
2 cups all-purpose flour
3/4 cup water
1 tsp. of baking soda
1/2 tsp. salt
2 tsp. ginger

Directions: Cream shortening, add sugar gradually, creaming well. Beat egg and add to shortening and sugar, add molasses. Sift the flour with the baking soda, salt, and ginger. Add dry ingredients alternately with the liquid to the shortening, sugar, and egg. Pour into a greased 9×13 baking pan. (Momma doubled this recipe because of the size of her family.)

And after about 35 or 40 minutes, stick a broomlike straw into it to see if it would come out clean. If so, you know it is done. (Momma's cast-iron stove didn't have a temperature gauge; she probably just stuck her hand inside the oven and judged the temperature with her hands.)

*Suggested Icing Vanilla*

2-2/3 cups powdered sugar
2 tsp. of vanilla extract
3 tbs. of water

*Fried Apple Pies*

3 tbs. of butter
5 red apples (from Poppa's orchard) thinly sliced and peeled
1 cup of sugar
½ tsp. of nutmeg
½ tsp. of ground cinnamon

*Pie Dough*

2 cups of flour
½ tsp. of salt
3/4 cup of shortening
3 tbs. of cold water
Toss lightly with fork until dough forms small balls.

Direction: Add butter to a large cast-iron skillet; add the apples, sugar, nutmeg, and cinnamon.

Cook over medium heat until the apples are soft. Remove from heat and cool. When the filling is cool, cut out crust approx. 9 in. for each pie. Place 3-4 tablespoons of pie filling into each cutout, brush the edge of crust with water. Fold the circle over the filling, seal by pressing the edges together by using a fork, carefully adding the pies to the preheated hot oil until golden brown.

*Teacakes*

1 cup of butter
2 cup of sugar
2 eggs
1 tsp. vanilla flavor
½ tsp. of salt
1 tsp. baking soda
6 tbs. of milk
4 cups of all-purpose flour

Direction: Roll out on floured cutting board with tin can that has top removed. Bake in hot oven until browned (10-12 minutes)

*Our Momma's Biscuits*

8 cups of sifted plain flour
2 1/2 tbs. of baking power
2 tbs. of salt
2 tbs. of sugar
2 1/2 cups of milk
1 1/2 cup of shortening

Knead dough on floured cutting board. Cut biscuits out with a cleaned medium-sized tin can with the top of can remove. Place in a very hot oven on baking sheet. Bake until golden brown for 10-12 minutes.

Looking Back

*Baptism*

*Beatrice age 46*

*Roberta at The Great Wall of China - Beijing 1999*

*Church of the Holy Sepulchre - Jerusalem, Israel 1988*

*South Korea*

*Roberta with a Masai Tribe, Kenya Africa - 1992*

*Pauline (Bowen) Bridgeford (Beatrice Sister)*

*Egypt - Ramses II - Roberta in Egypt 1988*

*Sam and Beatrice Gathing*

*Roberta (Gathing) Wright*

*Samuel Wesley Gathing*

*Sam Gathing*

*Roberta with Africa Village in Senegal Africa - 2000*

*(L-R: Alfred, Obadiah, James, Lloyd and Sam Jr.)*

*(L-R: Cynthia, Cozetta, Ruth, Christine, Iola,*
*Alberta, Roberta, Betty Jo and Peggy)*

# *Appendix*

Gathing Family Tree

Chapter 14—Gathing Family Tree

(A)William "Grandpa Bill" Gathing, b. 1828 in Anson County N. Carolina, died March 20, 1017 in Lewisburg, MS.

William first union was to Isabella Arrington, b. 1845 in Campbell County, Virginia, died 1897 Lewisburg, MS.

From this union 8 children were born (b) Julia 1861, (a)Fannie 1862, Mary 1866/died 1909, Kizzie 1872, Elizabeth 1872/ died 1909, Willie 1877, Henry 1879 and Eugenia 1882.

William was married again, Susie Collins, and from that union were John Wesley(Sr.), December 1857/died 1924 and Mattie b. 1867 d. 1951.

William also married Sallie, b. 1855. To this union were 3 sons, Peter, March 1887; Taylor Olanoh, May 1882; Andrew, June 1891 and 1 daughter, Perola, February 1887.

John Wesley Sr. was married to Mollie (Dasher), b. 1869. From this union were 5 sons John Wesley Jr., May 1880; Cary L, Oct 1881; Dave, June 1882; Lucious, 1889 and Hilliard (adopted); and 4 daughters, Cora & Dora, February 1885 and Jessie, August 1893 and Georgia.

John Wesley Jr. married January 2, 1904 to *Cynthia Nesbit, b. 1884. From this union 2 children were b. 1906 and Samuel Wesley, April 25, 1908 and Lilly Bowen, b. 1889. Cynthia died approximately six-months after Samuel was born.

John Wesley Jr. married **Millie Bowen and from this union were 2 sons, Emerson, 1911 and Booker T, 1912.

John Wesley married a 3rd time to Etta; also known as Mae Ella Baker or Big Momma and from this union Iola, b. 1915.

*Simon Nesbit, b. 1848, married May 17, 1880, Mary Spencer, date of birth unknown. From this union were 6 children, William, Mary,

259

Charles, Jerry b. 1883 (married Lena; daughter Gillie b. 1896), Cynthia, b. 1884, and Lilly, b. 1886.

**Millie Bowen was the aunt of Beatrice Bowen, wife of Samuel Wesley Gathing.

Samuel Wesley and Beatrice were married December 22, 1929 and from this union there were 14 children:

Cynthia, Samuel Wesley Jr. (died 2010), Obadiah, Cozetta, Ruth, Christine, Alfred, Iola (died 2004), Alberta, Roberta, Lloyd, James, Betty Jo and Peggy.

\*\*\*\*\*\*\*\*\*\*\*\*\*\*\*\*\*\*\*\*\*\*\*\*\*\*\*\*\*\*\*\*\*\*\*\*\*\*\*\*

The author is indebted to the following:

- James Mabley for the material on the family tree
- Corrine Davis on the history of Mt. Sinai Church
- Elnora Jackson on the information on Pastor Royer Person
- Marilyn Hickey, *Breaking Generational Curses*
- My sister Ruth Wilson for the information on BI
- Stephen B. Oats, *To Purge This Land with Blood: A Biography of John Brown*
- Phillip Dray, *At the Hands of Persons Unknown: The Lynching of Black America*
- Langston Hughes, "The Mourner's Bench," "Salvation"

# About the Author

Roberta was born Roberta Gathing, the tenth of Beatrice and Sam's fourteen children, in 1943 into Jim Crow laws in northern Mississippi.

She writes about how difficult it was to watch their father having to act like a "boy" and being called a "boy" by the southern whites.

Even though Reverend Gathing was pastor four churches and was the moderator of Sardis East Baptist Congress, the confederation didn't change whites' way of addressing him as "boy." Roberta, like her father, appreciated reading and travel. The many books she read and the series of countries she's visited reflects that. This includes Africa, Asia, China, Egypt, Israel, and South America.

Roberta left Mississippi after graduating from high school to live with her sister Ruth, her husband, and their three small children in a second-story three-room apartment in North St. Louis City, Missouri.

She retired from Mallinckrodt Chemical after thirty-seven years.

During this time, she also sold real estate and owned a small ice cream parlor, which her daughter Pam managed for her.